GREAT JOBS
FOR EVERYONE 50+

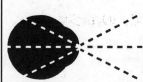

Great Jobs
for Everyone 50+

FINDING WORK THAT KEEPS YOU HAPPY
AND HEALTHY . . . AND PAYS THE BILLS

Kerry Hannon

THORNDIKE PRESS
A part of Gale, Cengage Learning

GALE
CENGAGE Learning·

Detroit • New York • San Francisco • New Haven, Conn • Waterville, Maine • London

GALE
CENGAGE Learning·

Thorndike Press® Large Print Health, Home and Learning.
The text of this Large Print edition is unabridged.
Other aspects of the book may vary from the original edition.
Set in 16 pt. Plantin.

LIBRARY OF CONGRESS CATALOGING-IN-PUBLICATION DATA

Hannon, Kerry.
    Great jobs for everyone 50+ : finding work that keeps you happy and
healthy — and pays the bills / by Kerry Hannon. — Large print edition.
        pages cm. — (Thorndike Press large print health, home and learning)
    ISBN 978-1-4104-5725-7 (hardcover) — ISBN 1-4104-5725-7 (hardcover)
    1. Job hunting—United States. 2. Older people—Employment—United
States. 3. Middle-aged persons—Employment—United States. I. AARP
(Organization) II. Title.
    HF5382.75.U6H363 2013
    331.702084'60973—dc23   2012050726

Published in 2013 by arrangement with John Wiley & Sons, Inc.

Printed in the United States of America
1 2 3 4 5 6 7 17 16 15 14 13

For my Dad, who showed me the joy of helping people find the work they love

CONTENTS

INTRODUCTION

Cheryl Champagne was 60, with 25 years as a finance manager, when she took an early retirement buyout package from downsizing Hartford Life Insurance Co. in September 2009. She received 18 weeks of severance and spent eight weeks gardening, taking yoga classes, and thinking about the rest of her life. "More than anything, what came out of that experience is that I realized I love to work," she says.

Not everyone wants to work simply for the pure love of it. Some of us *need* to keep working for the income. Others, who have saved enough to retire and choose to work, just *want* to stay mentally engaged.

While we all may have a common desire to keep working, what motivates us to work and what each of us calls a "great job" is as individual as we are. "Different flavors of ice cream," as my sister likes to say.

There's no doubt, though, that work at an

older age is becoming increasingly common. "Growing old in the 21st century is not what it was in the 20th," says Marcie Pitt-Catsouphes, Director of the Sloan Center on Aging & Work at Boston College. "As life expectancy continues to increase, older adults are healthier and more active than in the past."

In 2012, 70 percent of workers (up from 61 percent in 2001) said they expected to work for pay in retirement, according to the Employee Benefit Research Institute's (EBRI) Retirement Confidence Survey. "Even people with retirement savings see earning a half-time income as a safety net," says Beverly Jones, who advises 50- and 60-somethings as a career coach at Clearways Consulting in Washington, D.C.

The vision of people 50+ spending their retirement years gardening, golfing, and lounging on the beach is out. Meaningful work is in. Yes, some retirees have always taken part-time jobs out of financial need to shore up retirement accounts, or stave off boredom. What's different now is that baby boomers are either continuing to work much longer or approaching work not as an afterthought but as a pillar of their "retirement" plans, as oxymoronic as that sounds.

The Numbers Tell the Tale

More and more 55+ workers are in the workforce, according to EBRI. "This upward trend is likely to continue," says EBRI's Craig Copeland, co-author of the report.

In fact, between 2010 and 2020, people 55 and older are projected to be the fastest-growing segment of the U.S. labor force, according to the 2012–2013 *Occupational Outlook Handbook,* a jobs forecast by the U.S. Bureau of Labor Statistics. EBRI researchers also found that the percentage of workers who expect to delay retirement until after age 65 has increased from 11 percent in 1991 to 37 percent in its 2012 survey. That's a seismic swing.

Today's 60-year-old might reasonably plan to work at least part-time for another 15 years, figures Marc Freedman, author of *The Big Shift: Navigating the New Stage Beyond Midlife* and founder and CEO of Encore .org, a nonprofit that promotes second acts for the greater good. "That changes the entire equation about what you want to do, what's possible to do, and whether it is worth investing up front for additional education," he says.

I like his thinking. To me, it's exciting, inviting, and empowering. For many retirees, "working in retirement" is quickly becoming a new stage in career progression.

"The entire concept of you work and then retire is over for most people," Kevin Cahill, an economist with The Sloan Center on Aging & Work at Boston College, explained to me. "Retirement is a process. People gradually fade out of the workforce. About 60 percent of the career workers take on a job after exiting their main career. We call these bridge jobs."

And by the looks of it, there are more openings on the way for these kinds of jobs.

- A recent joint poll by the Society for Human Resources (SHRM) and AARP shows that more than seven in 10 U.S. employers are worried about the loss of talented older workers and are beginning to do something about it. Many are offering flexible work arrangements, hiring retired workers as consultants, and designing part-time jobs to attract experienced workers.
- Further evidence: ManPower Group's 2012 Talent Shortage Survey found a significant percentage of U.S. employers are struggling to fill positions despite continued high unemployment. Why? They're having trouble finding

workers with experience. According to the more than 1,300 U.S. employers surveyed, the hardest jobs to fill include skilled trades, engineers, IT staff, sales reps, account and finance staff, drivers, mechanics, nurses, and teachers.

This is good financial news if you're 50+ and looking for a job right now, or planning for your next gig when you do "retire."

Let me remind you of the three money-wise reasons to stay in the workforce as long as you can:

1. The more earning years when you can build savings in a defined contribution plan like a 401(k) or an Individual Retirement Account (IRA), the better off you'll be down the road. Your monthly Social Security payment will grow, too, the longer you work (until age 70).
2. The longer you work, the longer you delay tapping retirement funds, which can continue to grow.
3. It can provide income to pay for health insurance until you're eligible for Medicare at 65. Fewer employers are offering their retired work-

ers medical benefits, and those who do are ramping up the amount retirees must contribute to the cost of coverage. Even better, you might even find a job that offers you access to a health plan.

Money aside, there's another big reason you may want to keep working in some adaptation: a sense of "well-being," according to The Sloan Center's Pitt-Catsouphes. The Center's 2012 report, *Life & Times in an Aging Society,* found that for people over 50, it's important to be *engaged* — not just involved.

Work gives us a sense of purpose, feeling connected and needed. It makes us feel relevant. It's hard to pin a precise paycheck to that, but it's real.

Moreover, it keeps our minds sharper. Researchers from the RAND Center for the Study of Aging and the University of Michigan published a study showing that cognitive performance levels decline faster in countries that have younger retirement ages. What? Brain cells dying from lack of use? You bet.

It's the old "Use it or lose it axiom." Many aging experts say that to stay healthy older adults, who are used to the demands of full-time work, have to learn new things, stay active socially, and exercise. When you stop challenging your brain with new experiences, you're in trouble.

Encore Careers

As many as 9 million people ages 44 to 70 in the United States are already in "encore careers" — those that combine personal meaning, continued income, and social impact, according to the 2011 Encore.org's study, *Encore Career Choices: Purpose, Passion and a Paycheck in a Tough Economy,* funded by MetLife Foundation. That's up from an estimated 8.4 million in 2008. And another 31 million people are interested in joining them. Together, those currently in encore careers and those interested in encore careers represent 40 percent — or two in five — of all Americans ages 44 to 70.

The motivation: Financial security and a bridge to tapping into Social Security. Without a defined pension, light on personal savings, and worried about future health care costs from living longer, it's little wonder staying in the workforce in an encore career is downright appealing.

The study found the most popular encore career fields (which I go into throughout this book) are:

- Education
- Health care
- Nonprofit organizations

More than half of those interested in encore careers figure they will be working at least part time after they retire from their earlier careers. On average, they envision working in their next act for about nine years after leaving their "midlife" jobs and working an average of 23.4 hours per week.

Three in five people interested in an encore career say it's very important that an encore career leaves free time for things you want to do, such as travel, take courses, or engage in other activities you enjoy. Indeed, many of those interested in encore careers appear eager to mix fewer hours of work per week with more years of work in total.

Now in my early 50s, I personally can't imagine *not* working in some form as a writer well beyond age 67 — the age the Social Security Administration considers to be my full-retirement age to start receiving benefits. I've been passionate about writing since childhood. I've been tickled to make a living at it.

And as I grow older, I appreciate that it's flexible. That is, if I'm open-minded about what kinds of assignments I accept. I'm certain that I will have to trade off pay, in some cases, for more control of my time, to write about something that really turns me on, but that's okay. I'm already planning for that when I estimate my sources of income in "retirement."

Perhaps your career offers that possibility, too. As you read through the following chapters, you'll meet a high school assistant superintendent who turned personal fitness trainer for the 50+ in Delaware, and a retired dog warden who has a hankering to drive and dons a cap to chauffeur kids to proms in Pittsburgh, Pennsylvania, among other part-time gigs. You'll read how a onetime Nevada state worker now plies his language skills as a Spanish translator and interpreter for Latinos in medical and legal settings in Reno, Nevada. And you'll smile as a retired Ohio pharmacist tells you how he has eased into retirement by working spring training with the Cleveland Indians baseball club in Arizona during the winter months.

Finding a job today starts with knowing where to look, what kind of work schedule you're shooting for, and what new skills and certifications you might need to add to your kit. The people you will meet in this book have done that successfully, and you can, too. My hope is that you will be inspired by why they love their jobs to find one you love, too, in this next stage of life.

Keep in Mind That Nothing is Forever
You may wind up doing lots of different jobs in your 50+ years. You may want a job for a season, for a few years to gradually unwind into retirement, or even for a few hours a week. Then too, you may be looking for a job that really does turn into full-blown second career.

I also wouldn't be surprised if you test a number of different kinds of jobs to find what you really shine at or want to do in the years ahead. You may even strategically build an income stream from a tapestry of work you enjoy and are skilled at doing.

Be patient. It can take a little time and you may need to re-train. For Cheryl Champagne, her hunt for her next job meant starting with a part-time job at one charity and a fellowship at *Encore!Hartford,* a workforce development program targeted to seasoned corporate and public-service professionals seeking to transition to professional and managerial employment in the nonprofit sector. That included a crash course in nonprofit management and finance (44 hours of classroom time at the University of Connecticut, two months in the field). She turned it into a position as a full-time fiscal analyst at Key Human Services, a Hartford nonprofit.

Work is not a four-letter word. It doesn't even have to be work in the traditional sense of eight-hour days. It can be, of course. But there are great jobs with flexible schedules that will keep you alive intellectually, financially, and spiritually.

Navigating today's job market can be tricky for older workers. I'm not going to sugarcoat that. Ageism is real and the job market in recent years has been challenging for workers of all ages. I'm here to help. With some smart planning and legwork, you can land the perfect job or weave together a quilt of jobs.

In these pages, you will discover the ultimate guide to great jobs, where to find them, pay ranges, and qualifications needed. I'll give you the action steps to take to find a job that works for you.

With that in mind, each chapter provides

short profiles of 50+ workers who have found a new stage of work life, sometimes in a new field, but many times by tweaking what they have already been doing, pulling from their skills honed in a previous work life. In doing so, they transition into meaningful work as a consultant, a temporary worker, or even an entrepreneur, finally breaking free to start a business.

I've divided the book into two sections.

In Part One, "Great Jobs," I provide 10 chapters that run the bases from part-time jobs, seasonal jobs, holiday jobs, and snowbird jobs to night owl jobs, retail and hospitality jobs, nonprofit jobs, work-at-home jobs, and more. As AARP's Jobs Expert, I have developed this material through extensive reporting and interviews conducted for my "Great Jobs for Retirees" column that appears monthly at AARP.org. The pressing need to find these kinds of jobs is evidenced by the more than one million visitors who click on the columns each month to find job suggestions and insider advice. Quite frankly, that's astounding to me.

There's something here for everyone, a virtual smorgasbord. You'll discover plenty of ideas to spur your imagination about how you can make the most of your talents to create work that, well, works for you.

Jobs held by older Americans tend to be more professional, according to an analysis done by Urban Institute researchers. More than one in three are in managerial, business, or other professional occupations. You'll find lots of those here.

But you'll also find a large selection of the jobs geared for someone who wants a little income, but doesn't want to do much heavy lifting.

You will find that many offer flexible schedules — a week, a month, a few months a year, or even on-again, off-again contract work — which means that three weeks at the lake house in the summer is still possible. If you want full-time work, many part-time positions have that promise.

Each job description follows this format: the nitty-gritty, median pay, hours, and qualifications needed, with a smattering of job-hunting tips tossed in. A handful of broad-based jobs may fall under two different categories. For example, tutoring in some iteration appears in seasonal jobs, as well as in great jobs for retired teachers. In truth, it could fall into the part-time category as well.

Pay ranges, which will vary based on factors such as experience and where you live, are derived for the most part from U.S. Department of Labor data. Don't be deterred by the "median" wage figures. Pay scales are finicky and vary widely from employer to employer and city to city and by your experience. They are listed here as a guideline.

The resource section in the back of the book is where you'll find a listing of web sites, job boards, and books to help your search.

In Part Two, "The Great Jobs Workshop" I deliver the professional advice and strategies I've been doling out as a career transition, retirement, and personal finance expert and journalist for more than two decades. Most recently, I've been fortunate to reach out to job seekers as a *Forbes* magazine contributing editor and Forbes .com "Second Verse" columnist. Some of the material here has been tested out there first. It has allowed me to get a conversation going with my thousands of readers to see what kind of advice they want and what really helps.

My tips also stem from the worries that I hear from audience members when the lights come up at the end of one of my keynote speeches, or when a listener calls into a radio talk show where I have been a guest to ask a question, or when someone calls or e-mails for one-on-one career guidance. These shout-outs for advice convinced me that there's a blazing need for this kind of straight-forward career guidance.

A portion of the new research found here emerged as part of my MetLife Foundation Journalists in Aging Fellowship, a project of New America Media and the Gerontological Society of America.

I have designed this section so you can dip in and out of the chapters as they apply to your situation. You'll find tips on resume writing, what you need to know to land a job at a nonprofit, and how to find a mentor (besides me) to guide you in this new chapter of your work life. While not every chapter will speak to your situation, I'm confident that you will find the direction you need right now.

At the very heart of it, I wrote this book to help you find the work you love. The rest will follow.

Bottom line: Brush off that resume. Let's go job hunting!

PART I
GREAT JOBS

Great. That's a word that fascinates me.

We all know what it means to have a great time. You can have a great time at a Rolling Stones concert, at a friend's 50th birthday party, or on a Caribbean vacation. But can you have a *great* job?

Is there work that's really great? You bet. But what constitutes greatness is up to you to interpret and define in context to your own life.

For me, it's something I lose track of time doing. Something that, well, doesn't feel like work. It doesn't have to be a passion, but it's nice if it is. It should be something that adds to your life — whether it's a financial or psychic boost.

Finding a job that works for you, rather than the other way around, is a goal worth pursuing. In the next 10 chapters, I will take you down that path of discovery.

You'll meet people who have retired and

are working in part-time jobs they take real pleasure in — jobs that help build the bank account until they no longer need, or want, to work. And you'll meet those who may have left one career, but have set off on another one with just as much determination.

Most of the people I've interviewed for this book told me that flexibility is *the* essential ingredient in a job. It's the ability to work from home, part-time, or for just a few months a year that they're after. As a result, I've geared several chapters to jobs that fall into that category. The lion's share of these jobs, however, can easily ramp up to full-time schedules, if desired.

The salary ranges I've listed are just that. Depending on your skills, where you live, and your previous work experience, what you might get paid could be quite a bit higher. I've used these figures to give you a general idea. Qualifications, too, will vary from employer to employer. The details I suggest are standards in many occupations, but everything is open to poetic license, in my view.

So I encourage you to read through all the jobs I have profiled to see which ones capture your attention, fit with your personality and skills. Be creative with your job search; be willing to experiment, to try something new, to be humbled by being a beginner again. Use this time to open your mind to possibilities.

There is an underlying theme here: A great job is not just something you imagine — it is something you can actually *do*. In the following chapters, you will learn how to jump-start your great job search, and you will realize that every job is an opportunity for inspiration. My aim is to generate ideas and "why not?" ideas for you.

CHAPTER 1
GREAT PART-TIME JOBS

A part-time job is just that, a few hours a day, or a couple of days a week or a month. The jobs I've listed in this chapter tend to be available year-round and can even be ramped up to full-time positions in some cases.

But if the possibilities listed here aren't quite what you're after, keep reading. You might find one that you can negotiate for part-time duties that calls out to you in Chapter 2, "Great Seasonal Jobs," Chapter 3, "Great Holiday Jobs," or Chapter 4, "Great Snowbird Jobs." In general, though, from my experience, the jobs you'll find in those narrower genres will lean toward full-time for a short burst of a few months a year. In today's job market, anything is negotiable. So don't be afraid to ask, or create your own hours on the go, as bloggers Jose and Jill Ferrer did.

When the Ferrers retired from telecommunications careers that spanned nearly three decades at AT&T, they sold their townhouse in Randolph, New Jersey, for about $360,000 and hit the road.

Since 2005, they've traveled full-time, from Oregon to New Mexico to Florida and points in between at the wheel of their 40-foot Country Coach Allure motor home (paid for with cash). A Harley-Davidson Heritage Softail motorcycle, a Saturn car, and two bicycles are also on board.

"We're living a lifestyle that enables us to move around as we choose," says Jill. "We usually take our time — spending at least a few days and more likely a week or more in an area. We fully intend to get to all of the national parks."

The couple planned carefully for retirement. For five years before retiring, they lived off one of their $100,000-a-year salaries, saving the other one. They contributed the maximum to their 401(k) plans and rolled them over into Individual Retirement Accounts (IRAs) once they retired. They expect to eventually supplement their savings with Social Security. "We're hopeful that we have saved enough to last us in a retirement that includes frugal living and part-time work," Jill explains.

For the road warrior couple, that part-time work is a web site and blog dedicated to the RV lifestyle. "We were seeking something we could do on the road to make some extra income," says Jill. "We created Your RV Lifestyle (your-rv-lifestyle.com) as a site where we could share tips, lessons learned, and travel experiences."

And it has worked. With both a laptop and a desktop in the motor home, they use a wireless data plan with an air card for Internet access. On average, they try to do something on the site every day: a blog, a new page, or an updated page.

The payoff: They earn a small commission on products sold through the web site — affiliate programs related to the RV lifestyle, such as the Good Sam Club, the Family Motor Coach Association, RVBookstore .com, and so on — that are promoted on the site. They also get a cut when visitors click on Google Adsense ads displayed on the relevant pages.

"For now, as we balance various aspects of our life, we are happy to earn a little extra money — about $700 a month — from the site," Jill says. "And we know the potential is there to grow our web site business further."

For a less nomadic approach, consider Sue Walbert, who retired in her early sixties from her position as head librarian at Fauquier High School in Warrenton, Virginia, but wasn't ready to quit working altogether. "I was okay with the idea of retiring, but I didn't want to not work at all," she says. "And I definitely wanted to keep my earnings going."

Her solution: a part-time job at the library. Walbert arranged to clock in two days a week through a job-sharing arrangement with a colleague who also wanted to cut back on hours. The sweetener: her pre-retirement hourly wage and pay for sick and personal days.

She also picked up work as a part-time bookkeeper helping out with monthly billing for a local horse boarding and training business, where she stables her own horse. "I've always been good with numbers, so I enjoy it," she says. Working on the computer, she admits, has been challenging.

Using your expertise as a consultant is another big draw for part-timers who go the self-employed route. When Kate Carmel retired at age 62 from auction house Phillips de Pury & Co. in New York City, she hung out her shingle as a certified art appraiser, serving buyers, sellers, and collectors who need special appraisals to claim tax deductions for donations of art.

Surprisingly, even with a graduate degree in art history and 35 years in the art world, including a stint as chief curator of the American Craft Museum (now the Museum of Arts & Design), Carmel needed more education to get certified. So at the urging of a co-worker (who was, fortuitously, president of the Appraisers Association of America, which issues a certification recognized by the IRS), she began taking courses at New York University well before she retired from the auction house. It took her two years of part-time study. "Many people claim to be appraisers and aren't," Carmel explains. "There are legal documents that you have to know how to prepare. The IRS pays attention. It requires a rigorous attention to detail to not raise any red flags."

Today, Carmel charges $250 to $350 an hour and her business is still growing. Her specialty is 19th- and 20th-century decorative art, a field with a finite number of genuine authorities, which gives her an edge.

The workflow is erratic, which can make travel planning difficult. "There are times when I'm really stressed, say, two or three estate clearance projects go into warehouses. I can spend six weeks with someone uncrating, photographing, and measuring. Then there will be a quiet period," she says.

But Carmel isn't complaining. The appraisal business, she says, gives her days structure and focus and provides a way to stay current with the art world she loves. "I can't imagine not working," she adds.

All of these "retirees" have found a unique way to make money without the full-time constraints holding them back from savoring their new stage of life. If you're like me, their stories have sparked some ideas of ways you can start planning what you might like to do, too.

Next: Here are great part-time jobs to consider.

Librarian Assistant/Aide

The nitty-gritty: Duties might include fielding questions, shelving books, helping patrons check out, tracking overdue material, and sending notices, as well as cataloging and keeping an eye out for lost and damaged items.

The hours: Schedules vary widely. Big libraries, or those on university campuses, tend to keep the doors open 24 hours a day, while small, local libraries might offer limited day and evening hours.

Median pay range: Small libraries can be cash-strapped and rely on volunteers, but at colleges, large city locations, and specialty niche libraries, pay generally ranges from $7.69 to $17.82 per hour. Those figures can more than double, depending on experience and where you live.

Qualifications: Experience working in libraries is desirable, as is an undergraduate or master's degree in library science. Larger libraries favor research skills using library resources, databases, and other tools, along with the ability to get along with the various denizens of the library. Some skills that will help: Knowledge of word processing, data entry, and online searching; ability to keep accurate records; understanding of library operations; and general secretarial skills. Love of books is a given.

Next: Do you have a knack for managing a budget?

Alumni Event Planning

The nitty-gritty: Multitasking can take on a whole new meaning in this position. This is detail-oriented work that requires lots of behind-the-scenes labor leading up to a major event, such as a class reunion or campus conference. You could be scheduling speakers, drafting a program agenda, registering guests, coordinating transportation, and setting up audio/visual equipment. You might handle contract negotiations to book off-campus venues and hire outside parties such as photographers, musicians or florists. Now and then you might take the show on the road to alums in their hometowns.

The hours: These can really pile up as the big day approaches and during the event itself, which is often on a weekend or evening.

Median pay: $21.76 per hour.

Qualifications: Ease with computers, including social media such as Facebook and LinkedIn, and a knack for managing a budget. Experience in hospitality, catering, or public relations will help. Some colleges offer continuing education courses in event planning; the Convention Industry Council offers the Certified Meeting Professional (CMP) credential, a certification for meeting and convention planners.

Next: Handy with a calculator? You'll excel at this next job.

Bookkeeper

The nitty-gritty: In small businesses, bookkeepers handle a full sweep of financial recordkeeping. You might take care of purchasing office supplies and processing payroll. Other duties can include establishing and maintaining inventory database systems, tracking accounts receivable and accounts payable, maintaining checking and savings accounts, producing financial reports, following up on delinquent accounts, and overseeing audits and reviews.

The hours: Vary by business. Frequently limited to one week mid-month and one at the end of the month for invoicing or bill-paying functions.

Median pay range: Generally $10.23 per hour to $24.25, but $50 or more is possible, depending on advanced training.

Qualifications: A degree in accounting is desirable. A Certified Public Accountant (CPA) certification is best. Relevant experience or formal training in accounting/auditing services is a plus. But experience with managing a broad range of financial matters for a company, nonprofit, or other organization can qualify you. This is a skill that transfers seamlessly from one industry to another. Other key skills: data entry, detail-oriented, and adept with financial and related computer software.

Job hunting tips: Check out the American Institute of Professional Bookkeepers, aipb.org, for job listings. The group also offers a bookkeeper certification, as does the National Association of Certified Public Bookkeepers (nacpb.org). Community colleges and universities in your area are good places to look for continuing education offerings. New York University's School of Continuing Education and Professional Studies, for example, offers a Professional Certificate in Bookkeeping.

Next: CPR training and a good bedside manner are a plus for this next job.

Personal and Home-Care Aide

The nitty-gritty: Personal care and home health care aides are projected to be the two fastest-growing occupations through this decade, according to the U.S. Bureau of Labor Statistics' 2012–2013 *Occupational Outlook Handbook.* Those positions are relatively low paid — with median annual salaries of around $20,000 — and entry-level jobs don't require a high-school diploma.

You typically help elderly, ill, or disabled people with everyday activities ranging from bathing and getting dressed to running errands and taking clients to appointments. Other duties might include light housekeeping, companionship, grocery shopping, meal preparation, and medication monitoring. A word of caution: Some positions require lifting patients and lots of time on your feet. If you have physical limitations, ask about the requirements of a specific client before signing on.

Jobs for private families, assisted living facilities, and hospices are often booked through a home-care agency.

The hours: Vary, depending on what

the clients and their families need. If you're working at someone's home, three or four hours a day, two or three days a week, might be all that's required.

Median pay range: There tends to be a lot of turnover, so job openings are plentiful, especially helping the elderly in-home, as well as at assisted living and hospice facilities. Expect generally $7.36 per hour to $12.45, but $35 or more per hour is possible, depending on experience and certification.

Qualifications: Some employers may require a Certified Nursing Assistant (CNA) certification. CPR training and a driver's license are helpful, too. Good bedside manner is a must.

Every state has different requirements for a CNA certification, so check with your Board of Nursing for details. A CNA may also be known as a nurse's aide, home health aide, or even a patient care technician. Nursing homes and health care facilities may offer classes, as do community colleges and the Red Cross (redcross .org). You can check with your local Red Cross chapter to see if it offers classes. In Philadelphia, Pennsylvania, for example, the Southeastern Pennsylvania Chapter of the American Red Cross offers a four-week Nurse Assistant Training program for $1,300 in Philadelphia and in the suburb of Lansdale.

Next: If you like working with your hands, this next job is for you.

HandyJack/HandyJill

The nitty-gritty: If you tackle this as a self-employed, fix-it-up service, figure on a smorgasbord of odd jobs that range from tightening loose door handles to repairing running toilets. It can be a mix of woodworking, plumbing, electrical, and even painting projects. You'll find more structured opportunities with building owners who hire part-time workers to perform basic maintenance. This is one job, even on a part-time basis, that requires a certain level of fitness and stamina. You'll also want to be on a first-name basis with the manager of your local hardware store!

The hours: If it's your own business, you can call the shots, even working weekends-only. Part-time schedules for building maintenance will depend on the owners' needs. Some employers might prefer to have you on call for emergencies, while others might like to have you on-site and available to residents during specific hours.

Median pay range: $10 to $20 an hour, and up to $50 for certain custom work.

Qualifications: Be competent in various aspects of home improvement, have your own tools, be self-motivated, and have good customer-service skills. Some states may require you to have a contractor's, electrician's or plumber's certificate, depending on the project. And clients might require you to be licensed, bonded, and insured.

Job hunting tips: If you want to formalize your business, tap into the U.S. Small Business Administration (sba.gov) under licenses for help on how to get started.

Next: Have a knack for medical terms? This next job might just click.

Medical Assistant
The nitty-gritty: Administrative tasks in doctors' offices are usually the bulk

of the workload. In essence, you're performing front-office duties, such as checking in patients, verifying insurance information, answering telephones, scheduling appointments, and typing. You may also be the one who maintains supplies. Some assistants help physicians with procedures and prepare medical records. If you have the training, you may perform direct patient care such as conducting an EKG, collecting specimens, caring for wounds, administering medications, and checking vital signs.

The hours: Varies by practitioner, but generally weekdays.

Median pay range: Generally $9.98 to $19.21 per hour, but can go up to $25-plus depending on location and experience.

Qualifications: Some employers permit you to learn on the job, but a certificate of training from a nationally recognized Medical Assistant Program or national certification as a Certified Medical Assistant is preferred. Related experience can sometimes serve in lieu of formal training and/or certification. Knowledge of medical terminology is useful. The sight of blood shouldn't make you squeamish.

Next: Have professional expertise in a specific area? Try consulting.

Project-Based Consultant

Nitty-gritty: This requires top-level expertise and self-starter initiative. Most independent contractors parachute in to problem-solve or work on a specific project. You might work for an intense period, then take time out for several weeks or even months. Small and fast-growing companies looking for experienced employees who can tackle a range of duties are great sources of work. Drawback: slow payments at times, and projects that run longer than expected or don't begin on schedule. This line of work is best for those who aren't afraid to jump into the deep end and start swimming fast.

Median pay range: $65 to $125 per hour.

Qualifications: Consultants with a track record in finance, management, health care, and information technology are sought after, but even more esoteric areas like art appraisal can fall

46

under this job description.

Job hunting tips: The trick to landing a project is tapping fearlessly into your professional network. Past employers are a good first stop when you're looking for a consulting gig. Contact ex-colleagues and clients for help finding great opportunities. For leads, you might get involved with the local Rotary or a regional small business association.

Next: Inspired by an eco-friendly job?

Green Building Consultant

The nitty-gritty: If you're genuinely interested in building a post-retirement career with a green bent, it's worth the time and effort to head back to the classroom. In general, a background in architecture, engineering, and construction will provide a firm foundation. Older buildings, in particular, are getting serious facelifts. States, counties, and cities are offering incentives targeted for green building projects. You probably need a grasp of (or the burning desire to learn) the technical aspects of building construction, say, the nature of leaky windows, the best ways to use natural lighting, energy-efficient heating and air-conditioning systems (HVAC), plus water-smart features such as low-pressure faucets and toilets.

Median pay range: Hourly rates can run between $35 to $150-plus, according to Indeed.com.

Qualifications: The Leadership in Energy and Environmental Design (LEED) organization offers a certification program that leads to a credential as a green building specialist. That's your calling card to offer strategic advice on a wide range of building projects. The Green Building Certification Institute provides information, as does its parent organization, the U.S. Green Building Council (usgbc.org).

Next: Are you a passionate writer with a knack for computers?

Blogger

The nitty-gritty: Most bloggers are making very little per month. Little wonder. There's lots of competition out there for eyeballs. By the end of 2011, there were 39 million Tumblr blogs and 70 million WordPress blogs

48

running on the Internet, according to Pingdom.com, which tracks Internet growth, and the number is growing exponentially. By the end of July 2012, WordPress users were producing about 500,000 new posts a day, according to the wordpress.com web site.

It is possible, though, to break through. An income stream comes from steadily building a following through referrals and generating income from the ads on your page. You can also make money by selling merchandise directly — from books to T-shirts. You can sign up for Google AdSense (Google.com/adsense), which allows Google to place ads on your web site, depending on your blog content. You get paid a small fee for each time someone clicks on an ad. With an Amazon Associates affiliate program (https://affiliate-program .amazon.com), you can create an online store for Amazon products, and you get paid an advertising fee when someone makes a purchase through your site's link. Chitika is another income stream to check out.

How much income they produce varies by blog. Developing traffic flow (and money) to your blog is time-consuming. You can't just come up with a few pithy posts on a whim every so often and expect visitors to show up with any consistency. It takes discipline. Use Facebook, LinkedIn, Google+, and Twitter to get the word out.

The hours: Flexible. It's tough to measure how long it takes someone to write a post of around 800 words. It might take three or four hours. The real money-hungry bloggers log in full-time schedules of 40 hours or more a week managing their blogs. While that's heavy duty, you should plan to blog at least three times a week. You also need to keep tabs on the business side — managing display ads and product sales adds up to a few hours a week.

Median pay range: The majority of bloggers make less than $100 a month from their sites. But the opportunity is there to earn more. Some bloggers produce more than one blog, which antes up income. There are bloggers who pull in more than $100,000, but they're the exception.

Qualifications: At the heart of it you'll

need passion about a micro-niche that you really know something about, decent writing skills, and the commitment to keep feeding your site with fresh content. If you have the chops, there are broad-based media sites, for example, that will give you a place to hang your hat and pay you a fee based on the number of page views your blog gets each month, a set monthly fee, or a per-word payment. As a professional financial journalist, for example, I have been able to establish a blog on Forbes .com and another on NextAvenue.org to generate monthly revenue. But you don't have to be a journalist at all to blog. You just need expertise and something to say . . . with attitude. For Forbes, which now has more than 1,000 bloggers, that can be in the areas of financial planning or accounting, travel savvy, even horse racing.

A successful blog is built on subject matter that's valuable to people interested in the precise topic. Computer skills are a must, and knowing how to post photos legally and YouTube clips is helpful. You have an edge if you know how to use keywords and other online links to lure people to your web site via search engines such as Bing, Google, and Yahoo.

Next: Enjoy helping others? You may like this job.

Personal Assistant

The nitty-gritty: Name it and you might be asked to do it: organize bills, papers and appointment calendars; accompany someone to doctor appointments; pay bills; handle laundry duties; run errands; cart around children; walk the dog; track and file medical bills and insurance payments; make meals; shop for groceries. The list of to-dos will depend on your client's needs. In essence, you're a one-stop shop. You might be hired by adult children who live out of the area to be their eyes and ears, and keep track of how their parents are doing.

Median pay range: You can probably charge hourly fees that range from $9.57 to $24.96, according to payscale .com.

The hours: Flexible, depending on your client's needs.

Qualifications: There are no formal training courses or certifications for this business. You might need to be physically fit to handle some requests you'll get. People with Alzheimer's will need special attention, so some nursing or caregiving skills are useful. Emergency medical technician training might come in handy. If you'll be behind the wheel, you'll need a driver's license in good standing. All in all, the key is building trust and being patient, flexible, and reliable. You may be asked to be bonded for the client's protection if you will be providing services in someone's home. Many clients will request a background check and references.

Job hunting tips: Advertise your services in community newspapers, online neighborhood list-serves, craigslist, even bulletin boards in apartment buildings, retirement or adult community residences, grocery stores, and libraries.

Next: Are you good with kids and have a love of sports?

Athletic Coach/Umpire/Referee
The nitty-gritty: This one's for the kid in all of us. Check into a coach, referee,

umpire, or scorekeeper posts, in high school programs, various youth and amateur leagues, parks departments, recreational and church leagues, and soccer clubs. Expect plenty of time standing, and for outdoor sports, prepare for the elements. Travel is usually part of the job, but it's probably a scoot across town. If you're blowing a whistle, you better brace yourself for the possibility of verbal strip downs (parental ire).

The hours: These fluctuate widely by sport and organization. Coaches can figure three hours or so for late afternoons, five days a week, plus weekend days in season. Umpires, referees, and scorekeepers usually work two to three hours per game. Figure on once a week for two or three games in an afternoon or evening.

Median pay range: For a coaching position at a school, $3,000 to $5,000 per season is possible. Umpires and referees can make $30 to $50 per game Independent leagues or private travel teams might pay $50 to $75 per game.

Qualifications: You need to be good with children, possess moderate physical fitness, and have an overall knowledge of the game. Specific education, training, and licensing requirements for coaches and officials vary greatly by the level and type of sport. Some entry-level positions for coaches require only experience gleaned as a participant in the sport. Umpires and referees usually are required to attend a training course and pass a test. You can gain experience by volunteering for intramural, community, and recreational league competitions.

If you have a hankering to umpire, check out your local umpire association. For American Legion high school games, contact your local division and attend a certifying clinic. There are one-day refresher classes and full courses with several sessions, plus an American Legion exam. Some leagues require that certification be renewed periodically. Estimated cost: $50 application, plus $7.50 for a rulebook, $5 for a flipping coin. You may need to pass a background check and applicable drug tests. Ask your local high schools, parks departments, recreational and church leagues, and soccer clubs if they offer a club-certified referee or umpire class. For soccer, you might need FIFA certification.

For additional resources, contact the National Association of Sports Officials, naso.org.

Next: Do you have teaching experience and a lot of patience?

Teacher's Aide

The nitty-gritty: Kid-central. This post can take some nerves of steel and patience, but the rewards are plentiful. It can be frustrating for some aides to have to defer to the guidance of the teacher in charge, so you need to have a good rapport and working relationship. The teacher needs to respect and value what you bring to the classroom. If not, it's a bust. Be prepared for some grunt work — clerical duties such as grading papers, recording grades, setting up equipment, and entering computer data.

One of the best aspects is one-on-one tutoring for a student who needs special help, or has a disability that requires individual attention. These are bonding moments of giving back that are worth more than a paycheck. While some of the school day is spent standing, walking, or kneeling, the lion's share is sitting while working with students. Teacher assistants also supervise students in the cafeteria, schoolyard, and hallways, or on field trips. About 37 percent work part time.

The hours: Three to five days a week, six to seven hours per day during the traditional school year (eight to nine months). Summer school hours may be available in some districts.

Median pay: $23,220/school year.

Qualifications: On-the-job training combined with a high school diploma. Some states or school districts may require additional education beyond high school. A college degree, related coursework in child development, and previous experience helping special education students can open up job opportunities. Self-starters who can multitask and work independently are highly valued.

Fluency in a second language, especially Spanish, is in demand. Many schools require previous experience in working with children and a valid driver's license. Most require you to pass a background check. For more information, go to American Federation of Teachers, National Education Association, and National Resource Center for Paraprofessionals. The promise: Gold stars.

Next: Do you like to impress others with enthralling historical facts?

Tour Jobs

The nitty-gritty: Imagine steering a group of curious tourists around historical monuments in Washington, D.C., on a sunny, cherry-blossom day in April. That's particularly fun if you're a history buff and have a knack for storytelling and showmanship. You need to have a mind for remembering dates and historical facts. You also must interact easily with everyone — from excitable school kids on a field trip to older people hailing from all over the globe.

Tour guide jobs pop up in various places that attract visitors. You might lead visitors through points of historical or local interest, pretzel factories, wineries, breweries, and more, doling out tidbits of information in a narrative format. The downside is that it can be hard on the feet and the vocal cords, and the patter can become stifling rote. Your job is to dig down for a fresh and energetic performance each round. Many of these jobs are walking tours, although you may land one where you drive a vehicle, or go with a group on a park shuttle or monorail system.

Depending on the assignment, you might have to stand up to eight hours per day, or walk, and climb stairs. Plus, you'll need to be sharp-eyed to visually monitor guests to ensure compliance with security and safety rules. Less demanding openings, such as ticket-takers, program sellers, or cashiers, are also generally available.

The hours: Varying schedules including days, evenings, and weekends. It might be difficult to receive time off around peak tourist times, such as holidays and school vacations.

Median pay range: Hourly wage: $7.72 to $18.87.

Qualifications: Tour guides often receive on-the-job training. The academic background required for a position varies according to the venue. Best skill: the ability to hang on to historical facts, dates, and anecdotes, and relate that information to visitors in a compelling way.

Some cities require licensing, and applicants may have to pass a written exam covering factual knowledge of specific locations and city history. Some community colleges and universities offer online and short-term courses in tour and travel-related occupations.

Your hidden gem: Knowing where George Washington really slept.

Next: Are you a charming people person with a flexible schedule?

Convention Center Jobs

The nitty-gritty: Convention centers in major cities can be well-springs for a wide range of part-time jobs with various skill requirements. The panoply of shows rolls in and rolls out. Set 'em up and tear 'em down. Each week, the venues play host to various industry events from exotic food to car and boat shows, as well as concerts and even sports competitions.

The demand for workers is a moving target — the perfect scenario if you're looking for the occasional paycheck.

Some part-time jobs include nurse, parking lot attendant, parking lot cashier, set-up worker/cleaner, usher, and information booth attendant. Many of these jobs require little to no physical labor. There are also food service opportunities for banquets and special dining events. The center's kitchen facility often hires line cooks and servers on an as-needed basis.

In some towns, outside vendors will lease space inside a convention center and staff-up for each event. These positions can range from being a barista for a coffee stand to working at a concession stand. Sign on with one of these businesses, and the vendor will call and ask your availability depending on weekly needs.

The hours: The work schedules are irregular, and no minimum number of hours is guaranteed. Work is typically available on all days of the year, including holidays. Evening and night hours may be required depending on the job.

Median pay range: Typically $10 to $20 an hour.

Qualifications: It's all about the customer, so people skills matter. Working knowledge of the event industry —

including trade shows, conventions, consumer shows, concerts, athletic events, and meetings — is a plus for some positions. Pre-employment drug screening and background checks are common.

Job hunting tips: Many convention centers outsource their personnel management to companies that specialize in doing this for large convention and event centers, and hire locals to come in and do specific jobs for individual events. You might stop by at an event and ask booth operators about future openings. Your local convention and sports and entertainment agency should be able to provide employment information.

Next: Not afraid to get your hands dirty? Read on.

Pet Groomer

The nitty-gritty: Primping a pooch (or cat) runs the gamut from bathing to nail-trimming and brushing, to cleaning ears and clipping coats. You've got to be detail-oriented and love the down and dirty work. It takes some stamina, too. The work can include kneeling, bending, and lifting. The result is worth it when you tie that bright bow on a collar and see the owners' smiles when their pal rushes out to greet them. You might work out of a kennel, pet shop, your own home, or even a mobile grooming van.

Median pay range: $7.76 to $17.80 an hour, but an experienced groomer might earn $25 to $30 an hour, grooming eight to 10 dogs per day. Tips are an extra perk and will vary.

Qualifications: Although pet groomers typically learn by training under the direction of an established groomer, they can also attend one of 50 state-licensed grooming schools, according to the Bureau of Labor Statistic's *Occupational Outlook Handbook.* The length of each program varies depending on the school and training offered. The National Dog Groomers Association of America offers certification as a groomer and can provide a list of state-licensed schools.

Next up, for every season, there's a job.

Chapter 2
Great Seasonal Jobs

Not ready or willing to commit to year-round employment? Plenty of jobs run the course of a season — spring, summer, fall, or winter — and can pay bills and keep you busy.

Sixty-something Jim Brush drives a stretch limo filled with tuxedo-clad prom goers in the spring and decked-out wedding parties in the summer. Pay is typically $18 an hour, and the extra cash is welcomed. Although he and his wife have two grown children, and he receives a pension, they need a little more to meet their mortgage. Brush, who lives in Pittsburgh, retired five years ago from his position as a Pennsylvania state dog warden, where he had worked for 25 years. In his preretirement days, Brush spent plenty of time in the car cruising county roads to inspect kennels and patrolling for stray pets. Knowing his way around comes in handy today.

Besides driving, Brush fills his year with other seasonal employment. Snow removal is in high demand in Pittsburgh's blustery winters, and he does landscaping during the spring and fall months. He's not set on seasonal gigs, though. He also chauffeurs passengers for nonseasonal events, such as airport runs. And he even tends bar from time to time. "I want to keep busy earning money while I still have the energy and the desire," he says.

If summertime work suits you best, from national parks to ballparks to amusement parks, seasonal hiring heats up at a whole host of summer vacation playgrounds. For many retirees, this is the perfect time to scoop up short-term work that lasts anywhere from a few weeks to a few months.

Rich Bartkowski's work, for example, extends through the baseball season. A couple of days a week from April to November, the diehard baseball fan dons his Baltimore Orioles polo shirt and heads from his home in Perry Hall, Maryland, to Oriole Park at Camden Yards, where he leads 75-minute walking ballpark tours. Bartkowski, 68, recites fun stats and team facts as he strolls through the stadium. "It's dream job time," he says. "I get paid to be outside and talk about baseball."

Bartkowski started working for the Orioles as a tour guide in 2002, not long after he retired from a 34-year career with Constellation Energy. "My wife didn't want me sitting around the house, and I wanted something to do," he says.

You have to be fairly fit and like to walk . . . and, of course, not be bothered by all kinds of weather, he says. The best part of the job: meeting and talking to people. "Everyone's a kid when they come to the ballpark," he says.

Now Bartkowski trains most of the new guides and leads two tours a day. Until last year, he also worked in the box office. The Orioles' front office employs 25 tour guides during the season; most of them are retirees, Bartkowski says.

While the $8.50-an-hour pay isn't eye-popping, the perks can be. He gets free tickets for about 20 nonworking games, free parking, and free Orioles shirts and other discounted merchandise to wear on the job. And, yep, all the game day giveaways you desire. Can you say bobbleheads?

While you might not have the passion for baseball or the experience or stamina to sign on as a ski instructor in Squaw Valley or a white-water rafting guide in Colorado, great seasonal jobs are out there that are right for you. Here are some great ones to consider.

Limo Driver

The nitty-gritty: Limo drivers can find work year-round, but their dance card fills up during prom and wedding season from April to June. Routine duties include keeping the car shipshape each day. You'll help passengers into the car, hold open doors, provide umbrellas if it's raining. Loading and unloading heavy luggage can call for some strong muscles. Other drawbacks: Driving for long periods can take a mental toll, especially in crowded city streets. Then, too, remaining seated for several hours at a time isn't as easy as it sounds.

The hours: For weddings and proms, drivers are busy from April to June and usually book in three- to five-hour increments. Proms are evening and night shifts. Weddings vary from morning to night bookings. Other trips are often booked by the hour.

Median pay range: Pay can range from $7.67 to more than $16.84 per hour, though figures vary widely depending on experience, where you live, the number of hours worked, and customer tips.

Qualifications: Most limo companies provide on-the-job training. A good driving record is vital — no more than two moving violations in the past five years, and no reckless or drunk driving violations. If you're 70 or older, insurance restrictions might be a stumbling block. Patience, punctuality, and level-headedness are de rigueur. A basic understanding of auto mechanics can also be useful. To spruce up on your driving skills, check out at AARP's Driver Safety Program.

Next: Do you like cruising college campuses?

Shuttle Bus Driver on Campus

The nitty-gritty: If you like to drive, climb aboard. During the busy fall and spring semesters, the demand for university transportation ramps up, and driving jobs are plentiful. You cruise the campus byways in university transit wheels. The routes are clearly set, and you keep to a regular schedule. You might occasionally have to give directions or help someone on or off the bus.

Heavy traffic is not usually a problem unless it's a city campus. Bad weather can make road conditions dicey. If you drive the night shift, your riders might get a little exuberant. You'll usually be the one in charge of checking the tires, lights, and oil.

Median pay: $13.51 an hour. Range: $8.45 to $20.98 per hour.

Qualifications: You must have a commercial driver's license (CDL) in good standing and undergo some short training that will include a driving course and practice of various maneuvers with a bus. The qualifications for getting a CDL vary by state, but normally include both knowledge and driving tests. Your vision and hearing will be checked too. States have the right to withhold a license from someone who's had a CDL suspended by another state.

Next: Number crunchers, tax season is calling.

Tax Preparer

The nitty-gritty: To prepare annual income tax returns for individuals or small businesses, you typically will want to be an enrolled agent with the Internal Revenue Service. Your job is to help filers avoid penalties, interest, or additional taxes that could result from an examination by the Internal Revenue Service.

The hours: Expect to book plenty of hours between January and the April 15 tax deadline, particularly if you sign up with a tax preparation firm.

Median pay range: $8.70 to $34.35 per hour.

Qualifications: A degree in accounting is helpful, but not required. Computer use is mandatory. You are required to use IRS e-file if you prepare 11 or more returns. Under new IRS (irs.gov) rules, any individual who, for compensation, prepares or assists in the preparation of a tax return or claim for refund must have his or her own Tax Preparer Identification Number, which costs $64.25 per year. Check with the IRS for more guidance. Next, you must pass a competency exam — mandatory for most, but some certified public accountants and others are exempted — to become an IRS registered tax return preparer. Additionally, you must take continuing education courses.

Job hunting tips: Large tax firms, for instance, H&R Block and Jackson Hewitt Tax Service, hire thousands of tax preparers each year to come on board from January until May 1. You usually need to take the firm's income tax course in the fall to prepare. You apply via individual stores. Refresher courses are offered each season. To get your toes wet, you might start by volunteering with the AARP Foundation Tax-Aide Program (aarp.org/money/taxes/aarp_taxaide/). It can offer good experience for those who want to graduate to a paying tax preparer job. Bean counters should apply.

Next: One way to share your teaching expertise outside the classroom.

Tutor

The nitty-gritty: If teaching experience is in your bag of tricks, then you'll find plenty of opportunities in working as a private tutor throughout the year, although the fall opening of school and before major tests is when many opportunities ramp up. Retired teachers, go to Chapter 6 for more information.

71

Some prep firms hire tutors to help teens and adults with standardized tests and professional certification exams. The firms provide tools and training materials. Fall and spring are the top seasons for college-bound kids to take the SAT and ACT aptitude tests. A demand also exists for ongoing private tutoring in a range of subjects to boost student grades.

The hours: Tutoring sessions can last anywhere from an hour after school to three hours on weekends. Private sessions can take place at your place, theirs, the library, or online. Plan to work at least four hours a week.

Median pay range: $10.27 to $24.21 generally, but landing rates higher than $65 and up an hour isn't unusual, if you have expertise.

Qualifications: A background in education and working with students in a classroom is generally a prerequisite. A certified teacher is preferred. That said, professional experience can open doors. There is no certification to be a private tutor. Experts in a range of fields from nursing to finance to law and business may find opportunities, as can those with foreign language skills.

Job hunting tips: You might get your foot in the door by volunteering at a local library. Create a "Tutor" business card and drop it off at nearby school counseling offices to let them know you are available. You might want to post a classified ad in a community newspaper, supermarket jobs board, or online news board. No chalkboard needed.

Next: Expertise in history or geology can help you land this job.

Park Service Employee

The nitty-gritty: Each year the National Park Service as well as state and local parks hire temporary and seasonal employees. You might be in charge of basic tasks like collecting fees at the entry gate, answering visitor questions, and passing out maps and brochures. With a little homework, you might find yourself teaching brief educational programs about the park ecosystem from bear habitats to flora and fauna. Those of you with a fit physique might step it up with trail upkeep responsibilities or guiding tours.

Parks with lodges hire part-time employees to accept reservations, provide concierge-type information, check in guests, and perform other booking functions. Other responsibilities may include maintenance and office work, equipment rental, housekeeping assistance, food and merchandise sales, fee collection, and other general support services.

These types of positions are usually available at most parks and forests and wildlife management areas. There are also guest service and hospitality jobs at park stores and restaurants via Aramark, a national firm that provides facility and concession management under authorization of the National Park Service.

State parks, too, pump up rosters during the tourist months. Each year, for example, the New Jersey State Park Service hires approximately 600 people to fill seasonal jobs from May through September. State park jobs include collecting fees, issuing permits and passes, and directing traffic. Community parks also need help with managing recreational activities such as softball, volleyball, craft programs, and summer day camps.

You might also find jobs at touristy gift shops and restaurants near the parks.

Median pay range: National Parks: $13 to $26-plus an hour. You might opt to work as a National Park Service volunteer, too, where your only pay may be free housing or a pad for your RV.

The hours: From Memorial Day through Labor Day, hiring ramps up. Specific times will vary, but expect regular eight-hour shifts at peak times.

Qualifications: Training is provided for most jobs. A knack for working smoothly with park visitors of all ages may be the most important criterion. A teaching resume or public speaking skills help. Expertise in a particular field — such as history, botany, or geology — can get you in the gate. If you're interested in pursuing a nature guide job, then flora and fauna identification skills are a must.

Job-hunting tips: Keep in mind that if you actually work for the National Park Service and not one of the outside vendors, you will be applying for a federal government job. You may be subject to a security background check. The best way to find a job at a National Park is to go to each park's individual web site, or USAJobs.com, and click on "Employment Opportunities." For a state park opening, check with your state's division of parks and recreation. Hear the call of the wild.

Next: Got a green thumb?

Nursery Worker

The nitty-gritty: It's all about getting dirt under your nails, tending plants, and answering customers' gardening queries. More physically demanding tasks may require cutting and stacking sod, staking trees, packing plants to fill orders, and digging up or moving shrubs and trees.

The hours: Spring and summer are the busiest times. Expect weekend hours.

Median pay range: $7.94 to $12.12 an hour.

Qualifications: Training is on the job. It helps to know the difference between an annual and a perennial, of course, and what plants do best in the shade versus the sun. You might consider taking a master gardener class to boost your resume.

Next: Green gardening, anyone?

Eco-Landscaper

The nitty-gritty: Gardening is not for sissies. It's mostly outdoor work in all kinds of weather. From a purely physical perspective, it means bending, squatting, lifting, and pulling — unless you can hire a brawny assistant to handle those chores. The goal of building these types of "sustainable" gardens is generally to create landscaping that's cheaper to maintain over time, a lofty environmental goal. To do it right, you'll be able to make money-smart choices based on a deep understanding of native plants. Beauty is in the eye of the beholder, so you'll work closely with your clients to create a space that works best for them and the environment.

Median pay range: $8.16 to $17.90-plus an hour. $50 to $90 an hour is possible, depending on experience. Most landscapers opt for a flat rate for an initial design, and then add hourly fees for execution and maintenance.

Qualifications: Understanding of horticulture, including a wide-ranging knowledge of plants and diseases. Drafting a design by hand is generally accepted, although some clients might want to see a computer-design via CAD software. You might consider taking a Master Gardener class to boost your resume. The Ecological Landscaping Association holds an annual conference with workshops and educational sessions. The site provides links to seminars and events held around the country.

Many community colleges and universities offer certificates and degrees in sustainable landscape design. George Washington University's program, for instance, is offered on a series of weekends, and there is an annual landscape design career fair. Check out garden centers in your locale for classes and certificate programs. In Pittsburgh, you can earn a certificate in sustainable horticulture at Phipps Conservatory and Botanical Gardens. The Association of Professional Landscape Designers offers certification to members who have at least four years of experience and submit three projects they have completed for review.

Next: Do you have a love for America's favorite pastime?

Ballparks

The nitty-gritty: The boys (and girls) of summer are calling. Ballparks around the country are scouting for seasonal ushers, ticket takers, box office attendants, ballpark guides, cashiers, bartenders, suite attendants, in-seat servers, concession stand workers, and more. In general, these jobs are not for fans longing to stretch out in the bleachers and marvel at the action on the diamond. Pausing to watch a line drive is permissible, of course, but you're frequently on the move. You'll need to know your way around the ballpark. Some positions can require standing for long stretches and facing the mercurial elements that Mother Nature throws out.

The hours: Flexible schedules are offered. Availability for the majority of home games is often a prerequisite. Days, nights, weekends, and holidays are possible. Average shifts: 3 hours for in-seat food and beer vendors; 4-1/2 hours for guides.

Median pay range: $8 to $11.50 an hour. In-seat food and beer vendors might pull in a minimum $7.40 an hour, plus commissions, for an average $25 an hour.

Qualifications: Managers like signing workers with a love and knowledge of the game. Advance training is provided. An outgoing and fan-friendly personality is essential, especially if you're in a position of meeting and greeting fans as you scan tickets, ushering people to seats, or giving directions to the nearest concession stand. This is show biz. Ticket sellers are expected to understand the seating layout of the ballpark and ticket prices. Background checks will be performed.

Job hunting tips: Tap into your hometown team's official web site for openings. Team-by-team contact information can be found at Major League Baseball's site. Look for your city's team-sponsored job fairs in the spring. Play ball!

Next: Love the open road and the great

outdoors? Look no further.

RV Campgrounds

The nitty-gritty: Got a recreational vehicle (RV) and want to roll? As vacationers flock to campgrounds at theme parks, national and regional parks, marinas, and resorts, RVers can work at a campground in exchange for a free or discounted campsite and full hook-ups. Jobs might include office work, guest check-in, reservations, security, restaurant, groundskeeping, maintenance, handyman work, housekeeping, running social activities and rentals, interpretive guides, and retail sales. Some of these opportunities can be found at government employers, such as Alaska State Parks, U.S. Fish and Wildlife Service, U.S. Bureau of Land Management, and U.S. Army Corps of Engineers.

You might work four days a week at Buffalo Bill Village in Cody, Wyoming, for instance, and have three days off to explore nearby Yellowstone and Grand Teton national parks. Work at the Atlantic Oaks campground on Cape Cod and spend your free time enjoying the beaches, Provincetown, and other seaside communities, with side trips to Martha's Vineyard and Nantucket.

The hours: Vary widely. Some employers might require a four-week to three-month commitment or an agreement to work eight hours a day, two to four days per week.

Median pay range: There are a variety of arrangements in this semibarter opportunity. Pay is typically $7.50 to $10 an hour, but compensation is usually a combo of campsite, hourly wages, store discounts, and laundry allowance.

Qualifications: Past experience in the type of work available helps. Expect on-the-job training if necessary.

Job hunting tips: Go to Workamper .com, a web site and organization that promotes the concept of RVer jobs, connecting prospective employers and employees. Job site CoolWorks.com is one place to start your job hunt. The site has a special section for RVer jobs. This type of job is best for rambling road warriors 10-4.

Next: Enjoy cotton candy and rides? Get paid for reliving your youth.

Amusement Parks

The nitty-gritty: Still got rollercoaster rushes racing through your blood or a cotton candy sweet tooth? Thousands of seasonal gigs are available at amusement and theme parks across the country each summer. But be warned — you may have to elbow out earnest teenagers for the slots.

Jobs run the gamut from rollercoaster ride technician — you make sure riders are seated and strapped in safely and stop and start the ride — to waiting tables to hawking souvenir shirts and unwieldy stuffed animals. There are crowd control and security patrol openings, custodial work picking up trash and repairing benches. And the list goes on from ticket-selling at the entranceway to parking lot attendants and grounds maintenance (such as watering, planting, and pruning). If you have entertainment chops, you might score a role as a dancer or storyteller, even a musician.

The summer heat and humidity can sap you. Expect to slather on the sunscreen and drink lots of water. You may also be required to walk around the park or stand for stretches. In the heat of the day, loud clanging rides filled with screaming passengers, combined with tired and testy customers, can be nerve-jangling.

The hours: Part- and full-time shifts and night and weekends are available.

Median pay range: $8 to $13 an hour. Employees normally have access to free admission and are often given free tickets for friends and family. Discounts on food and beverages, merchandise, and hotel stays, depending on the venue, may be offered, too.

Qualifications: Hiring managers will typically look for areas where you have experience or education. A pleasant and outgoing personality can sweep you to the front of the line. On-the-job training is standard. Good communication skills are prized. Expect background checks and drug tests.

Job hunting tips: Look for local job fairs sponsored by the theme parks in your region. Web sites such as Job-Monkey and CoolWorks have sections dedicated to amusement/theme park jobs. Adrenaline junkies wanted.

Next: Check out this job if you're an animal lover.

Pet Sitter

The nitty-gritty: If you prefer catering to pets rather than people, give me your paw. Pet sitting is a legit business these days. Nearly two-thirds of U.S. households have a pet, and last year they spent an estimated $52 billion on them, an increase from $17 billion in 1994, according to a survey by the American Pet Products Association in Greenwich, Conn.

As vacationers head off for school breaks and summer frolic, someone's got to tend to those members of the family that can't fit (or fit quietly) in the suitcase. The upside: This is a pampered clientele that will be tail-wagging happy to see you.

The level of activity depends on your charge. If it's a canine client, you'll need a certain level of fitness and a love for walking, and perhaps an aptitude for Frisbee tossing. Not so strenuous playtime is required for cats, and less so for hamsters and fish. Clearly, you can't be squeamish about cleaning out kitty litter boxes and picking up after any waste or mess the pet has created on your walks. That comes with the territory. A level head able to handle any veterinary crisis is vital. With animals, you need to be prepared to deal with the unexpected.

Work arrangements differ. If it's a dog or two, the owner may be willing to allow the dog to stay at your home. Other owners will prefer that you make visits to their home once or twice a day to feed and walk dogs, dole out treats, and clean litter boxes, if applicable. Depending on how footloose you are, you might opt to stay overnight at the owner's home. Of course, you'll toss in gratis picking up newspapers and mail, watering plants, and flicking on lights as part of your service. You can work for a pet sitting company or advertise as an independent contractor. Local vets, grooming salons, and pet stores can get the word out about your service.

The hours: Flexible. They can be as little as an hour or two a day, depending on the number of and type of pets you're caring for and the arrangement. Summer vacations, spring breaks, and holidays are peak demand times.

Median pay range: The charge for a single visit to a pet ranges from $10 to $22, depending on the location, and

$45 or more for overnight care. You might charge $25 or so a day if the pet stays overnight at your pad. Expertise with administering medications pays a bonus.

Qualifications: Animal instincts and a reputation for being a responsible pet owner in your own right go a long way in this world. This tends to be a word-of-mouth service. There are no required certifications. That said, if you're interested in getting certified, you can. The National Association of Professional Pet Sitters, for example, offers an at-home certification course online. The course consists of pet care, health, nutrition and behavior, business development and management, and a complete pet first aid course. DogWalker.com, an online directory of dog walkers around the country, offers educational resources for those starting out. You'll probably want to carry personal liability insurance and possibly business insurance and bonding coverage, too. Pet sitting associations such as Pet Sitters International, PetSit LLC, and the National Association of Professional Pet Sitters offer access to plans. Compare rates with an insurance broker.

Job hunting tips: You might consider joining the National Association of Professional Pet Sitters. In addition to certification, the roughly 8,000-member trade association offers a national listing service searchable by ZIP code for pet owners looking for a reliable sitter. You might also consider signing up with a national franchise operator like Fetch! Petcare (fetch petcare.com), or check with your local pet-sitting services advertised in your neighborhood or community paper. Another good way to get the word out is to post your services on a community news board for opportunities. Call this puppy love.

Next: Got team spirit?

Athletic Event Ticket Services

The nitty-gritty: Team spirit counts. If you live near a college or university, these openings tend to pop up during fall and spring semesters. You don't have to dress up as the mascot, but you'll be the one juggling urgent ticket requests from well-heeled donors, eager alumni, university staffers needing a last-minute favor, students and die-hard fans. The work may be by phone, Internet, regular mail, or in-person at a customer service window. The key is a knack for solving the customer's troubles fast. You must also be up to speed on rules — national ones or your own university's. You might supervise interns and student workers. Be sure to clear your weekend social schedule for home games.

Median pay: $10 to $20 per hour.

Qualifications: A background in customer service, administration, and clerical duties; strong oral and written communication skills; basic computer skills.

Next up, hiring shifts to high gear around the holidays.

CHAPTER 3
GREAT HOLIDAY JOBS

When holiday hiring is kicking into high gear, for many retirees, in particular, it's the perfect time to stay busy while pulling in some extra cash for gifts and quite possibly finding employment that'll last beyond New Year's Eve. The retail industry, of course, is a key employer around the holidays. Sales clerk positions at stores and seasonal kiosks are the usual suspects for job hunters, but there are other job opportunities that may not be as obvious.

Bob Dunn's blue eyes twinkle and his cheeks grow rosy when he talks about his seasonal job. No surprise, he's Santa Claus. The 74-year-old retired seafood salesman travels from his home in Dover, Delaware to Norman, Oklahoma to commandeer the jolly man's chair at the Sooner Mall for the holiday season.

He's got the obligatory white beard and hearty "ho-ho-ho." Plus, Dunn has a knack for putting jumpy kids at ease. "I'm a people person. The job is pure joy," Dunn says. "For 46 weeks out of the year, you're just another old man with a white beard, but for that six-week period, you're Santa Claus!"

The contracted pay is enough to keep his reindeer flying in style too. He might fill his stocking with anywhere from $10,000 to $15,000, depending on the contract, for the stretch of 10-hour days (with two meal breaks), which starts the Saturday before Thanksgiving and runs through Christmas Eve. The only day off: Thanksgiving. His hotel room, rental car, and airfare are also covered.

For the past two years, Dunn has been employed by Cherry Hill Photo Enterprises Inc., a privately held company based in Cherry Hill, New Jersey. The company is one of the big players in the Santa business. Last year, it placed more than 350 Santas in malls and department stores in 44 states. The firm negotiates the contract with the venue and provides three costumes per Santa. It also runs its own "Santa University" to train new St. Nicks on how to do the job and prepare for the potential pitfalls.

What does Santa need to watch out for? "Kids throw up," Dunn says. "They cough in your face. There are messy diapers. Some cry, and others pull your beard. Your glasses break. And you've got to protect your nose."

He doesn't mind the fact that the Santa's sleigh takes him away from home and his wife, Kathleen. "The hours are so demanding that it's to my advantage," he says. "I can focus on the job."

Kathleen agrees. "I could join him there," she says. "But we'd have to put the dog in the kennel and pay for someone to keep an eye on the house. It would impact our bottom line."

Dunn's sales training is clearly an asset. Being Santa Claus, he says, "you're still in the sales business." To be a successful Santa, you need to have an upbeat personality and a darn good memory. That's because one of the keys to the job is returning year after year and building a clientele that comes to see you. "The kids remember you, and if you can remember them too, it helps," Dunn says.

Underneath all the packages and tree trimming, though, this is a business of selling photos. That is not Santa's job per se. No bonuses come Dunn's way from the number of "Me and Santa" images sold, but he knows why he's there — to make kids smile.

Last Christmas season, he had his picture

taken roughly 13,200 times — and it wasn't always children. Enlisted military stationed at nearby Tinker Air Force Base stopped by for pictures with Santa to send home, and brawny football players from the University of Oklahoma arrived at his North Pole set. "I sat on their laps," chuckles Dunn.

Ann Heckart, 62, took on a more solitary holiday paycheck. She was hired to work for specialty retailer Brookstone's distribution center in Mexico, Missouri. The job: an 8-hour shift, five days a week in quality control, checking each package to be sure that what's in the carton, say, a Boogie Board, LCD writing tablet, or iPod stand, matches the order slip.

The job suits her. She's detail-oriented, comfortable with numbers, and is able to lift moderately heavy packages, perhaps 15 pounds, if needed. Hours can swing each day, depending on the order volume, but Heckart expects that she'll be working seven days a week when peak shipping hits in mid-December, and then her hours will quickly taper off in early January.

Hourly pay is minimum wage, currently $7.25 per hour, but her checks can swell thanks to overtime. That said, it's neither the money nor the job duties, per se, that keeps her coming back to Brookstone for the holidays. "I just like working," Heckart says.

Whatever your motivation, there's a great holiday job out there that satisfies it, and there's always the potential to extend beyond the peak season. Here are several to consider. If one of these doesn't catch your fancy, you'll find others that fall tangentially into this category in Chapter 2, "Great Seasonal Jobs" and Chapter 4, "Great Snowbird Jobs."

Next: If you've got a jolly old soul, you may enjoy this job.

Santa Claus

The nitty-gritty: How's your kid-side manner? Wearing a Santa suit even made the Grinch grin. But it does have its challenges. For starters, it's not a gig for the weak-kneed. You can expect to have wiggling children of all ages climbing up on your knees to whisper a Christmas list into your ear. And the truth is that some of the little ones can be heavy to lift up and hold steady on your lap. Sitting for hours and smiling in a bulky red suit can be trying.

By all means, don't try to amble over to the food court for lunch. You'll be mobbed. If you're hired by an outside Santa distributor, a firm that places Santas at the thousand-plus enclosed shopping malls, you will probably travel to the mall assigned to you and spend 40-plus days camped out in a nearby motel room equipped with a small fridge and microwave. But if you're prepped, rested, and armed with breath mints, tissues, hand sanitizer, and a kind disposition, it's pure magic.

The hours: For contract Santas, typically six weeks starting at Thanksgiving, 10-hour days with meal breaks. Varies by job for private parties, events, and independent stores.

Median pay range: From $10 an hour to thousands of dollars per season. Contract pay for the 40-day season can range from around $10,000 for a rookie to more than $50,000 for a more experienced player, depending on the mall and location.

Qualifications: It helps if you look the part — older, plump, a white beard, and a jovial laugh. Santas can be of any race — depending on the venue — but they must be male. (There are some openings for Mrs. Santas and

Santa's helpers, too.) Having a natural beard is often a prerequisite. You can dye it if necessary. Padding can be tucked in to get that jelly belly. Expect a criminal background check and drug screening.

Job hunting tips: Contact smaller malls, department stores, photo shops, and special event party planners directly for openings. Check local classified ads. National staffing services typically provide Santa impersonators to the larger malls. Three of the bigger ones: Cherry Hill Photo Enterprises Inc., Worldwide Photography, and Noerr Programs Corp. You'll need to apply online and go for an in-person interview. If they like your look and attitude, you'll slip into costume and makeup for headshots, which are sent to the mall reps for selection. If you're picked, the service will negotiate your contract and send you to Santa school for tips on appropriate behavior and conversations, suggestions for calming kids, and makeup help. Don't forget your flu shot.

Next: Are you cheerful and good with money? Read on.

Retail Sales Cashier

The nitty-gritty: Cha-ching. Smoothly staffing the cash register is one of the most important jobs in the store, especially during the holiday season. While there's a great vibe when people are in the gift-buying spirit, it's often repetitious work. You'll need a grasp of basic math, keen attention to detail, and stamina to be on your feet for hours. At some shops, you'll fold and box items, too, and you might handle returns and exchanges.

Basic duties include entering charges for all items minus the value of any coupons or discounts; taking payment in cash, personal checks, and gift, credit, and debit cards; and requesting additional identification from the customer or calling in for an authorization is standard procedure. Scanners and computers make the job pretty perfunctory, but some registers require price and product data to be entered by hand. Depending on your shift, you might have to open or close registers, which can include counting the money and separating charge slips, coupons, and exchange vouchers.

Forgo fashion and pony up for comfy

footwear. Practice saying, "Did you find everything you were looking for?"

The hours: Variable. Plan on working evenings and weekends.

Median pay range: Pay can range from $7.15 to more than $12 an hour.

Qualifications: Cashiers need little or no previous experience, although that helps. Training is generally on the go with a more seasoned co-worker. Department and chain stores might offer a short training course to get you up to speed on customer service, security, the store's policies and procedures, and cash register operation. Employers generally run a background or credit score check to make sure you're trustworthy to handle money. You should be at ease with financial transactions and basic computer commands. Remember — the customer is always right.

Next: Make someone's shopping trip a little brighter.

Retail Salesperson

The nitty-gritty: It should come as no surprise that the heart of this job is having the customer at hello. You need to connect quickly with people in a warm manner. You're there to help them find what they're looking for, and that might mean a little sales razzle-dazzle, product demos, and knowhow of certain model features. It's possible that you'll be asked to reel off financing options if it's a big-ticket item.

In addition, you'll need to be at ease at the cash register and when packing up purchases. Depending on your shift, you may have to open or close cash registers, which can include counting money and separating charge slips, coupons, and exchange vouchers. In addition, you may stock shelves, mark price tags, take inventory, and prepare displays. Since you'll be on your feet for long stretches, it makes sense to spring for a pair of comfortable shoes.

The hours: During holiday crunch time, plan on working evenings and weekends.

Median pay range: Pay can range from less than $7.37 to more than $19.14 an hour although bonus pay is possible.

Qualifications: Previous sales experience helps, but it's not a deal-breaker.

Greenhorns can apply. Expect on-the-job training by a more experienced employee. This can be on the fly at this frenzied time of year. Don't be shy about asking questions. In department stores, training programs are more formal. Topics often include customer service, security, store policies and procedures, and cash register operation. Insider knowledge helps. If you're hawking computers, a sense of the technical distinctions between products is vital. People skills are de rigueur. Employers might run a background or credit score check on you to make sure you're trustworthy. Best arrows to have tucked in your quiver: patience and persuasion.

Next: If you're eloquent and outgiong, consider this job.

Product Demonstrator

The nitty-gritty: Don't be shy. This is "meet and greet" show time. Talk to people with snappy banter and product knowhow. You boldly step right up to a shopper and say with a friendly, earnest smile, "Would you like to try our apple cider?" You're not actually selling the elixir, but you're getting folks in the buying mood.

Demonstrators are typically standing or walking, and it can be fairly fast-paced. This is not a job for the couch potato. Think energizer bunny. Prepare to pass out food samples or product coupons or brochures. Performances might be on tap if you're assigned to demo a blender or new software program, or you could be asked to try your hand at in-store cooking. You might face some grunt work — setup and cleanup, as well as bringing the goods to and from the stores. Extra bonus: Tantalizing tidbits at your fingertips.

The hours: Vary by store. During holiday crunch times, evenings and weekends are the norm.

Median pay range: $8.28 to $21.19 per hour.

Qualifications: On-the-job training to glean sales techniques is standard fare. Smooth public speaking and communication skills and an outgoing personality will serve you well. This is a performance in many ways, so you'll want to channel your inner entertainer. Humor and friendly chit-chat attracts customers.

Past jobs in retail, sales, or customer service make it easier, but any volunteering or public speaking experience is noteworthy on your resume.

Job hunting tips: If you know a shop, even a "big-box" store, that uses demonstrators near you, stop by and ask if the store does the hiring directly. If so, put in your application.

You might also ask an in-store demonstrator during a break how he or she got the job. Some companies pay a kickback for bringing in a new worker. If the store uses an outside agency, get the contact information. If you're interested in a specific product, go to the company web site to check for openings and apply online. Kiosk operators in malls sometimes hire part-time product demo help. Pump it up.

Next: Do you take holiday decorating very seriously?

Holiday Decorator

The nitty-gritty: Do you have a passion for decking the halls with boughs of holly — or blue and silver Chanukah streamers? This job calls for creative flair and a way with bows and bulbs. You'll be making and setting up holiday decorations and displays. You might need to tap into your electrical smarts, too. Sometimes a touch of brawn and a strong back is required if you're responsible for moving large poinsettias, picking up boxes of ornaments, setting up Christmas trees, or stringing lights outdoors. You might have to clamber up ladders to get to rooftops and high trees if offering outside decorating services. Expect to get your hands dirty.

Demanding clients and last-minute flourishes can be a little nerve-wracking. Jobs range from adorning large offices and retail shops to hotels, restaurants, and private homes.

The hours: Potentially long and variable, but brief stints. November to early January. Some late night and weekend work required for installation and dismantling.

Median pay range: $8.14 to $17.23 per hour.

Qualifications: Past holiday decorating experience is a plus. Floral designer training helps. If you've got a flair for this type of work, a good attitude, and you're willing to learn, many florists and decorators will gladly train you as you go.

Many vocational schools and community colleges award certificates and degrees in floral design. You'll learn the basics of arranging flowers, including the different types of flowers, their color and texture, cutting and taping techniques, tying bows and ribbons, and proper handling and care of flowers. The American Institute of Floral Designers offers an accreditation examination.

Job hunting tips: Check with local florists and floral departments at grocery stores and event planning firms for openings.

If you're confident in your own decorating panache, you might opt to start your own business. You can land clients through word of mouth. Ask friends and family to help spread the word. For starters, decorate the homes or offices of a few friends or family members gratis or at a bargain price. You'll be able to build up a portfolio or web site with display pictures to show potential clients.

Next: Spread holiday joy with good food, drink, and your smile.

Bartending/Waiting Tables/Catering

The nitty-gritty: Smile though your feet are aching. Food and beverage service positions are in high demand during the end-of-year holiday party season. From restaurants to local pubs to private parties, typically a wide variety of places are hiring for the holiday season.

Patience, a good memory, and organizational skills are part of the job. It goes without saying, of course, that an amiable persona, charm, and an uncanny ability to smooth ruffled feathers of disgruntled customers are expected. A certain level of physical fitness is required.

Catering companies, too, search for bartenders and servers to work private parties. Caterers who handle food preparation are usually behind the scenes. You might be in charge of menu planning, food preparation, and setup.

The hours: Flexible schedules. Nights, weekend, and lunch times can peak during the weeks before New Year's.

Median pay range: Bartending: $7.33

to $15.11 per hour and up, plus tips. Wait staff: $7.54 to $14.41, plus tips. Caterers should expect an hourly range between $9.82 and $11.89, but can run up to $20 an hour, plus tips.

Qualifications: A pleasant personality and an ability to banter with customers are essential. Math and memorization skills come in handy, too. Past experience is helpful, but other positions where you've worked with people even as a volunteer are worth noting. Personal and professional references are valuable calling cards.

If you're considering bartending, especially as a postholiday part-time job, you might enroll in a bartender training school that offers two-week programs.

Catering will require more stove time in the kitchen to earn your culinary chops and references to back up your claims. You could face stiff competition from professional chefs. Expect upfront costs for sample menu preparation. Not for the hot and bothered.

Job hunting tips: Before you apply for jobs as wait staff or bartender, do your reconnaissance as a customer to see how the staff dress and get a feel for the venue and menu.

Next: Do you have the gift of gab? Look no further.

Call Center Representative

The nitty-gritty: If you're game to spend the entire day speaking on the telephone, this is your gig. Call centers heat up for holiday sales. You generally have your own workstation outfitted with a headset and computer. The bulk of your work is helping customers find a product, collecting payment information, and typing data in the system. Expect to answer simple questions or requests such as finding the status of an order. Be warned: Some customers are lodging complaints, so you'll need to stay cool.

Call centers can be cramped and noisy. The work is repetitious and, with brief breaks between calls, even stressful. Long periods spent sitting, typing, or looking at a computer screen can make your eyes and muscles ache. Smooth talkers should apply.

The hours: Many call centers are open extended hours or staffed around the clock. Peak times may not last for a full shift, so you may be slotted for part time or work a split shift.

Median pay range: Median hourly wages of customer service representatives range from less than $9.15 to more than $23.24.

Qualifications: Listening and verbal skills are key. For workers who correspond through e-mail, good typing, spelling, and grammar skills are essential. Basic to intermediate computer knowledge is vital. You'll likely be given training with background on the company and its products, the most commonly asked questions, and a review of the computer and telephone systems you'll be using. Hint: Companies favor folks who have a pleasant, neutral speaking voice.

Next: Are your gift-wrapping skills the envy of family and friends?

Gift Wrapper

The nitty-gritty: When it comes to wrapping special gifts, you need the creativity to make a present alluring. Much of the pressure comes from having a customer standing in front of you while you try to cut, fold, and tie a bow with precision. Some things you can't rush, but you do need to move rather swiftly with nimble fingers and not too much wasted paper. These wrapping table positions are usually found at gift shops, department stores, or booths in shopping malls.

The hours: In-store jobs track shopping hours. For distribution center jobs, night shifts apply.

Median pay range: The range is typically $8.60 to around $13 an hour.

Qualifications: The ability to fold and wrap paper so it's taut and neat around a package, plus a knack for deftly twisting ribbon in ways that the typical customer can't fathom. This skill is generally self-taught, but you may be given crash on-the-job training with a few test packages. Some community colleges offer classes for around $25 that teach the "creative art" of gift-wrapping.

Job hunting tip: Search online job boards for "gift wrapper associate" and stop by or contact the human resource department at nearby stores.

Next: Can you turn on the charm and control a crowd all at once?

Restaurant Greeter

The nitty-gritty: If you love to meet and greet and can cope with chaos, here's your chance. The restaurant business gets a boost with holiday parties and other festive entertaining during the holiday season. As a result, there's often an uptick in openings to keep things running smoothly on the front end. Think hungry diners crowding the entrance, tapping their toes to check in and be escorted to their tables.

It's a people-intensive and high-energy post. You'll need all your powers to smooth ruffled feathers of those kept waiting. You're in charge of creating the first impression for guests and have the power to influence the overall restaurant experience by how you deal with diners. If you're a fan of the food being served and know your way around a menu, you have a leg up.

The hours: Lunch and dinner shifts, generally no more than five hours.

Median pay range: The pay scale is generally $8.25 to $15 an hour, but varies widely by size and popularity of the establishment.

Qualifications: People and organizational skills are prerequisites. Some phone work. Prior time spent at a restaurant is valued. Warmth and a welcoming smile will serve you well. Your mantra: "Follow me. Your table is ready."

Next: If you're organized and can lift heavy boxes, this job might fit.

Shipping Clerk

The nitty-gritty: Around the holiday season, the big package shippers such as UPS and FedEx need your helping hands, but the small boutique around the corner selling hand-dipped chocolate-covered candies might, too. This behind-the-counter position calls for skill at fitting the right box or envelope to the item being shipped. Other duties: Explaining the various shipping methods and rates to customers, knowing how to pack an item so it arrives intact, taking inventory, stocking shelves, weighing packages, entering computer data, applying proper insurance coverage, affixing labels, working a cash register, and arranging pickups and accepting deliveries.

Plan on spending a good bit of your

time upright and on the move. You might have to lift boxes up to 55 pounds. Remember: Bend at the knees.

The hours: Flexible and partial shifts during the rush season.

Median pay range: The hourly wages run the gamut from $8.50 to $15 an hour based on experience.

Qualifications: You must be computer-literate. Retail experience staffing a cash register helps. Background check is standard for most positions.

Next: Not exactly Santa's sleigh, but you'll deliver the goods.

Package Delivery

Nitty-gritty: You don't have to bear the responsibility of full-time driver, but UPS and FedEx add thousands of part-time and temporary helpers and package handlers for their drivers during peak delivery period from Thanksgiving through New Years. It can require lifting and moving boxes, plus a smile for the customer if they happened to open the door.

The hours: Full 8-hour shifts to part time, depending on where you live.

Median pay range: $9 to more than

$14 an hour; tips and bonuses are possible.

Qualifications: You should be somewhat spry to handle the physical aspects of this job. At UPS and FedEx, there's typically a written test to gauge communication skills that may be called on when you come face-to-face with a customer. And some training is provided.

Job hunting tips: Check the big delivery company web sites online for openings.

---

6 Steps to Landing a Holiday Job

'Tis the season to earn a little extra money on the side.

Getting hired during the holiday season can be easier than finding work at other times of the year.

Opportunities exist for a variety of positions including gift wrappers, salespeople, shipping clerks, and call center reps. Try these six steps to find employment that's well suited to your skills and interests:

Stop by for a face-to-face. Many retailers offer online applications, but it's best to meet the manager in person.

Offer future help. If you think you might want to extend your hours after the holidays, or be willing to work during other hectic times of the year, tell the manager during the interview. It could sway the job your way, since employers are looking for ways to trim the cost of future hiring and training.

Be flexible. Holiday jobs mean adding and cutting hours at a drop of the hat, depending on the ebb and flow of demand during peak periods.

Network. Kick off your job search by checking with friends already working in places that typically add holiday workers.

Go where they know you. Check for openings at establishments where you are an existing customer.

Don't wait for a help-wanted sign. If there are shops or restaurants where you'd like to work, drop by during an off-peak time and meet the manager or assistant manager.

Next up, grab your suntan lotion and head south for the winter months.

CHAPTER 4
GREAT SNOWBIRD JOBS

Snowbirds are on the move in December and January. Biting cold in the North has sparked the annual migration of retirees and semi-retirees south for the winter. In parts of Florida and Arizona, especially, populations swell as warm-weather seekers make the seasonal shift. But changing locales for a few months doesn't mean you need (or want) to be in vacation mode the entire time.

While climate is the No. 1 motive, it's not the only draw. Unique employment opportunities await snowbirds who are interested in making money while they soak up the sun. Disney, for example, does brisk hiring for its theme parks during winter months, as do resorts, to handle the influx of tourists. The job possibilities, both full-time and part-time, don't end there.

When I interviewed Bill Armbrecht, a lifelong baseball fan, the Sandusky, Ohio resident had found work at the Cleveland Indians' spring training facility in Goodyear, Arizona. It's 18 miles from the Sun City condo where he and his wife spend winters.

Armbrecht's job title: Security. For the most part, that translates into making sure fans and reporters are respectful of the players and their time, but he has worked the parking lot and special events, too. "I do a lot of different things," says Armbrecht, who is in his 70s. "Whatever needs to be done."

The pay clocks in around $8 an hour, but it's not just about the money. "It's one of those jobs you would pay them to do," the retired pharmacist says. "As a child I went to Indians games with my grandmother. It's a hoot. The best part is rubbing shoulders with the big boys. Baseball, well, it's part of my heart."

For Mavis Rush, hunting for a warm weather job was driven by a sheer desire to keep active. She got antsy a week after arriving in Naples, Florida from Alexandria, Virginia. "I knew I wanted to be someplace where I wasn't cold anymore, but I couldn't stand playing leisurely golf and tennis," she says.

Truth is, Rush, 74, has never taken tennis leisurely. For a dozen years before she retired, she was the director of tennis for Worldgate Sport & Health, a large sport and health club in Herndon, Virginia outside of Washington, D.C.

So it's not all that surprising that when Rush retired, she wanted to stay active — even after hip replacement surgery. When she heard about possible openings at the Ritz-Carlton Resorts of Naples from a friend, she applied and was hired as a fitness attendant.

She wears lots of hats. She might teach a tennis lesson, dole out restaurant recommendations, or take a guest out on a catamaran for a sail. But her primary position is in the fitness center, where she commands the front desk.

She greets sleepy exercisers at 5 A.M., five days a week. She books appointments for guests with a personal trainer and makes sure they have peppermint-scented cool towels, and plenty of water within arm's reach. "I hope I brighten their day right from the start," Rush says.

Her pay: $13 an hour, plus tips and benefits. She has retirement savings and lives modestly. "I do it for the mental and physical engagement. I couldn't just sit around. But best of all, I make friendships, and I'm putting something in someone's life."

On a typical day, Rush signs out around 12:30 P.M. and heads home, two miles away, where she pedals off on a bike ride to unwind. "My job is about great service and making people happy," she says.

Rush hasn't lost her competitive edge, either. In her early adulthood, she competed in singles and mixed doubles in national tennis tournaments; in the Senior Olympics, she bumped up to contending in both tennis and race walking. She even ran the Marine Corps Marathon when she was skimming 60. Now, she's looking for more challenges to tackle on and off the job.

"I'm ambitious. I like to make at least two new friends a day. My next job, I want to bag groceries at Publix. . . . Look at all the people I'll meet," she says.

Whatever the attraction, the crack of a bat or the chance to work alongside Mickey Mouse, here are warm-weather jobs to consider. There are plenty of great jobs out there for you, and there's always the potential to extend beyond the peak season. You might even be able to take your own business with you on the road.

Resort Hospitality Worker

The nitty-gritty: When the snowbirds land in town, resort and hotel staffing expands to meet them, sometimes even doubling rosters. A broad sweep of jobs might be up your alley. These can range from greeting diners at restaurants with a warm, welcoming smile to bartending, waiting tables, driving a shuttle van to housekeeping, valet parking, working at the front desk, and more. The jobs, for the most part, demand a smooth, outgoing personality. Expect to spend time on your feet. A calm, take-charge attitude will come in handy when complaints must be dealt with quickly and professionally.

The hours: Part-time and full-time positions are typically available in all shifts. Weekends and school spring breaks are peak periods, when extra hands are needed.

Median pay range: The pay scale is $8 to $15 an hour, plus tips, but varies widely by type of establishment, size, and location.

Qualifications: The ability to communicate with people in a pleasant way, basic computer knowledge, and seamless phone manners are top of the list. In general, these are hospitality positions, so restaurant or service is a plus.

Job hunting tips: The tourist metro areas around cities such as Sarasota, Orlando, and Naples in Florida, or Tucson, Arizona and Taos, New Mexico in the Southwest are likely to have the most openings. First stop on your job hunt: large hotel chains such as Marriott, the Ritz-Carlton, and Westin Hotels and Resorts. Your catchphrase: Welcome to paradise. What can I do for you?

Next: Calling all pro shop attendants, gardeners, or fitness instructors. Read on.

Resort Services Worker

The nitty-gritty: Resorts of all shapes and sizes across the Sunbelt increase their guest services staff during winter months. You might find work in any number of capacities, from gardener to parking valet or room cleaner. Niche opportunities abound. If you love golf, there might be openings in the pro shop or as a groundskeeper. Boaters should check out marinas for odd jobs.

Gambling fans can investigate Gulf Coast casinos. Fitness professionals such as massage therapists and Pilates instructors may find seasonal jobs with a resort's spa operations. Be mindful of the physical demands of some service jobs.

The hours: Full-time and partial weeks available; weekend shifts, night shifts.

Median pay range: Anywhere from $7.33 to $15.11 or more an hour, plus tips, depending on the job; massage therapist, $8.30 to $33 or more an hour.

Qualifications: Experience is a must for certain jobs, say, boat mechanic or golf pro, but skills needed for entry-level service jobs can be picked up quickly. Most states require practicing massage therapists to complete a formal education program, pass an examination, and obtain a license. Pilates and yoga teachers must have proof of specialized training, too. Sun salutation, anyone?

Next: Do you believe in magic? There could be an opening for you.

Disney "Cast Member"

The nitty-gritty: Positions are available throughout Disney's resorts and theme parks in Florida and California. Seasonal openings include loading and unloading passengers from rides, doling out costumes at wardrobe facilities across the parks, staffing gift shops and concessions stands, and even portraying costumed characters. (The latter positions require auditions, and you must be willing and able to spend time on your feet signing autographs and posing for photos.) There are also openings for airport representatives who greet guests at arrival and usher them to waiting shuttles.

The hours: Part-time roles typically require a minimum of two to three days of full availability per week. Full-time positions are also available. Applicants who prefer weekends off or early shifts only may find opportunities limited.

Median pay range: $7.45 to $10.55 an hour.

Qualifications: Varies by category. Check the Walt Disney World web site for job openings in Florida; for California, see Disneyland's web site. Prerequisite: Believe in magic.

Next: Are you handy and don't mind doing a few chores?

Second Home Property Manager/Concierge

The nitty-gritty: In general, you prepare homes for their owner's arrival and close them up when they leave. The duties may include grocery shopping to stock the pantry, checking on the condition of the home's interior, inspecting for pests, running water in faucets, checking that all the kitchen appliances are in working order, flushing toilets, testing smoke detectors and air-conditioners, opening the pool, and checking the condition of screens. You set the house temperature and pool heater to the desired temperature just prior to the snowbirds' arrival. You can accept packages they send in advance. You might open the home for house cleaning services, pest control services, and maintenance workers. You also provide end-of-season house cleaning and shut-down.

This is one for entrepreneurial self-starters. You can extend your undertaking to provide a variety of maintenance chores from plumbing to electrical and painting projects throughout the months. You might offer your services as an errand runner or airport driver to ferry guests to and from the airport.

This is not a job for slackers. You'll need to be in reasonably good physical condition and adept at fixing things fast, or know whom to call who can. And don't forget the fresh flowers on the table — always a nice touch.

The hours: If it's your own business, you can call the shots, but it will depend on your client's needs. Part-time schedules for condo, townhouse, or retirement community maintenance vary. Some employers might prefer to have a handyman on call for emergencies, while others might like to have you onsite and available to residents during specific hours.

Median pay range: $10 to $20 an hour, but can be $60-plus, depending on your area.

Qualifications: Be knowledgeable in home repair, have your own tools, be self-motivated, and possess good customer-service skills. You will probably need to be bonded and have liability insurance. Laws vary by state. Some clients who don't know you personally may require a background check. Clients who vouch for your dependability are the keys to opening doors.

Job hunting tips: To build this business will take some selling on your part. Word-of-mouth will be your best means to drum up customers. This is a referral business, after all.

You might start with pitching your services to your neighbors in your winter haven, or market to northern connections who have second homes. Some real estate management firms, retirement communities, and time-share communities hire part-time workers to take on this advance prep and handle routine maintenance during the winter months.

Next: Can you cut hair like nobody's business?

Hairdresser

The nitty-gritty: Who doesn't dread leaving their hairdresser for months at a time? Why not go south with your clients? If you can nab some referrals in the area, maybe you can start a seasonal business. The essence of the job is shampooing, cutting, coloring, and styling. Ready for a new look?

The hours: Variable. Evenings and weekends are part of the mix.

Median pay range: $7.76 an hour to $19.97 and up, plus tips. A typical cut and color can easily top $120 per appointment.

Qualifications: All states require hairdressers to be licensed. Qualifications for a license vary by state, but generally a person must have a high school diploma or GED and have graduated from a state-licensed barber or cosmetology school. Some states have reciprocity agreements that allow you to transfer a valid cosmetology license. State licensing board requirements and a list of licensed training schools for cosmetologists may be obtained from the National Accrediting Commission of Cosmetology Arts and Sciences. Background checks are the norm. Good listening skills and stylish flair are your calling cards. Word-of-mouth marketing makes or breaks your success as a hairdresser.

Job hunting tips: You may work out of

your own home space. You may also find part-time work in a salon or a spa, hotel or resort. Many communities have full-service salons that rent chairs for a fee by the week or the month to freelancers.

Employment of hairdressers, hairstylists, and cosmetologists will increase by about 20 percent from 2008 to 2018, which is much faster than average occupations, according to the Bureau of Labor Statistics. Why? Baby boomers are hip to hair coloring and other sophisticated hair treatments, and are spurring the demand, according to BLS. Can you say cut and color?

Next: Show off your sense of style and love of fashion.

Retail

The nitty-gritty: Big chains and boutiques add part-time workers during the "season." You may have to open or close cash registers, count money, and separate charge slips, coupons, and exchange vouchers. In addition, you may stock shelves, mark price tags, take inventory, and prepare displays. While there are a variety of retail positions that can be as basic as greeting customers and folding sweaters, most have a physical aspect to them. You need to be prepared for bending, stretching, lifting, and walking around without plopping down in a chair for long periods. Plus, customers can be demanding, so cool demeanors come in handy. The underlying incentive: discounted merchandise. Sweet sale-o-rama.

The hours: If you're willing to work evenings and weekends, you might find more opportunities to flesh out schedules with year-round staffers.

Median pay range: Pay can range from $7.37 to more than $19.14 an hour, including commissions. Upscale shopping areas will usually pay top dollar.

Qualifications: Previous sales experience helps. If you're new to the game, on-the-job training is standard fare. Each store operator has its own way of selling and running things from security procedures to customer service peccadilloes, so even old hands have a learning curve. It helps if you have a passion or familiarity with the goods you are selling. Enthusiasm is infectious and opens wallets. Top-notch people skills are the underlying ingredient to making this a good fit for both you and the employer. Employers might run a background or credit score check on you to make sure you're trustworthy. Practice saying: "Did you find everything you were looking for?"

Spring Training Staff

The nitty-gritty: Spring training camps for Major League Baseball teams in Arizona and Florida have a range of possible positions: ushering, selling programs, fielding ticket inquiries, working concession booths, running cash registers in the team merchandise shop, and juggling other customer service duties. Teams may hire drivers to transport players and staff to and from the airport.

Some jobs require more expertise than others. For instance, the Pittsburgh Pirates had a recent posting for a seasonal sales assistant, who would take an active role in marketing and special promotions. IT analysts are called on to make sure wireless networks and computers run smoothly for press and players. While duties might be mundane, the chance to work alongside a World Series ring bearer is anything but.

The hours: Vary by team and demands of the job.

Median pay range: From $7.50 to more than $10 an hour.

Qualifications: Qualifications will depend on the post, but on-the-job training is standard in most cases. A valid driver's license and a fluency in Spanish might be necessary. Bestselling advantage: Love of the game.

Job hunting tips: To learn more, go to Major League Baseball's web site, click on the link to your favorite team's web site, then click on "job opportunities." You can also try contacting the training camp office directly.

Next: Take to the open road and earn some extra dough.

Car Transporter

The nitty-gritty: If rolling down long open highways catches your fancy, then delivering vehicles up and down the East Coast can pay your way to a warm weather getaway of your own. Busiest months are December and May, but departures and returns are staggered. In peak-demand periods you can snap up deliveries in rapid succession. You'll quickly get up to speed on shortcuts and construction detours, and maybe accrue frequent flyer miles in the process. Long hours on the road can take a physical and mental toll, so stopping to stretch and rest is a must.

It's possible to find seasonal driving jobs with a professional service, but drivers who want to work in snowbird season only may find it easier to drum up clients by word of mouth. Try posting flyers at senior centers, retirement communities, assisted-living facilities, libraries, pharmacies, and grocery stores. Build up a roster of repeat customers.

The hours: Expect to drive eight hours a day, but this is negotiable. Most one-way trips, however, can be done in two to three days.

Median pay range: This fluctuates widely, but a base pay of $200 a day, plus gas and tolls, is the ballpark.

Qualifications: A spotless driving record and impeccable character references. It helps if you know how to change a flat and have a working knowledge of car mechanics. You'll need a GPS and a cell phone to stay on course and connected to clients. Plus, be prepared to have some company on your way. Cars heading south tend to get crowded with precious cargo such as fragile personal belongings and even family pets.

Next: Are you a nurse who loves to travel? This gig might be for you.

Travel Nurse

The nitty-gritty: Registered nurses and licensed practical nurses are in high demand at hospitals and doctors' offices in Florida and Arizona during the winter months. The majority of travel nursing assignments run for 13 weeks — often with the option of extending the term to six months. You must have a travel-nursing license to practice in each state. These temporary licenses can cost $25 to $250 and are valid from one to six months. Plan ahead. Obtaining a temporary Florida RN license, for instance, takes an average of 30 days. Specific work responsibilities vary widely depending on specialty and facility.

The hours: Flexible and partial shifts during the winter/spring season.

Median pay range: From $21 to $45 or more an hour, plus housing stipends and health insurance are often part of the package.

Qualifications: A bachelor of science degree in nursing is a standard requirement, but an associate degree in nursing can open doors, too. You must pass a national licensing examination, known as the National Council Licensure Examination, to obtain a nursing license. Other eligibility requirements vary by state. Contact the state's board of nursing for details. A background check is standard. Compassion and care count.

Next: Love spending time on the open water? Read on.

Cruise Liners

The nitty-gritty: If you've got your sea legs and are up for a little adventure, a cruise line job can be swell. Some cruise ships hire married couples, so if you're escaping the cold with your partner, you both can set sail. Leading cruise lines, such as Carnival Cruise,

Disney Cruise Line, Princess Cruises, and Royal Caribbean International Lines, hire across a full array of jobs, including hosts, cruise directors and staff, disc jockeys, performers, swimming and other instructors, and shore excursion staff. Also needed: Pursers, photographers and videographers, wait staff, bartenders, cabin stewards, cooks, bakers, cleaners, gift-shop attendees, beauticians, medical staff, massage therapists, fitness instructors, and engine room technicians.

Tight quarters for accommodations can be a squeeze. If you're solo, you may share a small cabin and a bathroom. Plus, you will be afloat in all types of weather. If you suffer from severe sea-sickness, perhaps you can land one of the liner's landlubber jobs.

The hours: Long hours can be a drawback — 12 or 14 hours a day, seven days a week, typically for a period of six months.

Median pay range: Tipping personnel like bartenders and wait staff can earn $1,500 to $4,000 per month (including the tips), according to Cruiseline Jobs.com. The nontipping personnel earn from $350 to $500 per week. You get free accommodation and food and book some great gratis travel to boot.

Qualifications: Experience in the hospitality industry is essential for many of these openings. If you have an expertise in a particular area, say, personal finance and investing or technology, or you are an author, journalist, or college professor, you might be able to land a gig as a paid lecturer. Most employees will be required to pass a course on work safety and first aid. The most important job qualification, however, is good language skills — you must speak English effortlessly; if you're multilingual, even better. Your passport must be current.

Job hunting tips: When applying, it's best to target a specific job. Check out the cruise lines' web site career sections for more details; apply directly to the cruise line by following the instructions on the web site for the specific position being offered to avoid scams. Bon voyage.

Next up, is work from home sweet home calling?

CHAPTER 5
GREAT WORK-AT-HOME JOBS

Returning to work is an economic necessity for some and a personal choice for others. Either way, the prospect of long commutes and annoying co-workers can be off-putting. A good compromise might be to find a work-at-home job.

That's what Jackie Booley did. In 2007, she retired from her position as an AT&T call center manager. Her husband had recently died from chronic kidney failure, and Booley, then 61, was exhausted from serving as his primary caregiver while holding down full-time employment.

But retirement proved to be short-lived. Two years later, with her energy restored and nest egg depleted, she found a part-time job that allowed her to work from home. Now, when you dial Office Depot's toll-free number, you may be speaking with Booley in the spare bedroom of her Ocala, Florida home.

She doesn't work for the office-supply retailer, however. Rather, Booley's employed by Alpine Access, a call center service headquartered in Denver. Incoming calls to Office Depot are routed to her in Florida. Alpine has 4,500 work-at-home customer service agents in 1,700 cities.

Booley logs in anywhere from 18 to 30 hours each week answering questions and processing orders. At $9 an hour, she usually earns between $500 and $600 per month. It's not a fortune, but the extra money does allow her to go out to dinner and a movie without worry.

"I absolutely love it," says Booley of her work-at-home job. "It gives me flexibility. I feel like I'm my own boss, and I can fall out of bed and go to work in seconds." The topper: She's banked enough hours with her virtual employer to afford to take a vacation. She's going to England this year.

You might also opt to truly work for yourself, as Carlos E. Romo, 68, does. Like Booley, he can't argue with the commute to an office off the kitchen. But it's even sweeter when you have the freedom to set your own hours, as Romo's work as a translator-interpreter and mediator has allowed him to do.

The Reno, Nevada resident retired four

years ago from his administrator post at a local community college. When he stepped out of the day-to-day fray, he knew he wanted to keep doing something. And it didn't take long for him to find work that allows him to tap into a language he loves — Spanish. As a child, it was the language spoken in his remote hometown of Mora, New Mexico.

Taking on translating assignments that could be done from his home office was a no-brainer. "It's in my blood," Romo says. "I knew there was a need, and I wanted to put my skills and passion to good use."

The groundwork was in place. He had begun his career as an assistant professor of Spanish at the University of Nevada, Reno. Although he spent the bulk of his career working in various positions for the state of Nevada, ranging from administrator of the State Youth Services Division to assistant administrator for the Nevada Equal Rights Commission, he was careful about keeping up his language skills. Romo, who holds a doctorate, is also fluent in Portuguese from his days as a Fulbright-Hayes scholar in Lisbon, Portugal.

Because of the large Spanish-speaking population where he lives, Romo communicates with others in Spanish almost daily. Also, during his day-job years, he taught evening Spanish classes at the local community college in topics ranging from Spanish for travelers to Spanish for medical professionals.

When he decided to tap into the market for translators, he began by marketing his services the old-fashioned way, word of mouth. "We've been in the community for 39 years, so people know me," Romo says. He listed his background and contact information with the Language Bank at the Northern Nevada International Center. The bank provides translation and interpretation services in more than 60 languages to businesses and organizations.

The variety of work keeps it interesting. From the comfort of his home computer, he has translated workplace safety manuals and brochures for Spanish-speaking employees of area businesses from casinos to hospitals.

Other freelance assignments require that he venture out. Local lawyers hire him to help Spanish-speaking individuals who need simultaneous translation. As a mediator in job discrimination cases and community-related issues, for example, Romo translates from English to Spanish or Portuguese, and vice versa. He has worked as a translator with the local school district, which employs him to teach English as a second language to Spanish-speaking parents.

In general, the pay swings as widely as the assignments, ranging from $50 to $120 an hour. "If it's a nonprofit, I simply say 'how much can you pay?' One of my impetuses for working in retirement is to give back to the community," Romo says. "This is one way I can do that. If I'm asked to be in court for an indigent pro bono, I'm there."

The flexibility of the work permits Romo to pick and choose projects, which allows him and his wife, Nancy, 65, to travel, spend time with their grandchildren, and devote time to community and church volunteer projects.

The deeper reward: "It's the satisfaction you get from being able to help individuals communicate," Romo says. "In the courts, you have to be very precise. You translate the words the individual uses, and not what you think he's trying to say. . . . It can be a matter of their rights." In other words, "no ad libbing," he says.

While home-based jobs like translation services can be a boon, keep in mind that work-at-home scams have been around for decades. In the past few years, the Federal Trade Commission has seen the number of complaints nearly double. Legitimate work-at-home jobs exist, but you'll need to do legwork to avoid the unscrupulous operators.

Two glaring red flags to look out for: jobs touted via e-mail that promise to pay more than you ever dreamed, and firms that charge you a fee to obtain more information about a job. "Payment for the privilege of working is rarely acceptable, in our view," says Christine Durst, an Internet fraud and safety expert and co-founder of ratrace rebellion.com, a web site on home-based work that screens job leads.

Is the Home-Based Business a Scam?

- Check for complaints with the Better Business Bureau in your area and the area in which the company is headquartered. You'll also want to verify the company with your local consumer protection agency and state attorney general. For free information on work at home consumer issues, visit the FTC consumer information site at ftc.gov.
- Just because there aren't complaints doesn't mean the company is above board. Devious companies may settle complaints, change their names, or

move to avoid scrutiny. It's a good idea to enter the company name with the word "complaints" into a search engine to see if anything appears.

- Ask what specific tasks you'll have to perform, whether you will be paid by salary or commission, who will pay you, and when and how frequently you'll be paid.
- Never give any financial information like bank account or credit card numbers over the phone or online until you have done your research.
- Ask what the total cost to you will be, including supplies and equipment.
- Be wary of overstated claims of product effectiveness, exaggerated claims of potential earnings, and demands that you pay for something before instructions or products are provided.
- Be wary of personal testimonials that never identify the person so you can't investigate further.
- Get answers to your questions in writing.

Source: The Federal Trade Commission.

If you've set your sights on a work-from-home job, you might go straight to a company you would like to work for and see if it hires remote workers. A good place to start is the career section of its web site. There are also sites like FlexJobs.com that are focused on legitimate work-from-home jobs and prescreen each job and employer to be certain they aren't scams.

Following are some great work-from-home jobs to consider.

Translator-Interpreter

The nitty-gritty: You may brag that you're fluent in two languages, but are you really? It's easy to get rusty. Being a Spanish major back in college isn't going to be enough. Languages evolve, and being in sync with modern terms and slang is vital. Idioms matter. If you're going to be a Spanish translator or interpreter, for example, you need to know the difference between Spanish spoken in Spain, Mexico, Cuba, Puerto Rico, and different countries in South and Central America. Note: Interpreters deal with spoken words, translators with written words. Interpreters are the go-between for two parties, such as a doctor and patient, a client and lawyer, and actors or presenters and their audience. Translation work is generally done on a computer with files transmitted electronically back and forth. Online dictionary resources can be invaluable, but they don't replace expressions gleaned from interacting with others who speak the language frequently.

Spanish is the most in-demand language, but other languages are growing, such as Arabic. Specializing in a field such as the judicial system or health care and knowing the terminology will increase your job opportunities. This is precise work. Words have repercussions. If you don't know the vocabulary, don't take the assignment.

The hours: Flexible, based on the specific project.

Median pay range: $11.03 to $41.50 an hour. Depending on assignment and expertise, pay can top $100 an hour. Translation and proofreading projects are generally billed at a rate of 15 to 30 cents per word, depending on the skill level.

Qualifications: Interpreters and translators must be fluent in at least two languages. A subject area of expertise helps. No official certifications are required, although several are offered through trade organizations, such as the American Translators Association, which provides certification in 24 language combinations involving English for its members. Federal courts have certification for Spanish, Navajo, and Haitian Creole interpreters, and many state and municipal courts offer their own forms of certification. The National Association of Judiciary Interpreters and Translators also offers certification for court interpreting. The U.S. Department of State has a three-test series for prospective interpreters. The International Association of Conference Interpreters offers certification for conference interpreters.

If you have solid language skills, you can get translation training at community colleges and universities to prepare you for a translator certification. The American Translators Association has a list of programs it approves along with a job bank when you're ready. The All Language Alliance also connects job seekers and positions. Internships, apprenticeships, and volunteering via community organizations, hospitals, and sporting events that involve international competitors will build your resume. The ATA works with the Red Cross to provide volunteer interpreters in crisis situations. Working with a mentor and networking with native speakers will keep your skills fresh. The ATA also offers formal mentoring programs and has chapters in many states.

Selling point: A good ear for languages.

Next: Are you a pro at keeping cool in trying situations?

Mediator

The nitty-gritty: Arbitration and alternative dispute resolution (ADR) have steadily gained converts from those hoping to bypass lawsuits with onerous fees and often a drawn-out legal process. From divorce proceedings to housing and medical disputes, many people prefer to settle matters privately out of court. Some tense and sometimes frustrating debates can make your head throb, but mediators are the pros equipped with the calm voice of reason.

These jobs are not only for retired lawyers, mind you. An expertise in certain fields of business can be your ticket. Experience settling workplace discrimination issues, marriage counseling, and even a mental health background can land you a seat at the table to guide a sensitive negotiation.

In general, you work out of your home office, but may have to go to another location for the official meeting. You've got to be "all ears." Your task: Impartially hear both sides of a dispute, cut through the sometimes emotional verbiage, and intuitively hone in on the critical details. It's up to you to patiently direct and encourage both sides to keep talking in a civil fashion until a satisfactory resolution, or settlement, is struck. No taking sides.

The hours: Varies depending on caseload. Expect to put in the hours during negotiations.

Median pay range: $14.69 to $55.63 and up.

Qualifications: Many mediators have law degrees, but nonlegal backgrounds are acceptable. Specific training, license requirements, and certification vary by state. Mediators typically complete 60 hours of courses through independent programs or organizations, but some are trained on the job through volunteering at a community mediation center or teaming up with a practicing mediator.

Some colleges offer certificates or advanced degrees in dispute resolution. To tap into cases, network with local bar associations, insurers, realtors, and human resource departments at area businesses and hospitals. The American Bar Association Section for Dispute Resolution provides a trove of information relating to the dispute resolution field. Mediate.com is another source for international, national, and state conflict resolution organizations and more. You must have a gift for peacemaking.

Next: Artistic, collaborative, and tech-savvy? Read on.

Graphic Designer

The nitty-gritty: The canvas is wide. You might find assignments to design letterhead, business cards, and logos for local businesses. Bigger projects: marketing brochures, snazzy web sites, and e-mail marketing pieces. Most design work can be done via your home computer. You must be at ease with manipulating computer graphics and design software, and possibly know how to program animated graphics. You may, of course, find yourself sketching the old-fashion way with pad and pen as an inspired idea takes shape. It takes more than visual communication to shine in this field.

You must be able to translate your concept into words too. An underlying ability to perceive what appeals to your clients is essential. Sometimes they themselves don't know what they want. It's your job to help them see the possibilities. Skip the artistic temper. This is a collaborative process. Tweaking and redesigns come with the territory. Be prepared for hours at the computer and last-minute crushes for deadlines.

The hours: Hours can be irregular. You will need to adjust to client schedules.

Median pay range: $12.60 to $36.98 per hour and up.

Qualifications: Your success ultimately rests on your flair for design and ability to meet deadlines. That said, degree programs in fine arts or graphic design are offered at many colleges, universities, and private design schools. Most curricula include principles of design, computerized design, commercial graphics production, printing techniques, and web site design. Associate degrees and certificates in graphic design also are available from two-year and three-year professional schools. The National Association of Schools of Art and Design accredits about 300 postsecondary institutions with programs in art and design.

Job hunting tips: A go-to resource for career information is the American Institute of Graphic Arts and the extensive job board on the Art Directors Club's site. Other job sites to scroll through include Coroflot and Krop. Let the color wheel spin.

Next: If you are a detail-oriented writer, you'll love this job. Get paid for exceptional spelling and grammar skills.

Writer/Editor

The nitty-gritty: You don't have to be a professional writer or editor to find work in this arena. You do need a clear grasp of sentence and paragraph construction, spelling, grammar, and punctuation. Jobs run the gamut from copyediting to proofreading, from resume writing to technical editing, to writing marketing proposals, ads, even newsletters. If you have expertise in a particular field or genre, that's all the better for opening doors.

The hours: Freelance writers and editors typically set their own schedules based on deadlines.

Median pay range: Project rates may vary between $15 and $40 an hour. For creating a polished resume for a client, you might charge a base fee of $200. Some publishers pay freelance writers by the word or by the article, and that fluctuates widely depending on your background and experience; anywhere from 50 cents to $3 a word is not out of the ordinary. If you write for an online publisher, you might be paid solely based on the number of times Web visitors view your article or if the content is licensed to other publishers.

Qualifications: No formal training required. Employers often look for expertise in a specific field ranging from health care to taxes. If you're interested in resume and cover letter jobs, Certified Professional Resume Writers and Nationally Certified Resume Writers credentials might be required. For newsier publications, a grasp of the *Associated Press Style Guide* or the *Chicago Manual of Style* might be necessary. Plus, Strunk & White's *Elements of Style* never goes out of style.

Job hunting tips: Copyeditors, editors, proofreaders, or writers: Check out web sites such as eLance.com, Career-Builder and Journalismjobs.com. Cyberedit.com offers assignments via ResumeEdge and EssayEdge, which provide tutoring for high school students. You can also set up your own shop to provide these resume and essay-tuning services.

For more general writing gigs, Helium.com is another source to research. You might also reach out to local associations and organizations, community newsletters, and other regional publications. Ask if they need an extra hand on an assignment basis for online and print articles, brochures, and press releases.

Next: Are you a convincing wordsmith? Read on.

Grant/Proposal Writer

The nitty-gritty: You must have a knack for research and be detail-driven. Each funder has exact guidelines that you must follow to a tee. While your proposal must be persuasive in tone, this is a form of technical writing, so save the flowery lingo. Matching a nonprofit or for-profit with a foundation or government grant requires a solid understanding of the mission of your client's organization and grasp of the concept or program for which funding is being sought. You'll need to create a compelling pitch for why and how the requested funding can make a difference in the outfit's immediate needs and long-term goals. Former journalists often shine in this no-nonsense line of work. This is computer-based work that can hit high gear at deadline time.

The hours: Flexible.

Median pay range: $17.86 to $48.51 per hour and up; part of compensation may be based on the value of the grant obtained.

Qualifications: A bachelor's degree in communications, journalism, or English is often the baseline. Some jobs may be geared toward those with both experience and a degree or knowledge in a specialized field — for example, engineering or medicine. A working knowledge of computer graphics is helpful because of the increased use of online technical documentation.

The Association of Fundraising Professionals offers several options to obtain certification and a mini-grant proposal writing tutorial on the site. *Grant-Writing for Dummies* can help get you started. Many community colleges offer grant-writing certificate programs. Also check out the Foundation Center, which maintains a broad online database of U.S. and global grant makers.

Job hunting tips: Check online job boards like the Chronicle of Philanthropy for postings. Remember, it's not your job to get the grant, but to make the best case possible to suitable funding organizations.

Next: Have a background in accounting? You may qualify.

Financial Manager

The nitty-gritty: You're signing on for a variety of roles: part accountant, part tax expert, part cashier. Duties can run the gamut from processing payroll checks, to handling invoicing, accounts receivable, accounts paid, and other financial reporting. Buying office supplies may even be your bailiwick. Some firms may ask you to monitor checking and savings accounts and track credit card bills.

This is detail-oriented record-keeping work and requires a focused, organized approach. Tracking down delinquent accounts can be trying on the nerves. Delivering bad financial news to a client requires a matter-of-fact, business approach.

The hours: Vary by business; frequently limited to one week mid-month and one week at the end of the month for invoicing or bill-paying functions. Some firms will want you on call at least once a week.

Median pay range: $10.23 per hour to $24.25; $50 or more is possible depending on advanced training, degrees, and location.

Qualifications: A degree in accounting

or business is generally required. The most common certification is a Certified Public Accountant (CPA). The rigorous exam is administered by the American Institute of Certified Public Accountants. CPAs are licensed to offer a range of accounting services including tax preparation. Other certifications: A Certified Internal Auditor (CIA) is someone who has passed a four-part test, administered by the Institute of Internal Auditors. Relevant experience or formal training in accounting-auditing services is a plus. Other key skills to have in your kit: data entry and being adept with financial and accounting computer software such as QuickBooks (quickbooksonline .com).

Job hunting tips: The American Institute of Professional Bookkeepers lists jobs and offers a national certification for bookkeepers, which may help you land a job if you don't have prior practical experience. You might consider posting your resume to eLance .com and surf the big job boards. Networking with your local business groups, industry associations, or Rotary Club for leads is often your best approach. Bean counters, rev up your calculators.

Next: If you're good at talking and tapping into computer files at the same time, log in.

Customer Service Representative

The nitty-gritty: You must have an up-to-date computer (usually a PC), a high-speed Internet connection, a dedicated landline for your use while working, a telephone headset, and a quiet place to work.

In general, you're answering incoming calls, taking new orders, and tracking existing orders. In some cases, you'll troubleshoot and help out with technical support. Online chat sessions and e-mail may be part of the job. You'll need the ability to toggle seamlessly between several computer screen windows at a time. Employers usually offer paid training sessions.

The solitary work demands a good dose of "get up and go" gumption and discipline to keep from being distracted. It's not a bad idea to brush up on yoga stretches to do at your desk between customers. And don't skimp on buying a comfortable, ergonomically safe chair and headset. Remember, it's tax-deductible if you're an independent contractor.

The hours: Full-time, part-time, and split shifts are available. Employers may require at least 20 hours a week, plus weekend slots.

Median pay range: The typical hourly rate is about $9, but workers can earn more than $20 an hour with incentives and bonuses. Some firms provide health, vision, and dental benefits, or access to group plan rates. Paid vacation and matching 401(k) plans may be a perk, but you'll have to clock in enough hours to be eligible.

Qualifications: Job descriptions typically call for customer care or technical support experience. Think broadly. Prior experience in a retail store, as a bank teller, or in sales might suffice. Typically, an online test and a phone interview are required. Background, drug, and credit checks are standard. Some firms charge $30 to $45 for the screening tests.

Job hunting tips: Potential employers, such as Hilton, Marriott, and Best Western hotels (in some parts of the country), American Airlines, and 1-800-Flowers, might hire directly. Others use third-party companies, which then hire home-based workers. In addition to Alpine Access, other virtual call center operators include Arise.com, Convergys, LiveOps.com, WestatHome.com, and Working Solutions.

Next: Up to speed with Microsoft Word and Excel? Try this job.

Virtual Assistant

The nitty-gritty: Virtual personal assistants are increasingly popular for executives, small business owners, and others who need a helping hand but not an on-site staffer on the payroll. Duties range from making travel arrangements to sending out letters and other support services that can easily be handled remotely via e-mail and phone.

The job can involve sitting for long periods, so take precautions to prevent eyestrain, stress, and repetitive motion ailments such as carpal tunnel syndrome.

The hours: Flexible, including split

shifts and part time.

Median pay range: $15 to more than $30 an hour.

Qualifications: Employers increasingly demand knowledge of computer software applications, such as desktop publishing, project management, spreadsheets, and database management. You should be skilled in both Microsoft Word and, for financial statements, Excel. Two years' work experience in an office administrative function is helpful.

Virtual assistant training programs are available at many community colleges. While there's currently no set standard of certification for virtual assistants, the International Virtual Assistants Association (ivaa.org) does offer three certifications that require passing a written test: Certified Virtual Assistant, Ethics Checked Virtual Assistant, and the Real Estate Virtual Assistant. Hats off to the invisible workforce.

Next: Help students make the grade.

Online Tutor

The nitty-gritty: Private online tutoring sessions with students are a growing area in the uber-competitive march to college admissions. The subjects in demand are the core curriculum: world history, physics, science, math, and English. Foreign language specialties are also seeing an uptick, and help with preparation for standardized tests such as the SAT, GDE, and GRE is always in demand.

An online employer like Tutor.com, which offers one-on-one help to students, is set up so that when students need help with homework, they enter their grade level and subject into their computer log-on screen. The appropriate tutor (the firm has 2,200 on board) connects to the student inside the secure online classroom. The student and tutor chat using instant messaging, draw problems on an interactive whiteboard, share a file to review essays and papers, and browse resources on the Web together.

With individual accounts, sessions are saved so that students and parents can review them at any time. Coursework ranges from kindergarten to 12th grade, college courses, and adults returning to school or searching for a job. Other online tutoring firms include Kaplan and SmarThinking.com. Additional sites to market your teaching business: Skillshare.com, Teach street.com, and Edufire.com.

You might opt to tutor on your own. You probably will forgo the bells and whistles of the interactive whiteboard, but you can easily set up chat sessions and send files back and forth with your students, and you can develop an ongoing relationship that provides steady work.

The hours: Flexible. Firms ask you to plan on at least five hours a week between Sunday and Thursday from 4 to 11 P.M. during the school year, if possible, though earlier daytime hours are also available. Vacations are easy to schedule. The typical tutoring session is about 25 minutes long.

Median pay range: Hourly rates are between $10 and $14 an hour, based on experience, subject tutored, company, and grade level. Some private tutors, however, can make more than $65 an hour. Tutor.com claims the "most active" chemistry tutors earn anywhere from $800 to $1,600 a month.

Qualifications: A certified teacher is preferred, but not required. Professional experience opens doors. High-level math and science expertise is highly sought-after.

In general, with a tutoring company, you take an online exam in the subject you're interested in tutoring. If you pass, you will be given a mock session with an online tutor. Then you must pass a third-party background check and final exam. More than one subject is encouraged. Your computer must have high-speed Internet access and be able to run the classroom software provided. Mac users may be out of luck with some companies. And don't expect a shiny apple on your desk, either.

Next: Is crafting your passion?

Crafter

The nitty-gritty: It sounds divine. You carve out a workshop at home, and, inspired by your inner creativity, you churn out high-quality, handcrafted items and make some money at the same time. More people are peddling their homemade wares online, at craft shows, and at flea markets. But to really build a business beyond pocket change, you need to push out of your comfort zone of selling to friends and family and peddle to the masses on the online marketplace.

You can set up your own shop on the web site Etsy.com, which boasts more than 11 million handcrafted items for sale. Etsy charges 20 cents to list an item and lops off 3.5 percent of your sale. Other sites to market your merchandise: pinterest.com, madeitmyself .com, and silkfair.com. Some sites charge a small sales fee similar to Etsy. You might also launch a blog and your own web site and entice area boutiques to sell your creations, too.

Median pay range: Varies widely. It's possible to net a few hundred dollars a month in profit after you pay for your materials and figure your hourly wages. You can certainly boost that with a great product, super sales, and lots of elbow grease. You're the boss, so you set the pay scale. You're probably not going to get rich, but it's a fine way to earn money and love your job at the same time.

Qualifications: It's hard to set the bar here. In general, a sense of design and artistic bent will get you noticed. But the intangible skills of self-motivation and discipline, combined with a unique product and some sales chutzpah, is what will help you succeed. You should have a handle on bookkeeping, or hire someone part-time to help with record keeping. The IRS will want to know what you're up to, especially if you are selling online via credit cards.

Next: Got a flair for sales?

The Home-Based Craftsman

Working from home is getting to be big business. According to market researcher IDC, there will be 14 million full-time, home-based freelancers and independent contractors in the United States by 2015, up from 12 million in 2010. Between 2008 and 2011, the number of self-employed Americans between 55 and 64 years old rose by 5 percent.

"Some people start this kind of work as a side job while they are working elsewhere, but huge numbers of older workers and retirees are creating income for themselves in these ways," Art Koff, founder of RetiredBrains .com, says.

Mark Nelson is one of them. When Nelson, 60, retired in 2007 after three decades with the postal service, the bulk of it spent as postmaster in rural Boyceville, Wisconsin, a town of around 1,000 located about 60 miles from Minneapolis/St. Paul, he spent a year and change hunting, fishing, and fussing with his horses and mules. "But you get to the point when you've done all the playing," Nelson recalls. "You have to be productive." It might have helped that his wife, Lesley, a registered nurse, was still working part time on a nurse advice hotline at the local hospital.

A lot of things weren't possible for him to do, though. Eleven months after retiring, he broke his back falling 20 feet to the ground from a deer tree stand.

Leather-crafting had been his hobby since he got his first crafting kit the Christmas he was 13. And over the years, he made plenty of wallets and holsters while working his day job. "I had the best job in town as the postmaster," Nelson says. "It was rewarding, but frankly government work doesn't have a lot of outlet for creativity." His duties: sorting mail, waiting on customers, and managing the books — all structured activities. "I've always been a creative person, and leather-working as a hobby was a great outlet for that."

So when he was considering what to do next, leather-making came to mind. Then he took a step further; he turned to his old interest in saddle-making. That curiosity had been spurred back in his early 20s when he was working as a radio broadcaster and hanging out with a saddle maker in Ft. Pierre, South Dakota, during his spare time, watching him work.

"When I thought about what I would really love to do, that was it. I got the bug to make saddles, and not just any saddles," Nelson says. His love is for the old western saddles of the 19th century, the heyday of the cowboy era from 1866 to 1899, a time when the west was really the wild, wild west. That's his fancy.

Nelson's passion is historic reenactment of cowboy action. He even helped start a Cowboy Action Shooting club. "I wanted to know how to make saddles for my own use, but realized that I had to make some money at it, too."

That meant opening a tiny workshop shoehorned into a pole barn on his five-acre property, buying the equipment, which includes a heavy industrial sewing machine, a splitter to reduce the thickness of the hide, and other leather-cutting tools — some 100 years old — and shelling out $5,000 tuition to spend six weeks undergoing intense saddle-making tutelage at the Montana Horseman Saddle Building School in Belgrade, Montana.

During the course, he made three saddles, one for himself and two that he sold to team ropers in Montana. He was hooked. When he got home, he opened Way West Saddlery.

His custom-made saddles now start at $2,000 and take him around 40 hours or more to make. His primary clients: historic re-enactors and extreme cowboy competitors, who strive for the authentic costuming and accoutrements, including their saddles. He also builds custom Western stock saddles fitted for an individual horse and his or her rider.

The drawbacks: "There's a fine line between a hobby and an obsession," Nelson laughs. "A lot of us go over the line. One of my challenges is keeping myself out of the workshop when I'm home."

His saddle-making business is still growing, mostly by word of mouth. He admits that marketing is his weak point, not unusual for an entrepreneur working from home. His concern, though, is that he doesn't want to get to the point where he has six or seven saddles backed up and people waiting for their saddles. "I don't want to hire help," he says.

Nelson confesses that for now, he's not

making a lot of money. His upfront material costs usually top $800 per saddle. While his business slowly ramps up, Nelson is logging in two days a week as a caregiver at a nearby residential alcohol and drug addiction treatment center, earning $9.50 an hour. "After having been postmaster in a small town, I missed that contact with people all the time, and living out in the country it would be pretty easy to be a hermit," he says.

Nelson's gumption is noteworthy. Turning a hobby into paying work can ruin your passion for it, so you need to plan ahead and take it a step at a time. And if you need the income now, you might want to supplement your fledgling business with outside work initially as Nelson has done.

Direct Sales

The nitty-gritty: Selling for a direct sales firm like Avon, Cutco, Mary Kay, The Pampered Chef, Tupperware, and Silpada can be lucrative, and there are plenty of opportunities to do so. About 16 million Americans work in direct marketing, according to the Direct Selling Association. It's not about going door-to-door ringing bells anymore. You can market the goods straight from your home office via a computer, Internet access, and a telephone. But it requires plenty of legwork and some start-up costs, usually $200 or less for a "starter" kit of training materials and products. Legitimate direct selling companies allow you to "sell back" unsold products that are in good condition if you decide this isn't your bag.

You set your work schedule, so that's a plus. You'll usually sell a company's products through home or office parties and online sales. Earnings are commission-based. With some companies, you can ramp up your income by recruiting other salespeople to join your team. You then earn a commission for the products they sell, too.

Direct selling is not for slackers. You reap what you sow. You need to set monthly goals — how many new customers you will contact, how many parties you will hold, how many follow-ups with clients you will make. You can't be timid about asking existing customers for referrals, either. It's all about getting your name out there and growing your business.

An upside: Unlike starting a new business solo, where you're responsible for the whole ball of wax, for the most part, your job is purely selling. The company makes the product, delivers it, and has your back if you have customer complaints and other business questions.

For a list of direct selling companies with links back to each, go to Retired Brains.com. Contact the Direct Selling Association for information on any specific direct selling company. Beware that direct sales also encompass other types of businesses, such as multilevel marketing companies, also referred to as MLM. Visit business.ftc.gov for guidance. Many of these companies have been scrutinized for illegal practices or pyramid schemes. Check with your local Chamber of Commerce, Better Business Bureau, or state attorney general's office to see if there have been complaints about a company in the past.

Median pay range: You can earn around $300 to $500 a month part-time, up to $1,000 or more full-time. Compensation systems are commission-based — 25 percent to 40 percent generally. You buy the products wholesale and sell them at retail prices. You can increase your earnings draw by recruiting, training, and mentoring new representatives at companies such as Avon.

Qualifications: The core backing you need is your own passion for the product. If you use it and understand how it works yourself, it's easy to make a sales pitch from the heart. But some expertise can come in handy. If you're selling makeup, for example, it helps to have some background in cosmetics and be capable of confidently offering beauty and skin care advice. The same holds true with cooking utensils: knowing your way around a kitchen helps. This is a customer-centric gig, so you need smooth people skills and an ability to be at ease with one-to-one contact with your future customers. Creativity plays a role, too. Building sales stems from drumming up innovative ways to sell your product. Pull out the old soft shoe.

Next up, tapping teaching skills.

CHAPTER 6
GREAT JOBS FOR
RETIRED TEACHERS

After the last school bell rings, retired teachers have a leg up. Opportunities cut a broad swath, from tutoring to substitute teaching to jobs a little further afield, such as fitness training.

Teachers have a combination of tools in their kit that many other people 50+ don't — solid degree credentials, expertise in a specific field, and a passion for helping people learn something new.

That triple threat proved to be the ticket for Dave Kergaard, a former high school physical education and health teacher. When Kergaard, now 65, retired from his position as assistant superintendent of Kent County Public Schools on Maryland's Eastern Shore, he knew just what he wanted to do: set up a shingle as a personal fitness coach. "I've always worked out and been involved in sports," he explains.

As a young man, his football and wrestling

prowess earned him scholarships to college. And after graduating, he parlayed his bachelor's degree in physical education and a master's degree in psychology into a 30-year career in education. He kicked off a rewarding career by teaching physical education and health in public high schools and coaching high school sport squads in football, soccer, track, and basketball before segueing into administrative roles.

Kergaard has had both hips replaced, but this hasn't stopped him. Today, he usually clocks in 12 hours a week as a personal trainer at Club Fitness in Rehoboth Beach, Delaware, near where he and his wife moved in retirement. Trainers there can pull in anywhere from $30 to $60 an hour. The work runs the gamut from nutrition counseling to designing workout regimes with weights, bikes, balls, and resistance bands.

He has embraced his newfound career — helping a wide range of clients, including a 90-year-old woman who ditched her walker after gaining back her strength via the exercise regime he custom-designed for her. Kergaard also works with high school athletes and the 55+ crowd alike. "Some days I use my psychology degree more than my physical education one," Kergaard says with a laugh.

Beyond the moderate physical demands, the real challenge for a trainer is giving undivided attention to a student, er, a trainee.

"Many people won't push as hard unless you are there with them 100 percent," Kergaard says. "I love seeing the looks on their faces when they see the change in themselves that comes from what they're learning about fitness and health. You feel their energy and see the smiles — like the ones the kids had as they came down the hallways."

Sure sounds like a day in the life of a teacher.

Here are great jobs for retired teachers to consider.

Personal Trainer/Physical Conditioner

The nitty-gritty: Fit as a fiddle means something in this world. Expect sweat. You'll be demonstrating exercise techniques, bending to set machines, and lifting balls and weights. Prepare for some tough love. Honesty rules when helping clients gauge their physical fitness level and set reasonable goals. Creativity comes into play, too. The core of the job is teaching and motivation. Generally, you have free rein to design course plans for your clients' individual workout routines.

And it's not all mats and machines. You need grounding in nutrition and diet issues, which go hand-in-hand with a fit physique. Most trainers work at health and fitness club facilities. But if you've got an entrepreneurial bent, one-on-one training at clients' homes is popular. Senior living communities, wellness centers, civic associations, and even large nonprofits like the Arthritis Foundation are often on the lookout for individual or small group trainers.

The hours: Flexible. Mornings, evenings, weekends, you name it. You book your own sessions.

Median pay range: The median scale is $17 to $30 an hour. But in larger cities, rates can roll up to $60 to $100 or more. Most health clubs collect the cost for the session from their members and dole out a percentage to you.

Qualifications: Certification is not required by law, but most fitness clubs insist. Several national groups offer some type of credential. These include the American Council on Exercise, the International Sports Sciences Association, and the National Strength and

Conditioning Association. For credentials, you must be certified in cardiopulmonary resuscitation (CPR) and pass an exam that consists of both a written test and practical demonstration.

These exams aren't for slouchers. You'll need to be up to speed on human physiology, understand correct exercise techniques, know how to assess a client's fitness level, and know the ins and outs of proper exercise programs. The groups sell study materials, including books and CD-ROMs, and offer exam preparation workshops. Renewal every two years via continuing education classes is standard.

If you're an education junkie, you might step it up by enrolling in an adult education program at a community or local college to obtain a fitness training degree. In general, advanced certification will require an associate's or bachelor's degree in an exercise-related subject such as physical education or kinesiology. And as with many people-oriented jobs, a peppy personality and a physique that shows you practice what you preach will attract and retain clients. Gym rats need apply.

Next: Share your love for schoolbooks.

University Bookstore Retail Specialist

The nitty-gritty: Bookworms, take note. This job requires more than a passion for reading. You've got to be a cool and organized person to take charge in this venue. The campus bookstore is a central hub of campus life. There are all those textbooks to sell. And visitors stop in to purchase a T-shirt or pair of socks with the school's logo; on home game football weekends in the fall, the store can be a madhouse. Be prepared to be on your feet for long periods. You'll be directing shoppers and stocking the sales floor. Some lifting is involved. It's likely you'll be ordering merchandise, too, and at peak hours putting in time at the cash register.

Median pay range: $10.09 per hour. It is possible to find positions up to $20 an hour.

Qualifications: Basic computer skills and retail experience. Customer service skills, knowledge of merchandising, and ability to multitask.

178

Next: Put those teaching skills to good use and earn high hourly wages.

Tutoring

The nitty-gritty: For those of you who always wished you had more time to give personal attention to individual students, tutoring is a dream come true.

For test prep review, the most common method is by setting up sessions at the student's home or a local library. Public and private schools often pass along tutor referrals to parents, so let the guidance counselors at schools know you're available and your credentials. You can also post on community bulletin boards, or even create your own web site to market your business.

You might opt for online test prep tutoring jobs, arranged through a tutoring web site such as Kaplan, SmarThinking.com, and Tutor.com. These may not pay as much, but you also don't have to spend time trying to drum up business. Tutor.com, for instance, is set up so you work with the student inside a secure online classroom. You teach by instant messaging, drawing problems on an interactive whiteboard, and sending essays and papers back and forth via e-mail attachments.

While test prep is popular, there's a perennial need for private tutoring in a range of subjects to boost student grades and help adult learners. The subjects in demand are the core curriculum: world history, physics, science, math, and English. Foreign language specialties also offer opportunities.

For more on tutoring, see Chapter 2.

The hours: Online sessions may be as short as 25 minutes, but most in-person tutoring sessions range from an hour after school to three hours on weekends. Scheduling at least four hours a week during peak test prep times should be a snap. Fall and spring are the prime times for college-bound kids to take the SAT and ACT aptitude tests. Prep for a range of other standardized tests such as the GDE, GRE, and LSAT are in demand year-round.

Median pay range: Generally $10.27 to $24.21, but landing rates as high as $65 an hour isn't unusual.

Qualifications: A background in education and working with students in a classroom is generally a prerequisite. Some special areas to consider: A Wilson Language-certified trainer, who has mastered the Wilson Reading System, a program that specializes in teaching reading to children with dyslexia, is becoming a marketable tool for reading tutors. As more school districts and adult education centers across the country have added the reading and spelling technique to its classrooms, those who have the credential are sought after as private tutors to boost reading and language skills for students of all ages, especially during the summer months. You can add the certification through a rigorous program that combines online instruction plus observation and feedback from a Wilson trainer.

At Tutor.com, high-level math and science expertise is your best calling card. You'll need to take an online exam in the subject you apply to tutor, followed by a mock session with one of the firm's online tutors. If you sail through, there's a third-party background check and a final exam. As the saying goes, "When the student is ready, the teacher will appear."

Next: A master's degree might come in handy with this teaching job.

Adjunct Professor/Instructor/Lecturer/ Visiting Professor

The nitty-gritty: Still have a hankering for a classroom? Community colleges in your area can send you back to the front of the class with a short- or long-term commitment. You'll have an opportunity to teach a range of students, from recent high school grads to career transitioning adults adding new skills or updating old ones. Part-time faculty comes in under various monikers — adjunct professor, instructor, lecturer, and visiting professor. Technical schools also may have openings.

Most community colleges have online applications. Stop by the registrar's office or go online to obtain a copy of current course listings from the place where you'd like to teach. Do some sleuthing to discover what courses are missing in your field of expertise. Ask around to see if you know anyone in your professional network from boards, for instance, who might be teaching in the evenings and see if they can make an introduction for you. It might take some time to find the right course for you to teach.

If you're tech savvy and at ease teaching a class via a computer Web cam, a growing number of community colleges now offer online courses for their students. To learn more about community colleges, go to the American Association of Community Colleges' web site.

The hours: These vary widely depending on the number of courses you teach. Summer courses are common. Night and weekend classes are standard. Figure on one hour to two hours of classroom time per week for each course, plus your lesson preparation and grading time, for a total of, say, five hours a week.

Median pay range: An average of $30 to $40 an hour; $1,000 to $1,800 per class taught. The pay can pop up to $5,000, however, depending on your degree level, teaching experience, the department, and number of credits the course offers.

Qualifications: A master's degree within your discipline is usually preferred, but depending on your experience and the course, it's possible to land a post with a bachelor's degree. Of course, you'll need to be an expert in the subject area. You'll need to provide teaching references and probably perform a tryout session to demonstrate your teaching skills. Generally speaking, technical schools hire with only a bachelor's degree. As with most teaching gigs, expertise, passion for the subject, and experience trumps all else.

Job hunting tips: Stop by the college where you might like to teach and meet the head of the department where your expertise falls. Find out what might be missing from their offerings and if there might be any openings. Look for job listings on Adjunct ProfessorsOnline.com and Highered Jobs.com. The professor is in.

Next: A flexible schedule is your calling card for this opportunity.

Substitute Teacher

The nitty-gritty: Stepping out of full-time teaching but keeping a toe dipped in has long been a way for retired teachers to stay engaged and supplement income. Subbing can take on a fairly regular schedule, but it's your prerogative to just say no when the request comes in. The life of a sub can have its challenges. Picking up a course midstream takes some fancy footwork, memorizing two dozen students' names in a blink of an eye can be daunting, and quickly gaining the respect of students trying to test you takes some special mojo. Some teachers will leave a prepared class plan. But if you are filling in at the last minute, you may be in improv mode to keep the class on track.

Depending on your background, you may be tapped to teach a range of subjects in grade levels from kindergarten through 12. If you have a proclivity for special needs kids, you may find your services in demand. Never forget that flexibility is your calling card. School districts typically keep an active roster of substitutes on call who are willing to drop everything and step into a classroom with little advance notice.

The hours: Flexible half-days to several-week stints for the entire school day.

Median pay range: Each school district sets its own pay scale for substitute teachers. Currently, the pay rate for substitutes is $20 to $190 per full day. The national average for a substitute teacher is about $105 per full day, according to the National Substitute Teachers Alliance. Generally, the pay will match the length of the assignment and the area's cost of living. Some subs may get benefits.

Qualifications: Most substitute teaching jobs require a bachelor's degree from an accredited college or university. The National Education Association's State-by-State Summary provides the minimum requirements. Your state's education department has the details. Learn about the full requirements for substitute teachers in each state here. There are often fewer requirements at private schools. You should expect a background check. Baby sitters need not apply.

Next: Show off your research skills and earn money.

Market and Survey Researchers
The nitty-gritty: Combining research and people skills makes these jobs appealing to those who have mastered

academic life. In general, if you're a newcomer, you're often on the front lines conducting surveys of customers — either on the phone, online, through questionnaires via mail, or door-to-door. You might even find yourself working a shopping mall booth to help get the "man or woman on the street" snapshot of consumer preferences. Typically, you'll be asked to write a detailed report and provide an analysis of your findings. In some instances, you're sizing up potential sales of a product or service. Other times it's pulling together statistical data on competitors, prices, and more.

The list of potential employers runs the gamut from consumer products firms to university research centers to financial services organizations, government agencies, health care institutions, and advertising firms. You'll need to be a stickler for details since this kind of work tends to rely on precise data reviews. For information about careers and salaries in market and survey research, contact the Council of American Survey Research Organizations and the Marketing Research Association.

The hours: Flexible, project-based, full time for short assignments.

Median pay range: $17.01 to $53.80 hourly.

Qualifications: A bachelor's degree is the baseline. A background in liberal arts and social science courses — including economics, psychology, and sociology — is helpful. A master's or doctorate degree may be required, especially for more analytical positions. Quantitative skills are important for some survey research positions, so courses in mathematics, statistics, sampling theory and survey design, and computer science are helpful. An advanced degree in business administration, marketing, statistics, and communications may give you an edge. Check out the human resources section at university and college web sites for job postings. Having some training in survey research methodology can help you get a foot in the door. Curiosity doesn't kill the cat — it gets him work.

Job hunting tips: Check out the human resources section at university and college web sites for job postings.

Next: Guiding students beyond the ivy-covered walls.

Career Center Counselor

The nitty-gritty: This one's for your inner mentor. These centers tend to need staff during the busy fall and spring semesters. Think of yourself as a matchmaker: you put students and employers together with something they love through networking, suggestions, employer interviews, internships, and more.

You'll probably find yourself the interpreter of a battery of vocational assessment tests. You hone resume and cover letters with smooth wordsmithing. You dole out dress-for-success and etiquette advice for interviews. You rehearse your charges with mock interviews. Chances are, you'll be called to develop and present career education workshops for small groups and help run career fairs.

Median pay range: $25.67 per hour.

Qualifications: Familiarity with national career trends and labor markets. Experience in general counseling, career counseling, human resources, and education or career development.

The International Coach Federation has a list of certification programs and offers its own certification. Recognition as a National Certified Counselor or licensing as a professional counselor is sometimes preferred. Some employers might require a master's degree in counseling or higher education.

Need more information on counseling? The Bureau of Labor Statistic's *Occupational Outlook Handbook* suggests the American Counseling Association, the National Career Developers Association, and the National Board for Certified Counselors.

Next up, doing work that gives back.

CHAPTER 7
GREAT NONPROFIT JOBS

When Mattie Ruffin, 62, retired from her job as a program analyst at the U.S. Environmental Protection Agency in early 2010, she took a year off to relax. After working for the federal government for 27 years, it was a well-deserved respite. "I hadn't planned to retire, but my sister died suddenly," recalls Ruffin, who is also a widow. "I got to thinking . . . I'm not 21 anymore, and tomorrow is just not promised to me. So I'm just going to come on out of here and enjoy my life."

Ironically, that involved going back to work. Her ultimate working in retirement reward: "I'm a people person — I like helping people," Ruffin says. "And that's what I'm doing." That led her to nonprofit work.

Ruffin has the cushion of a federal government pension, but she didn't want to sit home indefinitely. "I developed a lot of good skills over the years, and computers are my thing," she says. Her specialties, for example, include administrative management and budgets and spreadsheets on Excel. "I didn't want to lose the technology skills," she says. "If I didn't do something to keep those up, then I felt I would have lost those skills."

She signed up for the 10-week Envision 50+ program offered through the Workforce Development and Continuing Education department at nearby Prince George's Community College in Largo, Maryland. In 2010, the college started the program, aimed at people over 50 who want to rewire either to change careers or continue to work in retirement. Funding comes from Encore .org's Encore College Initiative.

The course didn't involve too much heavy lifting for Ruffin, since the work could be done partially online. She gradually revamped her resume, brushed up on her computer and online job-hunting skills, and networked with potential employers as the weeks ticked by. A sweet bonus — since she was over 60, her tuition was free.

Ruffin learned about an opening at the nonprofit community college in its adult education department, and the part-time position was ideal for someone with her techie background. She works nine hours per week as an adult education administrative assistant. Ruffin helps adults from age 18 to over 40 register via computer to enroll in classes to earn GEDs and more.

She collects drilled-down data on how many students are being trained and their progress, then churns out detailed, monthly spreadsheet reports for the college and the Maryland Department of Labor, which partially funds the efforts. Her rate: $15 an hour. "It's not like I need the job to pay my bills. I call it my mad money. It's the money I use to go shopping, or hang out with my girlfriends, or go to dinner," Ruffin says.

While the hours sitting at the computer aren't a problem for her, she does feel the budgetary pinch faced by many nonprofit workers: "I was so used to having all the office supplies I needed to perform my job when I wanted them when I was in the government. Now, because of the college's budget constraints, I'm careful to reuse some office supplies."

There are plenty of great nonprofit jobs out there for you. For job-hunting help, you can start your search at web sites such as Bridgestar.org, Change.org, Encore.org, Commongood Careers (cgcareers.org), CreateTheGood.org, and Idealist.org. LinkedIn also has a job search section dedicated to nonprofit positions.

Here are some opportunities at nonprofits.

Administrative Assistant

The nitty-gritty: Can you say jack-of-all-trades? This position calls for a mixed bag of skills and an ability to roll with the punches. You'll be working with top management as well as consultants, contractors, customers, and donors. You'll typically be responsible for the down and dirty clerical work from word processing to updating databases. You may be in charge of scheduling appointments, making travel arrangements for professional staff and board members, coordinating meetings and seminars, and processing registrations for workshops. Generally speaking, you'll take incoming calls; order and maintain office supplies; fulfill orders for reports, books, and other materials; and organize materials and hand-outs for events. The occupation ranks among those with the largest number of job openings through 2018, according to the Bureau of Labor Statistics.

The greatest demand is from nonprofits that serve educational services, health care, and social assistance, according to BLS. At the heart of it, a versatile assistant is the point person who keeps things running smoothly with a lean staff, tight supplies, and a big agenda. Basic job description: good team player.

The hours: Part time and full time; some virtual work possible.

Median pay range: $13.82 to $32.21 an hour.

Qualifications: Computer literacy. Come armed with a broad knowledge of computer software applications such as Word, Excel, PowerPoint, and Constant Contact. Core word processing, writing, proofreading, editing, and communication skills are indispensable. You should also be at ease working with software for desktop publishing, project management, spreadsheets, and database management.

Familiarity with social media, including Twitter and Facebook, is a plus. Good customer service and organizational skills, and the ability to work independently will serve you well. Employers will be on the lookout for a proven track record of getting things done, problem solving, and pumped-up energy.

Don't panic if you aren't riding the cutting-edge technology; on-the-job skills can be gleaned with the help of other employees or equipment and software vendors.

Next: Have you always enjoyed volunteering?

Volunteer Manager

The nitty-gritty: Your first line of duty is recruiting qualified volunteers via meetings with local interest groups and businesses. You want to drum up awareness of the nonprofit's cause and hopefully flush out helping hands. Then you interview volunteers to find out where they can best help out.

Once they're on board, you direct training, coordinate schedules, supervise, and retain them. Keeping busy professionals who are willing to donate their time coming back to perform sometimes-routine tasks requires some finesse. You may need to jump into the fray from time to time if volunteers don't show up or a deadline is crashing. If the volunteers are providing their support overseas, you'll be in charge of making sure all have the proper visas, passports, and shots. In the end, it's up to you to know who's on first.

The hours: Part-time and full-time positions are typically available. Flexible schedules for weekends and evening work may be necessary to align with peak volunteer times.

Median pay range: An hourly wage for a part-time manager may range from $20 to $25 an hour. The average full-time salary for a director of volunteer services can range from $55,000 to $60,000, but salaries vary greatly.

Qualifications: A personal history of volunteerism goes without saying. Public speaking chops are paramount. A track record of delegating and monitoring many activities at the same time will get you noticed. And those "rah, rah" motivational skills will open doors for you. It's vital to have the know-how to bring people together from all sorts of backgrounds to work together for a cause, not a paycheck.

A background in social services helps, but proven leadership and managerial skills in previous positions trumps. Many colleges and universities offer classes in volunteer management as part of their graduate programs in public administration or nonprofit management. One credential available for volunteer managers is "Certified Volunteer Administration." The certification is backed by supporters such as The United Way Worldwide, Idealist .org, and VolunteerMatch.org.

Next: Do you have a great mind for marketing and media relations?

Marketing/Communications Manager

The nitty-gritty: Consider yourself the "cause" messenger. You're the voice of the nonprofit in many ways. Duties can range from drafting press releases about upcoming events or capital campaigns to media outreach for coverage in print, broadcast, and social media streams. You might be writing compelling blast e-mails, or mass snail mail letters requesting donations, or producing content for quarterly newsletters.

Under the public relations guise, you may be asked to give speeches, set up speaking engagements, and prepare speeches for the executive director and board members. A note of caution: Nonprofits are collaborative places, and anything that reflects the face of the organization to the outside world will come under close scrutiny. Higher-ups will want to put their fingerprints on anything you write. Learn to let it go.

The hours: Part-time and full-time positions.

Median pay range: The pay scale is $14.69 to $45.77 an hour, but depending on experience can be far higher.

Qualifications: In general, experience in media relations, writing, editing, and marketing are the prerequisites. A background in journalism can help. Bring a deep understanding of a non-profit's specific field — environment, medical, social issues — plus more extensive knowledge of the core issue at the forefront of the group's mission. A bottomless basket of media contacts is vital. A working knowledge of the ways of social media — Twitter, Facebook, LinkedIn, Google+, and other Internet platforms — is expected.

The Public Relations Society of America and the American Marketing

Association offer workshops, seminars, webinars, and boot camps on a range of topics you need to know now, such as social media, green marketing, crisis communication, and branding.

Tip: A new kid on the block, Empowered UCLA Extension, an online Internet-education firm (empowered .com), offers fast-track certificate programs for older adults looking for post-retirement careers to retrain or upgrade skills through UCLA Extension starting this fall. Taught via an iPad, tuition is $12,800 for a 12-month certificate program, and includes career counseling. Fields of study include marketing and new media, college counseling, health care management, financial planning, nonprofit management, and other growing fields.

Next: If you revel in event planning, you will love this job.

Fundraiser

The nitty-gritty: How good are you at asking for money? Fundraising is a key ingredient to a nonprofit's ultimate success and requires nurturing a rapport with donors and establishing a database of existing and potential donors. Prepare to confidently unleash your outgoing, persuasive nature.

It takes chutzpah to ask for money. You might ask for large gifts from individual donors, solicit bequests, host special events, apply for grants (see grant-writing jobs, p. 153), or launch phone and letter appeals. In a smaller nonprofit, you may very well be asked to dig in on all of these activities. If you're hunting down a large gift, you'll be on the front line — kibitzing over long lunches and meeting with potential donors in their offices and at their homes.

But this is a job that takes more than charm and a verbal soft shoe. Good listening skills are essential, too. A successful fundraiser knows how to build relationships and patiently wait for the right time to press for a gift — especially when asking for thousands of dollars. If you revel in event planning, organizing parties with purpose, so to speak, can be a cool aspect of fundraising, too. Think black-tie dinners, charity walks. There are behind-the-scenes jobs, too — drafting form fundraising letters asking for donations, writing grant proposals, and penning those all-important "thank you for your donation" notes.

The hours: From part-time consultant to full-time staff; evening and weekend hours may be required.

Median pay range: $23.90 to more than $80 an hour.

Qualifications: It's not unusual for fundraisers to transfer into the position from careers in public relations, sales, or market research. One way to sharpen your fundraising skills is to enroll in classes and certification programs offered by the Association of Fundraising Professionals and the Foundation Center. The AFP's Fundamentals of Fundraising course offers introductory-level sessions — seven workshops — to introduce the novice fundraiser to the fundamental concepts and techniques of fundraising. The Foundation Center offers free and affordable classes nationwide in classrooms and online that cover grant proposal writing and fundraising skills. Many colleges and universities offer courses in fundraising.

Planned giving specialists should have a grounding in gift and tax law.

There's no sweet-talking Uncle Sam when it comes to the requirements for a charitable deduction.

Exploring Nonprofits — Job-Hunting Tips

Despite the do-gooder aspect of the work, there can be some drawbacks — starting with lower pay scales. In the nonprofit world, you work hard and often lack the resources to get it all done as fast or as successfully as you would like. Simply put, you have to do more with less.

But there's a silver lining. An Idealist.org survey of 3,000 U.S. nonprofits concluded that jobs in this sector are opening up after a few years of cuts in services, staff, or both. Program or service staffs are top of the hiring lists. If you're a go-getter fundraiser and can whip up creative and diverse funding streams, they want you. Administrative, communications, accounting and finance personnel, and technology experts are also needed.

Here are some steps to take if you're interested:

Soul-search. What issues do you care about?
Skill search. What skills do you have to help move into the sector — computer, legal, sales, financial management?

Research. The nonprofit world is broad. Understand what you can do for the specific field you're getting into by having an understanding of the organization's goals and expectations. Volunteering first can give you an insider's view and networking contacts that may lead to a job.

Add to your skill set. Consider taking a course to fill in any holes in your background. Credentials help in the nonprofit world. A number of people complete a master's or certificate program in social work in their fifties. Course work includes nonprofit marketing, fundraising, campaigns, corporate philanthropy, ethics, and law.

Salary check. Be realistic about your salary, vacation, and benefits needs. Salaries tend to be 20 to 50 percent lower than in the for-profit arena.

Web search. Check out nonprofit web sites in the resource section.

Next up, health care workers are in demand.

CHAPTER 8
GREAT HEALTH CARE JOBS

When you scan the job market these days, one bright light is health care. Not surprisingly, some of these jobs top the *AARP Bulletin*'s list of 50 jobs for a second career. Have medical experience or willing to learn? These fields are in demand.

You don't have to be a surgeon or ICU nurse. There are hundreds of areas of specialization, such as paramedical examiner, school nurse, medical records administrator, medical assistant, or home care aide. Many jobs offer flexible work schedules.

If you have health care experience in your preretirement tool kit, you'll have a leg up. Stepping into this growing and ever-changing arena, however, may require new skills to score a certification or renew a license. Many employers prefer applicants who are certified by a recognized professional association.

The soaring demand for skilled workers,

though, will make the effort worth your while. Ideally you can plan ahead and add the necessary courses before you start job seeking to smooth the move.

For Denise Teifel, working part time as a paramedical examiner is the perfect financial safety net in her new stage of life. The bulk of her work for ExamOne, a subsidiary of Quest Diagnostics, is conducting medical exams to screen individuals for life insurance policies.

Her working hours are usually spent on the road, making house calls on applicants. She's fine with that — it's flexible work, and the pay amply cushions her retirement lifestyle.

The tools of her trade: a suitcase on wheels packed with a scale, tape measure, blood pressure cuff, and sealed lab kits stocked with sterile syringes and vials.

Her basic duties include drawing blood and obtaining urine specimens, then sending them off to the appointed lab for testing. She takes weight and height measurements and records medical histories. Depending on the age of the applicant, she may be asked to run a battery of mental and physical tests. In addition, she draws blood samples for cholesterol screens at health fairs for corporations such as Home

Depot and Safeway, and she conducts random employee drug tests for corporate clients.

This is an encore career for her. Seven years ago, Teifel, 58, an accountant by training, retired from her post as an executive assistant for the El Dorado County Department of Veterans Affairs in Placerville, California. Stress was the impetus for her early exit. Juggling accounts payable and receivable, budgeting, and hiring were getting to her. Combine that with a serious health scare, thyroid cancer, and she decided to pump the brakes.

Her husband, a manager for an environmental oil and gas company, was on board with the decision. Seeking a slower pace of life, the couple moved to Albany, Oregon, nestled in the bucolic Willamette Valley.

"I hadn't planned to work when we moved up here," Teifel says. The couple had adequate retirement savings and used the proceeds from the sale of their California abode to buy their dream home with mostly cash.

But for Teifel, not bringing home a paycheck was hard to adjust to from the get-go. "I had worked so many years bringing in money that I couldn't justify spending to even get a massage — the extras," she says.

"That's when I started thinking about what was I going to do."

Her two daughters, both working in the medical field, knew she could find a job in their world. "I was too old to go back to school to get my RN," she surmises, but they told her about the demand for phlebotomists, who make a living drawing blood. "At first, I thought, oh man, that's gruesome."

In truth, Teifel was pretty familiar with blood work because of her thyroid condition. "As a cancer survivor, I get my blood drawn all the time," she says. "I wanted to be a better phlebotomist than some of those I had come up against."

She enrolled in a phlebotomy certification program at an Oregon vocational school. It offered an intense course load — anatomy, physiology, and medical terminology — plus she learned her way around tricky veins. The price was right — around $1,600 for a six-week course, followed by an eight-week internship at a local clinic.

After attaining her certificate, she signed on as a contractor for the paramedical company, which supplied additional training. Continuing education is required to keep her skills current.

Appointments range from a snappy 15

minutes for a basic exam to over an hour when additional services are requested. She can earn anywhere from $300 to more than $1,000 every two weeks, depending on the number of assignments she accepts.

A basic exam brings in around $20. A full exam pays $35 to $40 an hour. She's reimbursed for mileage costs over 40 miles round-trip. Some weeks she may work six hours, not including drive time; other weeks she'll rack up nearly 20 hours. Flexibility is the name of the game. "I get new orders daily and can choose where I want to go," Teifel says.

It's not a job for introverts. The first thing Teifel does when she gets out of the car is look at what someone has in the yard, or in the house, to get a sense of the person's interests. That way she can strike up a conversation to put clients at ease before she opens her kit.

"You have no idea how many folks have white coat syndrome, or are just deathly afraid of needles," Teifel says. "I've had grown men start bawling like a baby when I try to stick them with a needle to draw blood. I say, 'Okay, put your big boy panties on,' " she chuckles. "I meet quirky people. A lot of friends have told me I should write a book: My Adventures in Examland."

You'll find useful details about health care jobs in the Department of Labor's *Occupational Outlook Handbook* and the American Medical Association's annual *Health Professions Career and Education Directory.*

Here are great health care jobs to consider.

Paramedical Examiner

The nitty-gritty: Don the scrubs, grab the medical kit, and prepare for soothing nervous people. You're generally hired as a contractor to perform routine medical tests that screen individuals applying for life insurance coverage. Most insurance companies require an applicant over 40 to have a medical exam before they will approve a policy. Depending on the amount of life insurance someone is buying and his or her age, these exams include visiting someone's home or office and taking a medical history, getting weight and height, drawing blood, taking blood pressure, obtaining a urine specimen, and perhaps performing an EKG.

In addition to house calls, you might be hired by corporate clients to perform random drug testing on employees or handle cholesterol screenings at health and wellness fairs. You're not expected to be Marcus Welby, M.D., but it can take some smooth talking to relax the blood- and needle-phobic. Make sure you have an up-to-date GPS.

The hours: Flexible. You schedule your own appointments. Expect evenings and weekends.

Median pay range: Contractors typically are paid by the job versus the hour and pay varies by experience and contracting firm. In general, a basic insurance medical exam pays around $20 to $25 per case. Additional tests may pay around $40 each. Firms typically cover transportation costs above a set mileage limit. You can work for more than one contractor. Median hourly wages for phlebotomists in other health settings: $12.50 to $13.

Qualifications: Paramedical examiners may have prior training as a nurse or licensed practical nurse. If not, you should pursue a phlebotomist certification, which includes practical experience drawing, collecting, and storing blood and a thorough knowledge of vein location and puncture points. Courses are offered through vocational and technical schools, as well as community colleges.

Look for a training program that is accredited by the National Accrediting Agency for Clinical Laboratory Sciences. Coursework covers human physiology and anatomy. EKG certification is strongly suggested. You'll need a valid driver's license. Background checks are standard. A prerequisite: a minimum number of draws ranging from 100 to 300 and up.

Job hunting tips: An array of job listings can be found at GetPhlebotomy jobs.com. Practice good bedside manners.

Next: Healthy eating can take some work.

Dietician and Nutritionist

Nitty-gritty: Foodies need apply. As the saying goes, you are what you eat. And for an aging population, staying healthy and strong is top of mind, and living longer is the mantra of the day. So it's knowing how to whip up mindful menus and more. Your job revolves around custom planning healthy food and nutrition regimes and monitoring meal prep. You'll administer nutrition screenings for clients and dole out advice on diet-related concerns such as weight loss and cholesterol reduction. You might find your services are called on by corporations who offer wellness programs, sports teams, even supermarkets. The lion's share of these jobs are contracted by hospitals, nursing care facilities, outpatient care centers, and offices of physicians or other health practitioners. You might have your own private practice, too.

Hours: Part- or full-time, depending on whether you work for a health care facility or are hired independently as a freelance consultant by individuals. Full-time dietitians and nutritionists work a standard 40-hour week, although some work weekends; about 20 percent work part-time.

Median pay range: $16 per hour to $36 and up.

Qualifications: In general, dietitians and nutritionists need at least a bachelor's degree in dietetics, foods, and nutrition; licensure, certification, or registration requirements vary by state. There are roughly 280 bachelor's degree programs and 18 master's degree programs approved by the American Dietetic Association's Commission on Accreditation for Dietetics Education. Although not required, the Commission on Dietetic Registration of the American Dietetic Association awards the Registered Dietitian credential to those who pass an exam after completing academic coursework and a supervised internship.

To maintain a Registered Dietitian status, workers must complete at least 75 credit hours in approved continuing education classes every five years. A supervised internship, required for certification, can be completed via 900 hours of supervised practice experience in accredited internships. These internships may be full-time programs lasting six to 12 months or part-time programs lasting two years. Those specializing in renal and diabetic nutrition or gerontological nutrition will be of value to the growing number of diabetics and the aging of the population. For more information, visit the American Dietetic Association.

Next: Provide first aid to school children.

School Nurse

The nitty-gritty: Got your first-aid kit ready? For registered nurses stepping away from a full-time nursing career, part-time or seasonal nursing assignments are a schoolyard away. In fact, there's a shortage of nurses in public schools around the country, according to the National Association of School Nurses. The job: administering basic first aid for elementary to college-age kids who are injured or become ill during school hours.

These "need to see a nurse" traumas can run the gamut from headaches to cleaning and dressing cuts and scrapes to administering medicine for stomach aches. The aim is to quickly and calmly treat and/or send them home to a parent or primary care physician for continued care. Other duties include meting out a student's medication per written physician's orders for daily prescriptions for such ongoing illnesses as attention deficit disorder, chronic asthma, or diabetes. Nurses can also conduct basic vision and hearing tests and teach classes in nutrition and first aid.

The hours: Flexible, from summer

school stints to nine months, 20 hours a week to full-time. Job-sharing is possible.

Median pay range: Salaries for school nurses vary greatly across the country, ranging from $12.23 to $37.98 per hour, according to PayScale.com. Some schools and universities offer insurance and vacation benefits.

Qualifications: A valid state registered nurse license is generally a requirement. Each state has different rules for school nurses. You'll need to check with your state nursing board. All states, however, require the National Council Licensure Examination to become a registered nurse. Nurse's aides may be considered in some situations.

Clearances will include criminal and other background checks. You'll also need a current certification in cardiopulmonary resuscitation (CPR) and first aid from a recognized provider such as the American Heart Association. You might bolster your qualifications by earning a professional school nurse certification. Contact the National Board for Certification of School Nurses for more information. Finally,

add one dosage of psychology 101 —
a worried parent may need as much
TLC as a sick child. Hidden job description: must be kid- and parent-
friendly.

Extra points: If you've worked shifts
in emergency care, or in pediatrics for
an elementary school post, that's a
plus.

Next: Click if you like both computers
and medicine.

Medical Records Administrator

The nitty-gritty: Techies with a medical bent, log on. As hospitals, nursing
care facilities, outpatient care centers,
and old-fashioned doctors' offices say
sayonara to mounds of paperwork and
rows of file drawers in favor of electronic health records, there's a soaring
demand to hire workers at ease with
computer-ese. The work entails trans-
ferring records of physician notes from
patient visits, medical or surgical
procedures, medical history, test results, and more into computerized files.

For the most part, this is a stationary
desk job, so there's not a lot of running around, standing on your feet, or

tending to last-minute emergencies. A hot specialty: coding. Medical coders convert the doctor's report of a disease or injury and any procedures performed into numeric and alphanumeric designations, or codes, to create a claim for insurance reimbursement. It can be tedious. If you miscode, either the patient or the doctor may be underreimbursed by an insurer. The devil is in the details.

The hours: Varies by medical facility.

Median pay range: $10.21 to $25.69 per hour.

Qualifications: You'll typically need an associate's degree in health information technology from a technical or community college. Online courses are offered, too. Coursework covers medical terminology, anatomy and physiology, health data requirements and standards, clinical classification and coding systems, health care reimbursement methods, and database security.

Passing a certifying examination is not always required, but employers prefer it. This certification is awarded by the American Health Information Management Association. Visit its web site for complete information, including accredited schools and certification details. The American Academy of Professional Coders offers coding credentials. The Board of Medical Specialty Coding (BMSC) and Professional Association of Health Care Coding Specialists both offer credentialing in specialty coding. The National Cancer Registrars Association, for instance, offers a credential as a Certified Tumor Registrar. To learn more about the credentials available and their specific requirements, contact the credentialing organization. Computer geeks, this code's for you.

Next: Lend a hand in home health care.

Personal and Home Health Care Aide

The nitty-gritty: If you're suited to it, there's plenty of need for paid workers at private homes, assisted-living communities, memory-care centers for Alzheimer's patients, hospice facilities, and traditional nursing homes. It's also possible to be hired directly by the patient or the patient's family. Your job is to assist elderly, ill, or disabled people with routine activities ranging from bathing and dressing to running errands.

Other duties might include light housekeeping, companionship, grocery shopping, meal preparation, and medication monitoring. While the work is rewarding, it can be taxing mentally and physically. Some positions require lifting patients and lots of time on your feet. Ask about the requirements of a specific client before signing on.

The hours: If you're working at someone's home, three or four hours a day, two or three days a week, might be all they require. These jobs are often booked through a home care agency. You might opt for a part-time position in an assisted living facility or hospice.

Median pay range: Thanks to high turnover, job openings are plentiful, especially helping the elderly in-home as well as at assisted-living and hospice facilities. Expect generally $7.68 per hour to $12.45, but $35-plus depending on experience and certification.

Qualifications: Short-term training is generally on the job by registered nurses if you're working for an agency or in-house facility. You will undergo formal training and pass a competency test to work for certified home health or hospice agencies that receive reimbursement from Medicare or Medicaid. Requirements vary from state to state. Some employers may require a Certified Nursing Assistant (CNA) certification. See Chapter 1 for more details.

A criminal background check is standard. CPR training and a driver's license are helpful too. Contact local care facilities for job openings and training requirements. For overall home care information and a nursing job board, go to the American Association of Home Care. Compassion, self-control, and a sense of humor are the nuts and bolts. Your motto: Lend a hand.

Next: Organized? Help run a doctor's office.

Medical Assistant

The nitty-gritty: Administrative tasks in doctors' offices make up the bulk of the workload. Mostly you're performing routine front-office duties, such as checking in patients, verifying health insurance information, staffing the telephones, and scheduling appointments. You're on the front lines, so rev up the people person persona. You may be in charge of maintaining supplies. Some assistants help physicians with procedures and prepare medical records. If you have the training, you may perform direct patient care such as conducting an EKG, collecting specimens, caring for wounds, administering medication, and checking vital signs.

The hours: Varies by practitioner, but generally weekdays.

Median pay range: $9.98 to $19.21 per hour; $25-plus depending on location and experience.

Qualifications: Many medical assistants are trained on the job, but others complete programs at community colleges. Some programs offer certificates in as little as eight months and teach students to assist physicians in routine duties as well as basic office tasks. The Commission on Accreditation of Allied Health Education Programs and the Accrediting Bureau of Health Education Schools have lists of medical assisting accredited programs on their web sites.

Even when employers permit you to

learn on the job, a certificate of training from a nationally recognized association such as the American Association of Medical Assistants and Association of Medical Technologists helps you stand out. You can become certified in a specialty, such as optometry or podiatry.

Tip: Bulging bunions shouldn't make you grimace.

Next: For the animal lovers out there.

Veterinary Technician

The nitty-gritty: If you love animals, have an aptitude for science, and the willingness to go back to school to ramp up the necessary skills, you've got a great chance of landing a job — especially if you live in a rural area. Employment of veterinary technicians is expected to grow 52 percent from 2010 to 2020, much faster than the average for all occupations, according to the Bureau of Labor Statistics' *Occupational Outlook Handbook.* Working alongside primarily small animal vets, you might perform duties such as preparing pets for surgery, performing lab tests, administering medication and vaccines, providing emergency nursing care, collecting blood and samples, and the more mundane tasks of recording pet histories and weighing your sometimes nervous patients.

Median pay range: The median annual wage of veterinary technologists and technicians was $29,710 in May 2010, according to BLS. PayScale.com sets hourly wages at $9.40 to $17.71 per hour up to $27.62 per hour overtime.

Qualifications: Veterinary technicians usually have a two-year associate's degree in a veterinary technology program. In 2011, there were 191 veterinary technology programs accredited by the American Veterinary Medical Association (AVMA). Most of these programs offer a 2-year associate's degree for veterinary technicians. Although each state regulates vet techs differently, in general, you must take a credentialing exam — the Veterinary Technician National Examination. You're often the point person to explain a pet's condition, or how to manage medication prescribed by a veterinarian to the owner, so clear and calm communication skills are imperative.

Next up, for night owls.

CHAPTER 9
GREAT NIGHT JOBS

If you are willing to forgo working 9 to 5, a smorgasbord of jobs can be sampled during the hours when most folks have dimmed their lights.

These range from baking pastries and breads to staffing the front desk at a hotel, selling movie or theater tickets, cleaning offices, or working in a variety of different positions in the growing, round-the-clock casino industry. Nursing jobs are a natural fit here, too. See Chapter 8 on health care jobs for more.

Blackjack dealer Manny St. Mary, a 63-year-old retired restaurateur, typically works from 8 P.M. to 4 A.M., three to four days a week. You can find him behind one of the 100 green felt tables scattered across the spacious gaming floor at the Rivers Casino in Pittsburgh.

St. Mary, a native of the Philippines, initially signed on as a chef in the casino's

Grandview Buffet restaurant when it opened in the fall of 2009 after he and his wife, Priscilla Almazan, also an accomplished chef, were forced to close their own eatery. Priscilla was in failing health at the time. "She retired, and I spent about two years taking care of her," St. Mary recalls.

But full-blown retirement wasn't in the cards for St. Mary. "I was lonely. I wanted to be busy. I was a little worried about money and scared that my mind would idle and dementia would set in," he says. "I needed to keep working."

Shortly after St. Mary started at the casino restaurant, his people skills caught the eye of management and he was asked if he wanted to train to be a dealer.

St. Mary breezed through the process. He had to pass a math test and sit for an interview. Then, after graduating from an intensive 12-week course and receiving the green light from the state-required background check, he stepped into the action.

It was new territory for him. "I didn't gamble in my life. I didn't know anything about three-card poker, blackjack, or splitting cards," he says matter-of-factly. But he was a quick study. The real secret? "Your hands must be nimble, swift, and very accurate," he rattles off rapidly. "You must be flamboyant in your language, amiable, talkative, and very kind-hearted. You must evoke friendliness and smile."

In other words, have a little razzle-dazzle. Casinos riff off a vibe of youth and energy. St. Mary has that energy in spades. "I love interacting with people. It makes me feel vibrant, and I guess I'm lucky. I look 40," he boasts with a quick chortle.

St. Mary admits a card dealer's job won't suit everyone his age. It takes stamina of a sort. Aside from the oomph of showmanship, this is on-your-feet work. There is no sitting on this shift — except for scheduled breaks.

The hours allowing him to spend his days with Priscilla were a big motivator for him.

Base pay is low: $4.50 an hour, in addition to health benefits, a 401(k) plan, and paid vacation. "Dealers depend on the generosity of the players," St. Mary says. "They aren't obliged to tip, so you never know what each night will bring."

It's possible to take home $15 an hour, he estimates. (Players often tip 5 percent of winnings; if they lose for the session, a $10 gratuity is not unusual). "Last night, somebody won $10,000! Ahh . . . it was amazing," he excitedly squeals. "They were so happy. Me, too."

Here are great jobs for night owls to consider.

Casino Worker

The nitty-gritty: Given the 24-hour, nonstop action at venues spanning the spectrum from flashy big-name mega-casinos like Harrah's and MGM Grand to riverboats and "racinos" at racetracks, the need for workers who like the night life is unending. Typical positions include card dealer, ticket writer, pit boss, security guard, and valet. The upside: An energizing workplace with nonstop action.

It's not all bright lights, though. Jobs that require you to work the casino floor front and center can be high pressure and fast paced. You've got to turn on the megawatt charm and stay calm when the clientele get unruly. The work can be demanding physically, too, particularly if you're standing for long stretches or pacing the spread-out playing arena. The noise from clanging slot machines and keyed-up patrons can be rough on the nerves. There's also the silent stress of being watched by supervisors and security cameras to make sure you're doing the job right.

Big brother or sister really is watching.

The hours: Flexible, from part time to full time to seasonal. Eight-hour shifts are the norm, but partial weeks or weekend evenings and nights are often available.

Median pay wage: $15 an hour for dealers. Slot positions that require verifying and paying off jackpots and resetting slot machines after payoffs range from $8.31 to $24.73. Security positions range from $9.85 to $23.87. Many jobs, such as valet, wait staff, and dealer, are low wage, and income is dependent on tips.

Qualifications: All gaming service workers must obtain a license from a regulatory agency, such as a state casino control board or commission. Applicants for a license must provide photo identification and pay a fee. Some states may require gaming service workers to be residents of that state. The licensing application process includes a background investigation and drug test.

Some of the major casinos and slot machine manufacturers run their own training schools, which last anywhere from four to 12 weeks. Almost all provide some form of in-house, on-the-job training. Most casinos also require prospective dealers to audition for open positions. Prior work experience in a hospitality-related field and strong customer service skills can help.

The American Gaming Association is a good resource to learn more about the industry.

Job-hunting tips: Your best approach may be to go straight to the source and log on to the career or employment pages of casino web sites, including headliners like Caesar's Entertainment or a local establishment in your town, and browse the latest job postings. If you thrive on never having a dull moment, roll the dice.

Next: Love to bake? Take your hobby to the next level.

Baker

The nitty-gritty: There's nothing quite like the wafting aroma of bread baking or the sweet pleasures of whipping up a batch of chewy chocolate chip cookies. If you can take the heat, get in the kitchen. Look for bakery jobs at local bakeries, schools, cafeterias, hotel restaurants, and in the bakery sections at grocery stores and chains such as Dunkin' Donuts and Panera Bread.

Baking chores are typically done at night or in the predawn hours so the goods are fresh at the start of the business day. Tasks can be routine. You measure, mix, mold, shape, and bake ingredients adhering strictly to recipes. The bigger the facility and larger the quantities needed, the more standardized the work will be. Kitchens can be hot and noisy. Plan on bending, stooping to grasp goods, and climbing ladders, as well as lifting or pushing and pulling carts with 75- to 150-pound loads of ingredients. You also have to be good with the old kitchen timer: No burned bagels, please.

The hours: Generally after midnight to early morning. Holiday shifts are usually in demand. Full shifts may run from 10 P.M. to 6 A.M. for a bakery with a morning clientele.

Median pay range: $8.13 to $17.94. Full-time bakers employed by large grocery store or restaurant and hotel chains generally receive benefits, such as paid vacation days and health and dental insurance.

Qualifications: The hop from home baker to professional takes practice. Your best bet is to find an apprenticeship or trainee position at an established bakery, or even offer to moonlight for free. You'll learn how to run a range of equipment used in the production process, and be sure your basic math skills — for calculating ingredient quantities — are up to snuff. If you have time to plan your path into late-night baking, consider scoring a certification through the Retail Bakers of America. RBA offers certification for four levels of competence ranging in price from $100 to $850. The American Institute of Baking offers online seminars covering baking fundamentals from cake baking to muffin-making for $75 a pop.

Community colleges offer one-year baking and pastry arts degrees that can be completed part-time for under $4,000 and are great launching pads for job placement. Betty Crockers, grab your spatulas!

Next: Are you an organized people person and a night owl?

Front Desk Clerk/Night Auditor

The nitty-gritty: Whether it's a boutique hotel or an RV park and campground, guests come and go at all hours of the night and day. The basic drill: Meet and greet with a smile. Check guests in and out, access their reservation in the computer system, run their credit card, assign rooms, hand over keys, and answer questions on hotel services. You'll even dole out directions. You'll be expected to answer telephones and schedule reservations.

But the underbelly is when something goes wrong: A reservation can't be found; there's a dispute over charges; the air-conditioning in the room is on the fritz. That's when patience and a cool head prevail. Some employers combine these desk clerk duties with bookkeeping, so be clear about what you are ready to tackle. If you have a knack for numbers, you might have a bit more to offer doing double duty as a night auditor who can balance accounts and perform overnight bookkeeping chores.

The hours: Seasonal and part-time schedules of 20 to 30 hours a week, or four days a week, are common. Availability to work evenings, weekends, and holidays is usually required. Overnight generally means availability from 11 P.M. to 7 A.M.

Median pay range: $7.73 to $14.15 an hour. More is possible depending on advanced degrees.

Qualifications: Hotel or retail experience is a plus, but on-the-job training is the norm. Each hotel or motel has its own reservation and billing systems. Most important, employers are always on the lookout for someone with a customer service sweet spot. A degree in accounting is desirable for night auditors. A certified public accountant (CPA) certification is best. Relevant experience or formal training in accounting/auditing services is a plus. Your room is ready!

Next: Have a knack for keeping a neat house? Read on.

Office Cleaning Crew

The nitty-gritty: Because office buildings, schools, and stores generally are cleaned while they're empty, evening and night shifts are standard fare. There are downsides: Noisy vacuum cleaners can be bothersome, and cleaning bathrooms and trash rooms is messy work. You'll spend most of your time on your feet, sometimes lifting or pushing heavy furniture or equipment. Many tasks, such as dusting, waxing floors, mopping, and sweeping, require bending and stretching.

Some employers add a glittery glow to the job. When you are hired for the Third Shift Custodial gig at the Walt Disney World resort, your cast member role is "preserving the magic." You maintain the beauty of the resort and ensure that the magic of Disney shines through. "Third-Shift Custodial Cast Members work throughout the night to ensure that the resort is ready to welcome guests every morning," Disney's ad reads.

The hours: Hourly, part-time, and seasonal, as well as full-time slots. Typical is 15 to 20 hours per week from 8 P.M. to 1 A.M. Weekend work is often available.

Median pay range: $8.58 to $19.02 an hour. At Walt Disney World, for example, part-time custodial hosts and hostesses, start at $7.80 an hour, plus an additional $1 per hour for the late-shift.

Qualifications: No special education is required for most entry-level janitorial or cleaning jobs, but previous experience is always helpful. Experience using buffers and carpet-cleaning equipment helps, too. Reliable transportation and a valid driver's license come in handy. Criminal background checks, drug screening, and a valid Social Security number are standard requirements. And you have to be in decent shape. Some jobs require the ability to lift 50 pounds or more.

If you're interested in a managerial position, a small cadre of cleaning supervisors and managers are members of the International Executive Housekeepers Association, which offers two kinds of certification programs for cleaning supervisors and managers.

Job hunting tips: Contact cleaning crews in your area, or search online for possible openings at Indeed or Simplyhired. Spit-and-polish buffs, grab your feather dusters.

Next: Enjoy going to the movies? Find fun opportunities.

Cinema or Theater Ticket Vendor or Usher

The nitty-gritty: There's something romantic about the silver screen, a movie theater as the lights dim, the playhouse when the curtain is set to rise. There's a certain excitement and anticipation that theatergoers arrive with that is, well, joyful. Your duties are more mundane, usually taking place behind bulletproof glass with a microphone that lets you cheerfully greet the next in line. You're in charge of the till from collecting the cash and rendering change to handling credit card transactions. Theater owners count on you to make sure the receipts match the tickets sold. A thick skin can come in handy when disappointed wannabe ticket buyers arrive too late to score a seat.

Be prepared to offer expert advice on alternative choices. Beware of the sly youngsters trying to sneak into R-rated movies without an adult. If you opt to usher, you'll have a little more heavy lifting since you'll be in charge of assisting patrons to find seats and searching for lost articles. Hopefully you're handy with using a flashlight in darkened theaters. This is not the time for "break a leg." Best part: First dibs on first-run showings or popular performances sure to sell out.

The hours: Shifts can start as early as 4 P.M. and run well past the midnight show time. Work often includes weekends, evenings, and holidays. Can be less than 20 hours a week.

Median pay range: $7.60 to $13.37. One possible perk: discounted tickets.

Qualifications: On-the-job training and basic math for sales transactions. Most of this is computerized, but you're ultimately responsible for careful accounting.

Job hunting tips: The best way to get a foot in the door is to contact your local movie theater chains and arts venues to see what might be available. Lights, camera, ready for action!

Next up, catering to an aging population.

CHAPTER 10
GREAT JOBS TO RIDE THE AGE WAVE

As the 50+ population explodes, so do the number of jobs that serve them, from fitness experts and retirement coaches to home health aides and geriatric nurses.

In Warrenton, Virginia, Terry and Tina Ross, both in their mid-50s, run a shop called Simple Comforts that sells a panoply of products that cater to the older crowd. The shop sells literally thousands of items that promote healthy and active aging.

I'm talking everything from pill organizers to large-print crossword puzzle books to ramps and rose pruners. "These products make everyday activities such as gardening, cooking, travel, golf, exercise, and just plain gettin' around a little easier," Tina says. "We have items for boomers who might have an aching back and for their parents."

Bingo — a small business that caters to an aging population.

By 2050, according to Pew Research

projections, about one in five Americans, 20 percent, will be over age 65, up from 13 percent of the U.S. population now. And the number of those 85 and older is expected to more than double to about 5 percent.

This demographic shift is already creating a wave of new fields and opportunities for workers of all ages. It's just a tease of what's to come. To get in, though, you might need to bolster your resume with new skills, preferably added while continuing to work full-time in your first career.

True, some of the positions do require a full degree program, say, an associate of applied sciences degree in gerontology. Employers and clients in many arenas, however, are increasingly accepting professional certifications, which are great for the 50+ worker — they're faster and cheaper.

Where are these jobs? There's high demand for health care workers across a wide gamut, despite the tight job market. The number of health-related jobs in hospitals, clinics, nursing and residential care facilities, and home-centered services is growing. Projections from the U.S. Department of Labor's *Occupational Outlook Handbook* forecast 3.2 million new jobs within existing health care job classifications between 2008 and 2018. It lists a variety of home and personal care health care jobs as fast-growing occupations.

You don't have to be a surgeon or ICU nurse; there are hundreds of areas of specialization, such as music therapists for Alzheimer's patients and occupational therapists for the elderly. (When my friend Carol visited her Uncle Bob in a New Jersey assisted living home, an instructor was leading a tap dance class to the tune of "Staying Alive.") Other positions include registered nurses, mental health counselors, social workers, physical therapists, physician assistants, dental hygienists, fitness trainers, and nutritionists.

The American Medical Association's annual *Health Professions Career and Education Directory* is a good resource for job seekers. Other helpful web sites include Health Professions Network, which features different allied health professions, and Health Care Workforce, which has a long list of links to other job-listing sites in the field. As the stream of new medical technologies arrive, trained professionals will be called on to step into those areas as well.

"As tens of millions of people live into their 80s and 90s, we'll need millions of others in their 50s and 60s and 70s to help care for them — not just within families, but through second careers," says Marc Freedman of Encore.org and author of *The Big Shift: Navigating the New Stage Beyond Midlife*. "They'll be able to fill millions of positions we will need to fill — as nurses, home health aides, health navigators, and roles we've yet to even define."

Last year, Encore.org, MetLife, and Partners in Care Foundation published *How Boomers Can Help Improve Health Care: Emerging Encore Career Opportunities in Health Care*.

The report is good reading, packed with deep research and forward thinking. It examines six new occupations identified by a panel of national experts in workforce and health care issues. The highlighted jobs are community health worker, chronic illness coach, medications coach, patient navigator/ advocate, home- and community-based service navigator/advocate, and home modification specialist.

Open your mind and consider the possibilities. There are many ways to get an angle into the needs of this growing market beyond health care.

In the Pew Research survey of 2,969 adults:

- More than nine in 10 respondents age 65 and older live in their own home or apartment.
- About one in six have trouble paying bills.
- Nearly a quarter say they got some type of vigorous exercise in the 24 hours before they were interviewed.

How does that translate into more great "age wave" jobs? There's a need for people who:

- Modify homes to make them safer.
- Are motivated fitness coaches.
- Are certified financial planners.
- Can offer monthly help with finances and bill-paying.

Here are some jobs that benefit from an aging population. Some of these jobs were also discussed in earlier chapters, but I've pulled them all together here. Many of these do require additional schooling or certification.

Health Care/Patient Advocate

Nitty-gritty: You're in change of helping patients navigate the complex medical system. You can get to the bottom of billing mistakes and contest insurance-coverage rejections. At times, you might lend advice in making medical decisions, help find a specialist or hospital, go with patients to doctor appointments, coordinate multiple doctor care, and pick up prescriptions. Knowing how to fill out insurance forms and even negotiate with doctors for better rates might fall under your jurisdiction. Job opportunities range from working privately for one person or a couple to working on staff as an advocate at a local hospital, nursing home, rehab center, or insurance company.

Median pay range: $15 to $50 per hour on average, but pay can rise with experience.

Qualifications: Community colleges and nonprofit organizations are developing training and certification programs to help more people tackle this post. Nurses, social workers, medical professionals, and insurance experts are in high demand for these positions. But if you've steered your own exasperating path through the medical system, you might be the perfect person to take on this role. Do take the time to add the necessary skills to get certified. No licenses are required to practice, but there are several credentialing programs. Contact the National Association of Healthcare Advocacy Consultants (nahac.memberlodge.com/), a professional group in Berkeley, California, and the nonprofit Patient Advocate Foundation (patientadvocate.org/) for more information.

Next: Help people stay fit as a fiddle.

Fitness Trainer

Nitty-gritty: Design clients' individual workout routines or teach group classes. It's not all stationary bikes and exercise balls. You might, for example, specialize in swimming or become certified to teach "accessible" yoga, which adapts techniques for people with chronic illness and disability. Instructors, for example, modify traditional yoga positions that can work for people, whether they are in a chair or wheelchair, or struggling with other limitations. Water aerobics is a big attraction.

The hours: Flexible, usually during the daytime or evening.

Median pay range: The median scale

is $17 to $30 an hour. But in larger cities, rates can roll up to $60 to $100 or more. Most health clubs collect the cost for the session from their members and dole out a percentage to you.

Qualifications: Certification is not required by law, but most fitness clubs insist. Several national groups offer some type of credential. These include the American Council on Exercise, the International Sports Sciences Association, and the National Strength and Conditioning Association. For credentials, you must be certified in cardio-pulmonary resuscitation (CPR) and pass an exam that consists of both a written test and practical demonstration. You'll need to be up to speed on human physiology, understand correct exercise techniques, be able to assess a client's fitness level, and know the ins and outs of proper exercise programs. You may also need liability insurance. For yoga instructors, that can run you roughly $145 a year if you teach less than six hours a week, $205 if you teach more than six hours a week.

Next: A kind heart and patience will come in handy here.

Personal and Home Health Care Aide

Nitty-gritty: Assist elderly, ill, or disabled people with daily activities ranging from bathing and dressing to running errands. Other duties might include light housekeeping, laundry, companionship, grocery shopping, meal preparation, and medication monitoring. This work can be physical if you're called on to lift patients.

The hours: Half-days, or a few days each week are possible.

Median pay range: Expect $7.36 per hour to $12.45; $35-plus depending on experience and certification.

Qualifications: Some employers may require a Certified Nursing Assistant (CNA) certification. A criminal background check is standard. CPR training and a driver's license are helpful too. A good bedside manner is a must. See Chapter 1 for more details.

Job hunting tips: There are typically openings in residential care centers and hospice facilities if you prefer to work outside someone's home. Contact local care facilities and home care staffing agencies for job openings and training requirements. Word of mouth within a community or area physicians who have an elderly patient population can offer job leads.

Next: Got a talent for putting people at ease, so they can listen carefully?

Audiologist

Nitty-gritty: Hearing loss and aging go hand in hand. You'll examine, diagnose, and treat individuals for symptoms of hearing loss and other auditory, balance, and neural problems. Most of these positions, about 64 percent, are in health care facilities.

The hours: Flexible, part- to full-time.

Median pay range: $20.48 per hour to $50 and up.

Qualifications: You will need a Doctor of Audiology degree. Career information and information on state licensure is available from the American Speech-Language-Hearing Association and the Audiology Foundation of America.

Next: Can you make things fit?

Move Manager

Nitty-gritty: Making it fit. Downsizing is your bailiwick. You are in charge of coordinating a move and configuring a new home setup. Your typical clients are relocating to smaller quarters, usually an apartment or retirement community. They need advice on choosing what furniture, artwork, china, collectibles, and household goods make the cut to head over to the new digs. And you tally up what can be sold, donated, or given to friends and family. You might even be in charge of shopping for new furniture that suits the new pad, or organizing and running an estate or yard sale. This job calls for configuring and cajoling. Must be handy with a tape measure.

Median pay range: Fees range from $30 per hour to $75-plus.

Qualifications: Knowledge of interior design is essential. An "in" with a local realtor can jumpstart your business, as well as provide a steady clientele down the road. A calm, but take-charge demeanor is a desirable personality trait — no drama queens or kings here. This type of move is fraught with emotion. For more information on courses and certification, contact the National Association of Senior Move Managers (nasmm.org). Must be compassionate, but ruthless.

Job hunting tips: For leads on jobs, stop by local realtors' offices and visit retirement and assisted living communities in your area to ask about their future residents' needs. Find out who is handling this type of work for them. The community's management office usually provides soon-to-be residents with suggestions for moving specialists to lend a hand with what can be a daunting endeavor for downsizers of any age. Hiring an unbiased expert can be invaluable. What do you need to do to be featured on their list of recommended helpers?

Next: Good at hand-holding? You'll probably need to tap into that skill.

Real Estate Specialist

Nitty-gritty: This sales job takes a bit of finesse. You'll need to gently smooth the emotions of selling the family home first and help locate a suitable step-down abode.

The hours: Flexible; part to full time.

Median pay range: 2.5–3.0 percent of the purchase price.

Qualifications: Certification is via The

National Association of Realtors. Hone your soft-sell side. Tea and empathy may rule the day. These moves can be wrenching, so you need to stay positive and keep the client focused on the upside of a downsize.

Next: Safety first, is your mantra.

Aging in Place/Home Modification Pro

Nitty-gritty: Your specialty is to create a home that will serve for the long term. A variety of experts can get into the act from contractors to architects and interior designers. The key is to figure ways to creatively convert or adapt homes with lighting, ramps, grab bars in the shower, and more to stave off accidents.

The hours: Part time or full time.

Median pay range: $40 per hour and up.

Qualifications: The National Association of Home Builders offers a course that teaches design and building techniques for making a home accessible to all ages.

Next: Must listen carefully.

Retirement Coach

Nitty-gritty: Are you a good listener? A problem-solver? With this job, you're the one in charge of counseling soon-to-be retirees on what to do with the rest of their lives. No surprise that retirement is one of the fastest-growing segments of the coaching industry.

Retirees are often looking for their "what's next" direction. They need a guiding hand to help them identify their passions, their skills, and the best kind of work at this stage of life. Should they invest in education? Should they start their own business — one they've always dreamed of? What about moving to a new locale or retirement community?

It can be life coaching and job coaching all mixed into one. This is a process and takes someone who is patient, intuitive, and good at coming up with creative solutions and action steps. This can be an awkward stage. We are living longer and healthier lives, so most of us want to stay active. The question is, doing what and where?

The hours: Flexible.

Median pay range: $50 to $400 per hour.

Qualifications: Career and life coaching is a self-regulated industry and emerging profession. Many coaches have been doing it for years without adding professional designations. If you have a corporate background in human resources, counseling, even teaching, this might be a natural next step for you.

To learn more about certification, go to the nonprofit International Coach Federation (ICF). The ICF is the only organization that awards a global credential, which is currently held by over 4,800 coaches worldwide. ICF credentialed coaches have met certain stringent educational requirements, received specific coach training, and achieved a designated number of experience hours, among other requirements.

For coursework, you can search the IC's database for a program. Some coaching courses are offered online. Others consist of a few workshop sessions. More intensive programs run over the course of a few semesters combining online and in-person study. You might check into programs such as the Coaches Training Institute (thecoaches.com), New Ventures West (newventureswest.com), or the Rockport Institute (rockportinstitute.com). Check your local colleges for course listings too. Universities such as Pittsburgh's Duquesne University and Washington, D.C.'s George Washington University and Georgetown University, for example, offer coach training programs. Tuition is all over the map from under $1,000 to more than $10,000. The tuition for the Professional Coaching course at New Ventures West, for example, is currently $9,500.

Next: No speed demons need apply.

Driver

Nitty-Gritty: Think of the movie *Driving Miss Daisy.* There is a growing need for drivers to transport elderly clients who can no longer safely drive to appointments, airports, activities, and longer road trips. College campuses, too, need people to drive shuttle buses and vans.

The hours: Part time to full time.

Median pay range: From $7.67 per hour to more than $20 per hour, plus car expenses if you use your own wheels. Those figures vary widely depending on experience, where you live, the number of hours worked, and customer tips.

Qualifications: A safe driving record is prerequisite. Background checks are standard. You might be asked to undergo a drug screening as well. To drive a shuttle bus, you must have a commercial driver's license (CDL) in good standing and complete a short training. Part of the training is spent on a driving course, where drivers practice various maneuvers with a bus. The qualifications for getting one vary by state, but normally include passing both knowledge and driving tests. States have the right not to issue a license to someone who has had a CDL suspended by another state. You'll need sharp eyes and ears, too. There are hearing and vision requirements.

Next: For the budget-minded.

Financial Planner

Nitty-gritty: Are you good with numbers and sharp when it comes to money matters? It's not unusual for seniors to start struggling with managing investments and even paying bills in a timely fashion.

There is a huge demand for experts who can help older people manage their money sensibly. A good planner can devise an overall financial plan that will recommend how to allocate assets and determine if someone has the right blend to meet his or her specific goals.

What's more, a planner advises on how to draw down funds from accounts when needed and handle estate-planning and tax matters. It's a trust relationship, so it can take some building and slow steps. There are also money management jobs that aren't as full-blown as a planner. Consider starting a job-paying or budgeting service that helps folks track their monthly inflow and outflow and make sure payments are met on time.

The hours: Part- and full-time.

Median pay range: $120 to $300 per hour, or a percentage of assets under management, generally 1 percent to 3 percent. $10–$50 an hour for daily and monthly bill and budget aides.

Qualifications: There are myriad of

designations from certified financial planner to fee-only planner, a designation offered by the National Association of Personal Financial Advisors (NAPFA). It's a virtual alphabet soup. Anyone can call themselves a financial planner or adviser. No minimum experience or education is required by law.

But don't fall into that trap. This job is too important. Nearly half of all investor complaints submitted to state securities agencies came from seniors, according to a recent survey by the North American Securities Administrators Association. As a result, the association is aggressively cracking down on unscrupulous brokers and others using titles like "certified senior specialist."

Several reputable national organizations require members to earn credentials by passing exams. The groups include the National Association of Personal Financial Advisors, the Financial Planning Association, and the Certified Financial Planner Board of Standards. The American Institute of Certified Public Accountants has a list of CPAs who've earned the Personal Financial Specialist designation.

To learn more about the training necessary, visit the Washington, D.C.–based Certified Financial Planner Board of Standards at cfp.net. The Certified Financial Planner (CFP) designation is a professional certification mark for financial planners conferred by the Certified Financial Planner Board of Standards, Inc. There's substantial coursework and a comprehensive, 10-hour exam required to attain this title. In general, you'll need a bachelor's degree or its equivalent in any discipline, from an accredited college or university. If you already have a Certified Public Accountants (CPA) or Chartered Certified Accountants (ACCA) credential, for example, you can register for and take the exam without having to complete the education requirements. You must keep current with the annual certification fee and complete the continuing education (CE) requirement every two years.

Bonus points: Bone up on Psychology 101. Where money matters, emotions must be handled with care.

Next up, Kerry's great job-hunting workshop.

PART II
THE GREAT JOBS WORKSHOP

Landing a job is not a matter of luck. It's that oft repeated phrase — it's when preparation meets opportunity.

I've written this workshop for people who want to think and plan ahead in order to find a great job. In these next chapters, you'll find tips on resume writing, revving up your web job-hunting skills, interviewing dos and don'ts, and how to find a mentor to guide you, among other job-seeking strategies.

My hope is that you will use my specific suggestions to learn new ways to job hunt with confidence — with an appropriate dollop of swagger — and to make thoughtful long-range decisions about the kind of work you choose to do. I will also help you make the best decisions with your personal finances. Why? Because when your financial world is in order, you'll have the flexibility and control to make the right career choices.

These steps pose challenging questions that I hope you will take the time to ask yourself as you read along.

In my previous book, *What's Next? Follow Your Passion and Find Your Dream Job,* I profiled peopled who radically and successfully changed their working lives in their 50s and beyond. I wrote about what they did to make the turn a winning one. Career change is an underlying theme for many people who are contemplating what they want to do in their next act.

So I decided to kick off this workshop with my advice on starting a second "career" rather than just landing a job to stay busy. My reasoning? Simple. I think dreaming big is a great launching place for any job-hunting journey. Whether you want to work part time, or a full schedule, trying something new might just be the ticket. This is precisely the time in our lives when we all start yearning for something that brings more meaning to life.

And it's not just the dreamers who are doing this. Even those with their feet on the ground have eyes on the sky. It intrigues me how that quest to do work we love inspires and pushes so many of us to keep at it long after what might have been a time to take it easy.

As great American jazz pianist and composer Dave Brubeck, who is 91 as I write this and still performing, explained to Hedrick Smith in the PBS documentary, *Rediscovering Dave Brubeck:* "There's a way of playing safe, there's a way of using tricks, and there's the way I like to play which is dangerously where you're going to take a chance on making mistakes in order to create something you haven't created before."

So let's get started.

CHAPTER 11
HOW TO PLAN FOR A SECOND CAREER

There are loads of reasons to pursue work in a new field. You've retired, but still want to stay in the workforce. You've been laid off. Or you are simply burned out in your current job. For many workers, switching careers has become a necessity thanks to a topsy-turvy job market.

Then too, a life crisis may remind you of how quickly life can be snatched away — a health scare of your own perhaps, or the death of a close friend, colleague, or family member. You pause and think twice about what really matters.

But changing careers and redeploying is not new. It's deeply rooted in the American spirit. Benjamin Franklin got his start making candles before turning to the printing trade, then writing and became a statesman, inventor, and scientist. The Wright brothers were in the newspaper business, followed by bike repair, before turning to aviation and the great blue yonder. Ronald Reagan was an actor before he became a politician. Martha Stewart was a stockbroker. The Zagats, who publish the eponymous restaurant guide, were both corporate lawyers. And the list goes on, from generation to generation.

If switching careers is calling to you, go for it, but please take your time. Career change is a process, and it takes confidence that comes from laying the groundwork. The most successful 50+ career switchers take a few years to learn new skills, network, and prepare financially.

When midlife career switchers ask me for advice on how to succeed, I always begin by saying, "Get a fitness program." You need to be:

- **Physically fit.** Physical fitness provides the strength and mental sharpness to deal with stress, especially when changing jobs or making big decisions. It sounds superficial, but an in-shape and energetic appearance is a bonus in the work world for those in "late youth," as author Anne Lamott calls the boomer stage of life.
- **Spiritually fit.** Mind-body balance helps you calmly roll with the punches and teaches you to quietly listen to the

inner voice that can guide your decisions.

- **Financially fit.** Economic stability gives you freedom of choice. It provides the nimbleness you need to start a new career, whether that means opening your own business, paying the tuition to go back to school, or making it easier to work in a job that you love — even if it pays less than your old one.

To be honest, this three-step fitness regime is good for most things in life. That said, here are the essential steps to planning for a second career that I recommend.

Go slowly. No one dives into a second career on a whim. You've got to have a plan and have saved money, added skills, apprenticed. Start working at age 50 on a career you might kick off in another five years. If you have lots of time, you can sample some ideas and possibilities.

Look at your skill set and past experience as transferable to lots of different challenges and fields. Search inside and answer some important questions: What am I best at? Ask friends and colleagues too. They might see things that you take for granted.

Think of it not as *reinventing* yourself, but

rather as redirecting or *redeploying* many of the skills you already have in place. Retired Navy captain Don Covington, who became the company manager for the Big Apple Circus in his mid-50s, told me: "When you think about it, the military and the circus are not that different." What he meant is that the leadership and management skills honed in his naval career translated to moving a circus troupe of 100-plus from town to town.

When James S. Kunen, author of *Diary of a Company Man,* was fired from his job as director of communications at Time Warner on the cusp of turning 60, he tapped into his skills as a wordsmith. He landed a paying job four nights a week, teaching a three-hour intermediate English literacy/civics class at a community college.

He's okay with making far less than he did in his old position. "Riding the G train home, I realize I am happy," Kunen writes. "I am good at teaching ESL (English as a Second Language). It's worth doing. And I'm appreciated. The trifecta."

Research. Look for jobs and opportunities that leverage experience. Check out job web sites like aarp.org/jobs, encore.org, retired brains.com, and workforce50.com to get a flavor for what others are doing and what jobs are out there now. Investigate fields like health care, the clergy, elder care, sustainability or "green" arenas, and education, which have a growing demand for workers. The Bureau of Labor Statistic's *Occupational Outlook Handbook* (bls.gov/ooh) is a good reference for researching the fastest growing occupations.

Shape up your financial life. Starting over can mean a pay cut, the cost of a start-up, tuition for training, out-of-pocket health insurance costs. Start by charting a budget. It's smart to have a cushion of six months of living expenses or more set aside for transition costs, as well as unexpected emergencies.

Pay off outstanding high-interest credit card debts, college loans, and auto loans. This can take some time, but starting a new venture with as clean a balance sheet as you can will make a difference. Pare back your discretionary living expenses to reflect a more realistic view of what you'll earn. What things can you give up? One person I know quit his two-pack-a-day smoking habit. That's good for many reasons, of course. Are you willing to make sacrifices like that?

Depending on your situation, you might

consider downsizing to a smaller home, townhouse, or condo, Refinancing your mortgage to a lower rate might be an option. Or perhaps you're able to move to an area that has a lower cost of living. You might even be able to write off moving expenses.

If you're opening your own business, keep in mind that start-up costs can easily top $10,000 for the average small business owner. Then too, your monthly nut — electric, rent, payroll, and other ongoing outlays — starts rolling in immediately, often before your revenues do. You will need operating funds to meet these expenses.

Keep your hand out of the cookie jar. It's tempting to dip into retirement accounts and tap home equity and other savings, but that has obvious implications for retirement security.

Invest in additional education and training. Research the skills or certifications required for your new career. Add the essential expertise and degrees before you make the leap. Check out offerings at community colleges for retraining.

Consider taking one class at a time. A host of certificate programs in a specialized field of study are aimed at adult students looking to retool their careers. Some of these programs offer graduate-level courses in the subject area that you can use as a start toward a master's degree if you have the time, desire, and funds to do so. Certain fields, say health care, counseling, and technology, require a certificate for specific jobs. A certificate can also show that you have a specialty in the area — sustainable landscape design, or grant proposal writing, for instance.

A growing number of community colleges are offering courses to train people over 50. Then too, many colleges are starting to offer second career workshops at reunions. Moreover, four-year colleges and graduate schools — from Harvard's Advanced Leadership Initiative to the Bainbridge Graduate Institute — are gearing up programs for folks looking for nonprofit opportunities.

Another new program: Empowered UCLA Extension, an online Internet-education firm (empowered.com), offers fast-track certificate programs via your iPad for adults looking to retrain or upgrade skills. Tuition is $12,800 for a 12-month certificate program. Fields of study include: marketing and new media, college counseling, health care management, financial planning, nonprofit management, and other growing fields.

For information on scholarship opportunities, go to empowered.com/scholarships.

If you have some advance time to get ready, you might start to take classes while your current employer is offering tuition reimbursement. Under federal law, employers may offer up to $5,250 a year in tax-free education-assistance benefits for undergraduate or graduate courses. You may not need to be working toward a degree. But gradually gearing up new skills and adding to your kit, while you're gainfully employed, will prepare you for your transition when the time comes.

For those of you who dream of opening your own business, SBA.gov and Score.org, a nonprofit group that provides small business assistance, are top resources for seminars and other help to ease you off the ground.

- **Use tax breaks for your education.** As for the expense, yes, budget for it, but look into what financial aid offerings and tax breaks might be available to you. Depending on your income, you might qualify for various tax credits, such as the lifetime learning credit, worth up to $2,000 each year for an unlimited number of years. That credit can be used for tuition and required fees.

If you think you might go back to school in a few years, consider opening a 529 plan. You may be able to deduct qualified tuition and related expenses that you pay for yourself. For more tips, turn to Chapter 22.

- **Shop for a student loan or grant.** Low-interest Stafford loans, the main federal loan for students, have a fixed interest rate of 6.8 percent through 2013 for graduate loans and as low as 3.4 percent for undergraduates. Go to FastWeb.com and FinAid.org for details and a list of education lenders. Look for scholarships and grants available specifically for older students that are offered by different associations and foundations.

Apprentice, volunteer, or moonlight. Do yourself a favor — do the job first. It's is a great way to get in the door and see what goes on behind the scenes. It's also a networking opportunity.

If you're job hunting in a new field, apprenticing, volunteering, or moonlighting can catch a potential employer's eye. LinkedIn members can now add a "Volunteer Experience & Causes" field to their profile. If you've spent some time helping out organizations such as Big Brothers Big Sisters, the Humane Society of the United States, or the American Red Cross, then put it on your profile.

"Professionals often have the misconception that volunteer work doesn't qualify as 'real' work experience," Nicole Williams, LinkedIn's connection director, says. "You may be a salesperson by trade, but if you organized your nonprofit's fundraising event, you can add skills like event planning or event marketing to your profile. Having those additional skills can potentially make you a more attractive employee and business partner." See Chapter 18 for more on volunteering.

One of my favorite examples of how this can work out is Anne Nolan, president of Crossroads Rhode Island, the state's largest homeless service organization. She started as a volunteer. She didn't know what she wanted to do when she lost her executive-level job. She had a year's salary and time to think her options through. She decided to volunteer at the shelter — not because she dreamed it would turn into a full-time job, but because it was an activity to get her out of her rut and do something besides worrying about what was next. She was asked to join the board and then was hired on as the president.

Check out sites like Idealist.org, Create TheGood.org, and Volunteermatch.org. Surf onto BoardnetUSA.org for anyone looking for a nonprofit board. Look around you. Where might you lend a hand? Opportunity often comes from places where you least expect it.

Then too, what might sound romantic and wonderful, like running a B&B or a winery, turns out to be not so much fun when it becomes your daily routine. VocationVacations (vocationvacations.com) is a Portland, Oregon–based company that lets you do a job, say, baker or sports announcer for up to three days, under the guidance of expert mentors. The mentors are typically small- and medium-business owners and operators, both for-profit and nonprofits. "It's a career transition tool either for people with an eye to the future or for people worried about being laid off," founder Brian Kurth says. Clients pay a fee ranging from $549 to $2,000 (airfare and lodging not included), though most pay under $1,200. For more on volunteering, see my advice in Chapter 18.

Set up a retirement plan. If you're starting a freelance business, or moving to a nonprofit or small firm without an employee retirement plan, this is key. One of the biggest mistakes you can make is not planning sufficiently for your retirement. Read about the "Best Retirement Plans for the Self-Employed" in Chapter 21.

Shop for health insurance. If you're heading off on your own, check out any industry or alumni associations you belong to for group policies. Don't drop your current job insurance (you can continue it for a time under a law known as COBRA) until you have a new policy in place.

It's always one of the first questions I'm asked when I tell someone I'm a freelancer: "What do you do about health insurance?" If you work for yourself, finding health insurance can be a big pain. While there's no holy grail, there are ways to navigate the maze and find good coverage at manageable prices. What you'll pay for that coverage depends on a myriad of factors — where you live, your gender, the age, and the health of who is being covered, your deductible, plus the type of policy you need, among other things.

Today, an estimated 42 million people — about a third of the U.S. work force — are technically their own boss. We're self-employed freelancers and independent contractors. Some workers who fall into this cadre are temps or part-timers. Others have already officially retired and are continuing to work a reduced schedule, or have accepted an early retirement package, then launched an entrepreneurial enterprise.

Regardless of the job description, the problem is the same: finding health insurance until you reach age 65 when Medicare kicks in for most — but not all of your coverage. You might be covered by a spouse's employer policy or be able to join a group policy from a membership you have in an association. If you do need to find an individual policy, you can compare a variety of insurance options in your area at the federal web site healthcare.gov. Check your state insurance department web site too, to see if it provides a listing of health insurance choices for residents. Individual policies can be expensive, particularly if you're 55 or older.

Options to consider: premiums, deductibles, co-pays, coinsurance, and the annual limit you have to pay out of pocket before insurance covers the remainder. Expect a deductible of $1,000, $2,500, or even $5,000 to keep the premium within budget. Premiums vary broadly based on your age and physical condition.

Other online sources to check for availability and get an idea of costs by comparing dozens of health insurance plans that are available in your area include eHealth Insurance.com, Netquote.com, GoHealth insurance.com, and Insure.com. You can also go directly to the insurer sites for quotes. Keep in mind that these quotes can be all over the map and are just there to give you a notion of what it might cost. It will ultimately depend mostly on your individual medical situation and age.

Focus on smaller companies and nonprofits. They're more likely to value your overall work experience. You can provide the depth of practical knowledge and versatility that's worth two junior hires. For nonprofit job-hunting help, go to Chapter 17.

Network. In this era of online resumes, it's all about who you know that can get you in the chair for a face-to-face meeting. People want to hire someone who comes with the blessing of an existing employee or colleague. Networking is about building relationships. One way you can do that is to join a networking group.

I'm a member of The Transition Network (thetransitionnetwork.org), a nonprofit networking group for women over 50. It's based in New York, but the group has a chapter with 600 members in Washington, D.C., where I live. There are also chapters in cities like Atlanta, Chicago, Houston, San Francisco, and Santa Fe. New chapters are forming in Phoenix, Fort Lauderdale, Florida, Portland, Oregon and Dayton, Ohio. Memberships costs $70 to $135 a year, $40 if you live outside one of the chapter cities.

You might also consider joining a peer group associated with your profession or your alma mater. For instance, my alma mater, Duke University, has Women's Forums in New York, Washington, D.C., Los Angeles, San Francisco, Chicago, Dallas, Houston, Atlanta, Charlotte, Seattle, Denver, and even London.

There are also a growing number of online networking organizations. Join Facebook, Twitter, and LinkedIn. It's great way to pull together your professional network. But don't ignore networking in unlikely places. You might find the mother of your son's friend can help. That's what happened to author James S. Kunen, and it led to his job teaching English as a second language.

Ask for help. Find a mentor or two working in your new field. Seek out mentees you have worked with in the past. Over time, things shift, and now they may be in a position to help you make your next move. Many corporations also offer career coaches and counseling on a limited basis to help employees who have retired or lost their jobs. Check out career centers at your alma mater and those operated by area colleges or local government agencies offering workshops on resume writing, career counseling, job fairs, and retraining programs. If you're interested in a particular industry, join an association affiliated with it and attend conferences. (These are also great places to connect with potential mentors). See Chapter 20 for more on mentoring.

Get up to speed on the latest technology. Social media platforms such as Facebook, LinkedIn, Twitter, and, most recently, Google+ have changed how you job hunt. To get into today's job market, you must be at ease with computers, basic software programs, the web, e-mail, and mobile technology. Chapter 14 has more on web job-hunting strategies.

Prepare to be a beginner. When you leave one career or job, you lose your identity. And it can be unnerving, unsettling. Then when you start again, you find you're the new kid, and the rules of the game are alien. You might long for your old job, where you were the expert. This can take some mind-set tweaking. All of a sudden, your paycheck is slimmer, and you might even be making some mistakes. Give yourself time — at least a year — to get comfortable.

Don't mess with your hobby. Be aware of the difference between a hobby, which is a breather from your working world, and an interest that brings in an income. I'm passionate about horses, for example, but a career training horses would never suit me. It's my escape and relaxation. If the barn became my office, I would lose that magic.

Career guru Nicholas Lore, 67, who founded the Rockport Institute (rockport institute.com) and developed a pioneer program in the career-coaching field, explained it to me this way: "Your passion is a clue," he says. "To find a job you love to do, you need to become a career detective looking for the clues about the fit between yourself and the working world."

It's not too hard to find those clues. They are what turns you on and what excites you, what matters, and what you do well. It's something you would do for free.

There are plenty of things, for instance, Lore is passionate about, like sailing. "But I wouldn't want to be a charter boat skipper," he told me. As a clue, what he learned is that when you're sailing, you're making hundreds of little decisions all the time. He likes constantly problem solving. "You need to put together a clues list that becomes a definite components list and then turns to career ideas."

Be prepared for setbacks. If you've spent the time laying the proper groundwork, you'll push through the bumpy patches. Having a supportive family, partner, or friends is key, though. We all need a fan base to remind us of why we took this path and why we're going to make it work.

Keep in good shape. When you're eating healthy and have a normal workout regime, you have more physical vigor and mental sharpness. You'll need that get-up-and-go to face the challenges ahead. And the truth is, change *is* stressful, and exercise can counter that beautifully.

Do something every day to work toward your goal. Changing careers can be nerve-racking. Begin with a mental picture of where you want to go, tape a photograph on your office wall of what it might look like, journal about your goals. Get things moving by taking small steps. That might mean making a phone call to ask for advice, or reaching out with an e-mail a day to make a lunch date to knock around possibilities. People like to do small favors. And it helps build a relationship that may lead to your next job.

Be realistic. Nothing lasts forever. You might have several new "careers" from here on out. Accept that thesis, and it makes a next move more manageable. And who knows, you might do a couple of things at the same time and be a Jack or Jacqueline of many trades. One 50-something woman I know is self-employed as an SAT tutor, a community college associate professor, a personal fitness trainer, and a caterer. Bon appétit.

Switching to Eco-Friendly Work?
The U.S. Conference of Mayors forecasts that as many as 3.5 million "green" jobs will be created by 2028. To learn more about employment opportunities and salaries for more than 200 green careers and other job-hunting tools, the Department of Labor's CareerOneStop.org site is a good place to start. It has a green career section that can help you explore some possibilities and the education and training required.

For more guidance, I asked Joel Makower, executive editor of GreenBiz.com, for his best tips.

Check out these job-hunting sites. Green Biz.com, SustainableBusiness.com, Idealist .org, LinkedIn.com's Jobs section, under industry categories "Environmental Services" and "Renewables & Environment" — all have information on green jobs.

Search keywords. The three words companies will list in online green job descriptions are energy, efficiency, and waste. Also search the words "green" and "nonprofit" in the jobs section of the big online job boards.

Network. Join a discussion group for environment and green careers or green business on LinkedIn.

Troll green conferences. There's a cornucopia of green forums and conferences around the country that can be tracked down with a basic query to a search engine. GreenFestival.com, for example, lists upcoming events around the country.

Contact nonprofit environmental groups. Ask whether local nature clubs or national and global advocacy organizations have any openings. Some may be volunteer or board positions, which can be a great way to get in the door and in line for a paying job.

See what's happening on campus. Check in at your local community college or university to see whether they have any environmental job fairs or lectures. Attend Earth Day events. You'll meet everyone from entrepreneurs and advocacy groups to local utility representatives and solar installers. Talking to them about job opportunities will give you great firsthand information.

Location can help. Vermont has the highest ratio of green jobs to the general work force, with 4.4 percent of all jobs in the clean economy, according to a Bureau of Labor Statistics green jobs report. The U.S. Conference of Mayors' report indicates green job growth in large metropolitan areas like New York, Washington, and Los Angeles; cities like Pittsburgh and Boston also make the list. More states are setting up web sites focused on green jobs, so check out your state's Labor Department web site to see if it has a green jobs page.

_____

Chapter 12
Strategies for
50+ Job Hunters

My friend Randy Rieland, 60, started looking for a full-time job when he was laid off from his job as a digital media strategist and senior vice president for the Discovery Channel. He had worked there for 14 years, and the abrupt wave out the door caught him by surprise.

He stayed busy, working part-time in media relations for an environmental non-profit, writing a blog for an online magazine, and sharing wisdom for money, which "crasser types refer to as consulting," he told me with a laugh. But his search for a full-time gig left him feeling that while the interviews go well, he had the sense that "the person across the desk was looking at his 'expiration date'."

His frustration was palpable.

But there's a happy coda. It took nearly three years, but he did it. He landed a full-time position as digital editorial director for

Remedy Health Media. "I was hired by the same woman who hired me at Discovery back in 1995," he told me with a tinge of gratitude. "She really didn't care about age because she knew what I could do."

If you're over 50 and pounding the pavement these days, you can face certain challenges. On average, it takes someone age 55 or older three months longer to find a job than a younger person.

Randy is not my only friend who has felt the disappointment at a gut level. Some are frankly furious, discouraged, and dumbfounded by their inability to land a job that suits their experience and desired salary.

Like Randy, they pick up part-time consulting jobs to keep afloat, zap resumes into the black hole of online resume bins, wait for a response, and pull their hair out. They have graduate degrees and once held executive and management positions.

I can't help but hear Rod Stewart's refrain in my head: "Spent some time feelin' inferior, standing in front of my mirror." If you're 50+ and looking for a job, feeling inferior isn't so unusual. You feel like a castoff in today's job market.

What are you up against? Some employers figure your salary demands are out of their ballpark, and that if they hire you for less, you'll resent it and probably jump ship if you get a better offer. They often perceive, true or not, that you're set in your ways, or lack the cutting-edge skills, or even the energy to do the job.

Then too, some hiring managers might surmise that you have age-related health problems, or are likely to, and that will be a problem if you take too much time off for periodic sick leave. And, of course, as my friend Randy so aptly put it, there's the nagging issue that you've got an "expiration date," and you're not in it for the long haul, even if that's far from the truth. Finally, there's reverse ageism — the employer thinks you won't want to take orders from a younger boss who is probably making more than you.

It's up to you to lay their worries to rest. "The vital first step in fighting ageism is to be physically fit, energetic, and positive in attitude," executive career coach Beverly Jones of Clearways Consulting counsels.

That's just the top-coat. You need to speak up about your flexibility in terms of management style, your openness to report to a younger boss, your technological aptitude, your energy, and your knack of picking up new skills.

Job search is difficult for everybody. And everyone seems to have a different take on what it takes to break through. It's not automatically your age that's holding you back. People want to employ people they know, or someone they trust.

And your experience does matter, but maybe not as much as you think it does. For many employers it's not about the candidate with the best credentials. It's about fitting in with a crowd, its culture, so you've got to make it *personal* on some level.

"You have to make the case why you are the person who is going to both do the job brilliantly and fit in," career pro Nicholas Lore of The Rockport Institute explains to me. The question an employer is asking is, "Can you do my job right now and are you a big risk?"

Most candidates don't think they are a risk, Tony Beshara, a Dallas-based recruiter and author of *Unbeatable Resumes,* tells me. "But if you hire somebody who made more money than this, had a bigger job than this, has been out of work for six months, has had three jobs in three years — these are all risks. Some of those risks come with age, but it's not the age itself."

The older worker syndrome is not new.
It's come to our attention now because
when the economy tail-spinned a few years
ago, employers shrewdly dangled these alluring sayonara packets to senior staffers,
with the knowledge that when things im-
proved, they could add younger staff at less
pay, if they chose to.

This happens in recessions. Many 50+
workers, perhaps you, accepted an early
retirement package, thinking why not take
the money and run? Morale stinks, you
figured. Why go down with the ship? This
money will give me some space to refresh
and find something I really want to do at
this stage of my life. I get it. At the time, it
made sense.

You now know that no matter how sweet
your going-away present was, it's not
enough to live on for the next few decades,
or you want the psychological engagement
that comes from working.

Fact is, you're probably too young to be
retired in the traditional sense. You're ready
to get back in the door someplace else, and
nothing is working. Is age discrimination
keeping you on the job-hunting trail?

Even with all those other factors at play,
I'd have to say that the answer is loud and
clear: You bet. This stereotype is so deeply

set in our society that it isn't likely to change anytime soon. I suspect that even boomers themselves, who are making hiring decisions, are biased against other boomers. In May, an AARP poll of 1,000 registered voters 50 and older found that over one-third reported that they or someone they know has experienced age discrimination in the last four years.

Does Your Age Shut You Out?

In the category of expectations vs. reality, the Employee Benefit Research Institute researchers have, without fail, found that workers are far more likely to *expect* to work for pay in retirement than to actually work. The percentage of workers planning to work for pay in retirement is a sizeable 70 percent, compared with just 27 percent of retirees who report they did work for pay in retirement.

I can't help thinking that age discrimination plays a big role. AARP surveys over the past decade repeatedly have shown that at least 60 percent of those interviewed say they have either personally faced or observed age discrimination in the workplace. And my 50+ friends who have been laid off and are out looking for work right now tell me about their roadblocks all the time.

"I bet there's a lawsuit here," my job-hunting pals complain. Inevitably, that's when for the tenth time, the job beauty contest whittles down to the final round of candidates, and they lose out. The brush-off goes something like: "Since we last spoke, we've changed our direction with this position," "We're reevaluating our needs," or some such excuse that somehow smacks of a soft brush-off.

For older workers who lose a job and want to keep working, the average duration of unemployment is more than one year, above the average nine months for workers under age 55. It's likely that not all workers who would like to work in retirement will find paid employment, the EBRI researchers conclude. They may be right. I don't have that answer. But I do know there are some things you can do to stay in the fight.

It's illegal for employers to discriminate based on age, but many older job seekers know it's a fact of life. The U.S. Equal Employment Opportunity Commission has heard testimony that age discrimination is causing the nation's older workers to have a difficult time maintaining and finding new employment, a problem that was exacerbated by the downturn in the economy.

My guess is that a lot of job-seekers 50+

don't know about the law, or figure it seems pointless to fight discrimination. They know that the proof is hard to nail down. Plus, there's an emotional and financial price to filing an age discrimination claim. Older workers would rather direct resources and energy to finding a new job.

Despite that, age discrimination charges filed with the EEOC now account for a nearly a quarter of all complaints. In 2011, the EEOC received 23,465 age-related charges, up from 16,548 in 2006. I'm not a litigious person. But I must say, the more I talk to older workers looking for jobs, the easier it is for me to see where the combative spirit comes from.

Confirming that it's your age that's holding you back is darn near impossible. It's a gut feeling that you have. The fact is federal age discrimination law is designed to protect workers 40 and older. But a 2009 U.S. Supreme Court decision, in fact, has substantially increased the burden of proof required to win an age discrimination case. Jack Gross, who was 54 and a vice president at FBL Financial, was among a dozen employees demoted following a merger. He filed an age discrimination suit against his employer, but lost.

In a 5–4 decision written by Justice Clarence Thomas, the court said a worker has to *prove* that age was the determining factor in an employment decision, even if there's evidence that age played a role.

Before that decision, if a worker showed that age was a motivating factor in an adverse employment decision, say, he was fired, even if other factors also played a role, the employer had to prove that it had taken the action for another reason, not age discrimination. After the *Gross* decision, workers have had to prove that the employer would not have taken the action *"but for"* their age — in other words, that age played the determining role — a significantly higher standard of proof.

State courts seem to be a better bet for winning age discrimination cases, according to Dan Kohrman of AARP Foundation Litigation. "Older workers have stronger prospects of success in court under state laws — like those in Michigan, New York, and California — that treat age like race and sex as a prohibited basis for employment decisions." The issue is getting some attention. In the spring of 2012, the Protecting Older Workers Against Discrimination Act, sponsored by Senators Tom Harkin, Chuck Grassley, and Patrick Leahy, was introduced. It's designed to fix that Supreme Court decision (*Gross v. FBL Financial Services, Inc.*) "This bipartisan legislation reaffirms the contributions made by older Americans in the workforce and ensures that employees will be evaluated based on their performance and not by arbitrary criteria such as age," Senator Leahy says.

It is hard to really provide facts that you didn't get a job because of your age, says Laurie McCann, AARP Foundation senior litigation attorney. Being aware of your rights is your best protection, she says.

If you are looking for a job, here are four tips from McCann:

1. **Stay on top of your game.** Make sure you have done everything you can to keep up with technology and changes in your field. And by all means, I would add, be physically fit and look and dress with an eye toward a vibrant, youthful appearance.

2. **Prepare for age-related questions.** Your potential employer might use being overqualified as a reason not to hire you. Have a good answer for that. You need to show why you are sincerely interested in

the job and aren't taking it as a placeholder to continue looking for new one.

3. **Explain that age doesn't matter to you.** Stress that you have the ability to work well with co-workers of any age. You look forward to learning from younger workers and vice versa.

4. **Don't hide your age.** Under federal law, an employer can ask you how old you are. Never lie. Don't leave the age question blank on an application. That makes it too easy to toss out the incomplete file. Online applications might not even be accepted if you skip it. If you're in an interview, preface your response by saying you don't see why it is relevant for the position, if it isn't.

The details. For more on age discrimination, the AARP web site has resources from legal definitions to first-hand accounts, to what to do if you've been a victim. You can also learn about the AARP Foundation Litigation team's work in this area.

If you feel you've been discriminated against, you have a limited number of days to pursue a claim with the U.S. Equal Employment Opportunity Commission (eeoc.gov). If you believe that you have been discriminated against at work because of your race, color, religion, sex (including pregnancy), national origin, age (40 or older), disability, or genetic information, you can file a Charge of Discrimination. All of the laws enforced by EEOC, except for the Equal Pay Act, require you to file a Charge of Discrimination with the agency before you can file a job discrimination lawsuit against your employer. In addition, an individual, organization, or agency may file a charge on behalf of another person in order to protect the aggrieved person's identity. There are time limits for filing a charge.

Note: Federal employees and job applicants have similar protections, but a different complaint process.

If you file a charge, you may be asked to try to settle the dispute through mediation with the help of a neutral mediator. If the case is not sent to mediation, or if mediation doesn't resolve the problem, the charge will be given to an investigator.

If an investigation finds no violation of the law, you will be given a Notice of Right to Sue. This notice gives you permission to file suit in a court of law.

It's not surprising that the number of age discrimination cases increases when the economy weakens. It's basic business to want to replace older workers with juniors as a cost-cutting move. Employers insist that it's the high salary — not age — that's the issue. And that *is* permissible by law. There's no getting around it, though, like it or not. Employers want to hire younger workers who will presumably work for less and with potentially more enthusiasm. "Some employers think older workers are less productive, less healthy, and more resistant to change," says my friend and go-to guy on these issues, Mark Miller, an expert on aging and retirement and author of *The Hard Times Guide to Retirement Security*. "Human resources experts and recruiters say older workers do often bring a false sense of entitlement to the workplace and resist adapting to changing business conditions," he says.

Then too, there's a perception that people over 50 or 60 will be just passing through as a transition into retirement. "Employers are loath to hire someone they think will be out the door in a year or two," says Encore .org's Marc Freedman.

Betsy Werley, executive director of the

Transition Network, a nonprofit networking group for women over 50, says, "The real issue is not age, but energy, curiosity, confidence and a desire to keep learning. If you display those qualities, you'll be attractive to employers." She adds: "If you don't feel confident, a networking group can help you understand what you have to offer."

The fact is that compared to their younger colleagues, workers with a few decades of experience under their belt are typically better problem-solvers and people-managers and have honed leadership skills over time. I know I'm preaching to the choir, but you need to show that to potential employers.

Here are thirteen strategies that can help you fight back against ageism:

1. **Ask for help and advice.** "Networking, as I like to say, is just one letter off from not working," one of my mentors, Joel Makower, executive editor of Greenbiz.com, tells me with a laugh. In this era of online resumes, it's all about who you know that can get you in the chair for a face-to-face meeting. When businesses are looking for candidates, they rely on employee referrals more than job boards or

any other source, according to a new report from CareerXRoads, a recruiting industry consulting firm. In 2011, employee referrals accounted for 28 percent of new hires, followed by job boards (20.1 percent), career pages on company web sites (9.8 percent), and recruiters. The findings were based on a January 2012 survey of 200 midsized and larger U.S. companies, which together hired more than 213,000 new employees in 2011.

Simply put, people want to hire someone who comes with the blessing of an existing employee or colleague. It makes their job easier. That's a card younger workers can't play as often. LinkedIn, for instance, is a great way to pull together your professional network. More on this in Chapter 14.

You have got to pick up the phone and call everybody that you ever knew, everybody that you ever worked with, every employer that you ever worked with, recruiter Beshara preaches. "That's the way to get an interview. If you don't establish any personal connection to the company, it's a waste of time."

2. **Brainstorm.** Sit down with a spouse and friends and ask for help. Write down the names of previous employers and former colleagues, immediate and extended family. Don't be embarrassed to call family members when you're out of work. Get over it. Call friends of friends, people in your place of worship, athletic club, volunteer organizations, parents of children's friends.

If there's a particular industry you're gunning for, join an association affiliated with it and seek out volunteer opportunities. Attend industry and professional meetings and conferences.

You never know who will know someone who is hiring. College and university placement offices are there to help no matter how long ago you graduated. Seek out career centers operated by area colleges or local government agencies offering career counseling, workshops on resume writing, job fairs, and re-training programs.

Canvas local lawyers, accountants, and bank officers in town and see if they know if any clients are hiring. Leave no stone unturned.

Don't be bashful. You have to take the risk of picking up the phone and having someone say no, and maybe, heck no, Beshara advises. No matter how good your resume might be, unless it helps you get face-to-face interviews with hiring managers, your efforts are wasted.

Getting interviews is hard work. It requires tenacity, persistence, determination, and courage to thrust yourself upon people, even if that doesn't come naturally to you. No one likes being rejected. The sooner you face this reality and prepare for rejection, the sooner you will be able to find a job.

3. **Market your age as a plus.** Think brand management. You are responsible for your own image. Workers 50+ tend to be self-starters, know how to get the job done, and don't need as much hand-holding as those with less experience. A great benefit to being older is that you have a good deal of knowledge and leadership ability. And whether you realize it or not, you have a network.

You have a lot more resources to draw on than people in their 20s and 30s. So pitch your age as a plus. You need to be able to articulate your value. Strut your stuff.

4. **Roll with the latest technology:** If you don't have core technical skills, check out your local libraries, community colleges, and other venues where training is offered. Here are some of the essential tools to have in your kit:

- **Smartphones.** If you still have a standard cellphone, trade it in for a smartphone — whether it's an iPhone, Droid, or BlackBerry — and take the time to get comfortable with it. With smartphones, you can communicate on the go by e-mail and texting (which your kids will explain, if you don't understand). Technology analyst Forrester Research predicts 1 billion mobile phones in the world by 2016, with 35 percent of the devices used for work.

- **E-mail.** Use an e-mail address that's professional and includes your full name. Not mymonkey@aol.com, or some such obscure name that means something to you and friends, but not the person in HR. You might opt for a free g-mail account that includes your name such as johnsmith@gmail.com, or one that includes your own domain name kerry@kerryhannon.com. This is an easy way to demonstrate that you are hip to the value of owning online rights to your own name. Add a signature to your outgoing e-mail messages that includes your contact information and links to any social network accounts. I include my web site, Twitter, and LinkedIn. Employers will tap into those links to gather more information on you.

- **Computers.** You should be at ease with desktops and laptops and the basic software programs needed for the job you're applying for. Mobile technology should not be a stumbling block.

- **Social networking.** LinkedIn and Facebook can help you get job leads and seek advice. LinkedIn, in particular, is a great way to build a professional network. Employers troll it for perspective hires. Add a video to your LinkedIn profile. Get

305

professional references. (More on this in Chapter 14).

- **Video interviews.** If the prospective employer isn't local, offer to do a Skype interview. All you'll need is your computer's Internet access and a built-in camera or webcam. Skype is easy to navigate. Go to Skype.com on your browser to get started. A few tips: Make sure you know where to look (hint: not at the screen but at the camera). If you have a built-in camera, set your laptop up above you, so you look up, and talk to the tiny camera embedded at the top of the screen. I put mine on a shelf slightly above my desk, but a few books will work. Also you want light on the front of your face. If your room has a window, face it, or put a small light on the desk in front of you. For the best video image, consider shelling out around $50 for an HD web camera. It will dramatically sharpen your video image. And image counts.
- **Web navigation skills.** These are non-negotiable. You should have a grasp of the primary business tools. New ones are always arriving. Be

familiar with Safari, Yahoo!, Google, Google+, Firefox, and other search engines and browsers before even looking for a job. Search for a few web sites that follow your profession and sign up for any electronic newsletters. LinkedIn also has industry and special interest groups you can join.

- **Employer web sites and Google alerts.** In addition to visiting the web site of any company you're interested in, search for blogs or news stories (both good and bad) about the company, and sign up for Google Alerts about the firm. You might even learn some personal details about the people interviewing you — there's an astonishing amount of info on the web.

5. **Change it up.** Look at your skill set and past experience as transferable to lots of different challenges and fields. If you're switching industries, you're *redeploying* skills you already have in place, not reinventing or retraining for entirely new ones.

6. **Reframe your experience.** You're selling how your deep knowledge

base and skills can solve business problems in the future regardless of the employer.

7. **Look for openings at small businesses or local nonprofits.** They're more likely to value your experience as someone who can help them. You can provide the depth of practical knowledge and versatility that's worth two junior hires, and the learning curve is not as steep.

8. **Keep your resume alive.** If you're unemployed now, do something. Try volunteering for a nonprofit organization or do pro-bono work in a job that uses your skills, advises Maggie Mistal, a career coach in New York City.

   You might also check with an employer that you're interested in working for, or one in a field that you would like to move into, to see if they offer unpaid internships for more experienced workers. It never hurts to ask. They might even refer to you as a "visiting professional." In the past few years, these internships for workers of all ages have broadened beyond just college students and new graduates.

As I see it, the rewards of volunteering are fourfold: It gives you an opportunity to network and get your foot in the door with future employers, it explains gaps in your resume, it feels good, and it helps someone else. You never know where you might meet someone who will lead you to a job opportunity. It bears repeating: Landing a job these days is all about *who you know.*

Use your skills to create your own business at home. Be open to consulting or short-term projects. You might find that creating multiple income streams is just what you are looking for and gives you the income, variety of work, and flexible control of your time that makes sense after decades of reporting into an office.

It's easy to get sucked into the mindset that a full-time employer is the only money-making option that's safe and worth your time, Mistal notes. If you can work freelance or as a consultant for several employers and not have all your eggs in one basket, that gives you flexibility, she advises her clients.

You might even make more money, if you know how to package and sell your skills. A good career coach might be able to help you focus your pitch. Of course, not everyone has the temperament or self-motivation to work for himself or herself.

Add some classes to boost your expertise in a new arena, say, non-profit fundraising, if that's an area that appeals to you. Travel experiences, too, show that you've been actively learning and growing. You'll probably bump up your list of personal or professional references at the same time.

This is where a well-crafted resume is key. Achievements trump titles and responsibilities. Kick off your resume with specific examples of what you have accomplished in various positions, not a list of job duties. Hiring managers want resumes that put into words concrete examples of how you've helped the companies you've worked for make money, grow, and be more efficient.

9. Fine-tune your interview skills.

It may have been a while since you have been on the other side of the table. Don't be nervous. It helps if you psychologically approach the interview as if you're a highly paid consultant called in to trouble-shoot. Think like an expert. If you're desperate and thinking, "I just need a job and want to make money for the next 10 years," employers are on to you. They are going to pick the best, most interested, most innovative candidate.

You need to be able to articulate your value. State clearly what you think needs to be done and why, based on your experience, you're the one to do it. By taking a genuine interest in the firm you're interviewing with, learning about the company's history and goals, and talking to people who work there, you can demonstrate that. In a nutshell: Focus on the company's needs, not yours.

If you have done your homework on the firm, and Google alerts have kept you up-to-date on the latest developments with the company and its competitors, you'll have lots to pull from in your conversation.

Refrain from throwing out names of powerful people you worked with two decades ago — that makes you seem ancient. And who really cares? See Chapter 15 for more on interviewing.

10. **Don't be a know-it-all with a chip on your shoulder.** Inevitably, the talk will turn to you. The interviewer needs to learn as much about you as possible, but steer clear of lengthy resume regurgitation. Answer questions with crisp, dignified responses. Take time beforehand to internally focus on your best moments and what situations you shine in. Be clear in interviews that if an employer put you in those situations, you will perform.

Don't badmouth past employers, even if you are bitter from being ushered out the door in a downsizing move. Zip your lip. No good will come from this, and it will only reflect back on your character.

Overqualified? Deal with it, if you want the gig. If you do, repeat after me: What matters to me at this stage is having the opportunity to work with exceptional people in a company whose values and products I believe in, and where my skills and knowledge can be used in a meaningful way.

11. **Shoot for the sky.** This is a little out there, but think about what the coolest job in the world would be, or who would be your dream person to work for. This is your time to do something fabulous, right?

"I tell my clients to play longshots," career coach Jones tells me. Great jobs often come from unlikely sources. Once you have done the obvious networking with people who already know you, or those within your industry peer group, "you have to pursue the off the wall possibilities, jobs, in theory, you have never done, but have the skills to do. I have found these are often the ones that pay off," she says.

You will need to be fearless about doing this, says Jones. "What's the worst that can happen? They don't call you back?"

There's more on conquering fear in Chapter 24.

12. Look your best. Interviewers do judge a book by its cover. Invest in some new duds, update up your hairstyle, find fashion-forward specs if needed.

At the very least, you should freshen up your hairstyle with a good cut and shaping. Don't, however, do anything too radical the day before, of course.

I'm a stickler for good grooming. Pay attention to your entire look — head to toe. I recommend a manicure for both sexes. Men, you can forgo the polish.

Always overdress. If you know someone who works at the company, ask them about office attire, providing that doesn't make you feel awkward. Alternatively, you might surf for a Google image on your computer of someone in management there, even the CEO. That can give you a sense of what dress for success might be appropriate at the firm. Importantly, even if you're told the office is casual work attire, don't go there.

You probably don't need a Botox treatment. They can be pricey, anyway. Okay, if it really makes you feel more confident, what the heck, try it. I personally wouldn't, but that's just me.

"You won't believe how many clients ask me immediately if they should dye their hair, as if that's the number one thing to do," Mistal says.

13. **Practice positivity.** In truth, one of the biggest stumbling blocks to landing a job is negativity. You probably don't need a Botox treatment. What works better is a faith lift. You've got to believe in yourself. When you do, it shows from the inside out. People dwell on the bad news. "I've been unemployed for too long. I'm too old." You have to have faith in yourself. After you have been out of work for a while, you forget your value. You take for granted your accomplishments and contributions.

Sometimes it's hard to toot your own horn. Self-promotion is uncomfortable, especially if you've always thought of yourself as a team player. Mistal advises her clients, "ask people who know you well, whose opinions you value and trust, to evaluate you in writing: your best skills and talents, your personality, the roles you have been really good at."

Guess what comes back? All the accomplishments, all the positives that you need to be reminded of to prove to yourself that you're a talented individual who has a contribution to make. Then when you're in the interview, networking, or doing informational conversations, you can say, "Well, people have said about me that blah, blah, blah."

All of a sudden you have all the words to use, and it's easier to talk about your attributes because you're using someone else's tribute.

CHAPTER 13
TIPS FOR A GREAT RESUME

"Can you take a look at my resume and see what you think?" If I had a dollar for every time I've been asked this in the past year, I wouldn't be rich, but I would have some extra dough.

It's true. Since I write about jobs and careers, it's not surprising that I've been fielding calls from friends and colleagues who want me to take a look at their resumes to see what's missing, give some pointers. I try to help. They agonize over the details. They're frustrated beyond belief. They shoot their resumes off in a flick of a button when they hear about a job opening, and then silence — no response.

Sound familiar? I offer my two cents to them. As I mention in other chapters, I remind them that their resume is their calling card. Your resume needs to capture the essence of who you are and what you have to offer an employer. But the trick is to boil all that down into a clear, sharp and engaging one-dimensional presentation. Challenging, I know, but doable. It's called editing. This is your highlight reel.

I tell them to keep their resumes concise, not to list any whacky jobs, and stay present as best they can.

In other words, refrain from listing every job you've held since hitting the working world. Watch out for gaps in your employment history. If they are there, fudge as best you can, or have a good experience to sub for it, say, time off for travel, to add a degree, or pursue other education.

Be sure to include any volunteer work that can be viewed as management experience, or fundraising and marketing, for instance, to show other ways you've used your talents and experience to help others or forward a cause. This will reflect nicely on you in more ways than you probably realize.

And by all means tuck in any special tech training or social media acumen you may have under your belt.

I think awards are sometimes nice to list, too. They can demonstrate that your work has been recognized by others in your field. Again, don't go too far back in your treasure chest. Employers want to know what you can do now, who you are today. But to get some deeper insight, I asked Tony Beshara, a top recruiter and author of *Unbeatable Resumes,* to share his secrets.

KH: *Why are people so obsessed with their resumes?*

TB: The primary reason people spend so much time, money, and effort in writing a resume is that this is the one activity within the job search that they can control. Instead of picking up the phone and calling a prospective employer to ask for a face-to-face interview — risking potential rejection — people agonize over their resumes. Here's the truth: It is rare to get hired by simply submitting a resume. The purpose of the resume is to help get you an interview. And at the interview, remember that 40 percent of a hiring decision is based on personality. You've got to get the interview and sell your patootie off.

KH: *What makes an unbeatable resume?*

TB: It has to be simple. No more than two pages. The average resume gets read in 10 seconds. Be sure the content is on a level any high school senior could understand. In other words, the person looking at your resume should be able to easily understand exactly whom you have worked for and what that company does. Just because you know the company, or it's a big name like IBM, Boeing Corp., or Ford Motor Co., doesn't mean everyone is familiar with what your specific division does.

- Avoid the fancy-schmancy layout, font, and other special effects. Stick to traditional font of Times New Roman, 9 to 12 point size, and black type against a white paper. You might try a different type size for your name and the companies you have worked for, perhaps your title. But try to be consistent. Go easy on boldface type, italics, and underlining.
- Prepare it in a simple Word format that can easily be viewed on most computers.
- Use a reverse chronological order. List your present or most recent job first, and then work backwards. You state the complete name of the company you work for, or have worked for, and what they do, how

long you were there — month and year.

- Then list the position you held and your accomplishments. You don't have to use full sentences. Begin with verbs. "Managed company tax reporting, finance, invoicing, purchasing," for example.
- Get rid of objectives and a summary and all that silly stuff. It's all fluff. Employers don't care about your objective. They care about theirs.
- Skip personal information such as married with three kids. Sounds stable to you. But to a hiring authority looking for someone to travel, it may keep you from being interviewed.
- Tell stories. Stories sell. Numbers, statistics, and percentages get attention if you put them in bold type. "Increased profit by this 28 percent. Came under budget by 30 percent." If you were born and raised on a chicken farm, note it on your resume.
- Avoid fuzzy key words and phrases. These include *customer-oriented, excellent communications skills,* and *creative.* These words lack meaning

and do absolutely nothing to help you get an interview.

- Use words that refer to titles — customer service, controller, manager, accountant.
- Get the photos off your resume. You are looking for a job, not a date.

KH: *And the biggest frustration when it comes to getting a resume noticed?*

TB: People overestimate who is reading it. Most of the time, the people who are reading the resume really don't have anything to do with the job and have no direct experience with it. It's an internal recruiter, somebody in Human Resources, the "Hiring Roadblock" department. Just know that if you get relegated to the HR department, your odds of getting an interview, let alone a job, are drastically reduced. That's just the way it is.

CHAPTER 14
JOB HUNTING
AND SOCIAL MEDIA

Two-thirds of adult Internet users now say they use a social networking site like Facebook, LinkedIn, or MySpace, more than twice as many as in 2008, according to a survey by the Pew Research Center. Among the boomer-aged segment of Internet users ages 50–64, social networking site usage on a typical day grew a significant 60 percent, between 2010 and 2011, from 20 percent to 32 percent. "Many baby boomers are beginning to make a trip to the social media pool part of their daily routine," says Mary Madden, a senior research specialist and co-author of the Pew report.

All ethnic and age groups drive the rise, but women stand out as the most avid users, according to the Pew Internet & American Life Project. Seven out of 10 women said they used the social media sites, followed closely by six in 10 men.

If you're one of the many older Americans

working, or planning to work, into your 60s, you may already be one of the new devotees. If not, get on board.

Most job searches nowadays are via the Internet. Yep, social media platforms such as Facebook, LinkedIn, Twitter, and most recently, Google+ have transformed how you job hunt. As I note in Chapter 12, "Strategies for 50+ Job Hunters," you must be comfortable with computers, basic software programs, web navigation, e-mail, and mobile technology.

There's a view out there that once you cross over the big 50, you resist learning new technology. Not cool. For those of you who are looking to switch into a new career or build a small business, it's even more important to prove them wrong.

In today's job-hunting world, it's typical to e-mail your resume to companies and to job boards found on sites such as career builder.com, indeed.com, jobs.jobs, monster .com, retiredbrains.com, vault.com, and workforce50.com. It's a given that you need a social networking profile. Online networking and rah, rah self-promotion through social media channels are increasingly important tools to finding a job. It's a little awkward for many of us, but with practice it gets easier.

You hear about it all the time, and may very well choose to ignore it. Do so at your peril. The importance of social media is not to be taken lightly. If you spend some time, you can really build out a diverse network of contacts. You should be doing this even when you aren't looking for a job. I try to add a few new contacts each week.

Most job searches these days are at least started on the Internet — specifically, social media platforms such as LinkedIn and Twitter. It's about more than trolling through the job boards. It's a way to help recruiters find you.

"Social media is one of the easiest ways to accomplish several key factors that help people land jobs," says Miriam Salpeter, a job search and social media coach, owner of Keppie Careers, and author of *Social Networking for Career Success: Using Online Tools to Create a Personal Brand.* As a pro in this area, she told me how she advises her clients. Here are Salpeter's tips:

- Grow a community of people who know, like, and trust you. This is nothing new; expanding your network has always proven crucial for job seekers.
- Learn new information. Social media is an ongoing source of professional

development opportunities. This is so important, as it allows you to keep up-to-date with what is new in a field. Social media is also a great tool to help job seekers who want to transition to a new profession.

- Demonstrate expertise. There's no easier way to showcase what you know to a broad audience of potential colleagues, networking contacts, and hiring managers than via social media. Be found. If you are "perfect for the job" and no one knows, you won't go far! Social media makes it easier for people to learn about you, and that's necessary to land a job.

I know from personal experience that it takes practice to be able to converse clearly and efficiently online. It takes the repetition of doing it every day. Start by taking simple actions. You can share your know-how by posting a link to a relevant article on your Twitter, LinkedIn, or Facebook page with your own short commentary, or chime in on a LinkedIn group discussion, even if it means merely checking the "Like" button.

When hiring managers see that you're using social media, it can help alleviate their worry about you as an older applicant who is woefully behind the times. If you're using LinkedIn, have a blog perhaps, and you're even semi-active on your Twitter account, it's going to be hard for people to think that you can't be taught new things. I'm not saying you'll have an overnight success in your job search by tapping social media, and it does zap your time, but in today's marketplace you'd be foolish to ignore it.

To help you steer through the latest landscape, here are eight must-do social media moves.

1. **Become a LinkedIn member.** I view LinkedIn as a key social media tool for every job seeker. For companies, it's where recruiters go these days when they have a job to fill. For you, it's a fast way to build a far-reaching professional network. And in a harsh job market, networking rules. I can't lay its importance on thick enough. Stay active on it. Join alumni and industry groups. Try connecting to a few new people each day.

   LinkedIn actually does help people in their job searches. It's easy to create a profile. For me, my LinkedIn profile is my working resume. It lets anyone who wants to know about my background, awards, interests, and so on see it all in a straightforward format that I can tweak easily.

Don't be bashful about posting your interests and volunteer activities. A well-rounded profile creates an impression of who you are and how you balance your personal and professional life. I list what I'm reading, thanks to an Amazon link, and I'm an active member of LinkedIn groups that relate to my current work, alma mater, past employers, and more. I comment on posts from others and add in my own. It's amazing how many new "Links" you can make, when you interact.

I recommend writing your own personal note when you send a request to someone to LinkIn with you. The site automatically pops up with a generic one, but it only takes a second to erase it and write your own. It's friendlier and a good way to remind someone of how you know one another in a more direct way than you were colleagues at such and such company or class-mates.

There's more window-dressing to apply on LinkedIn once you're up and rolling. You can add a Power-Point presentation and a video clip of you from a television interview or a speech via Slideshare. You can link a WordPress blog if you have one and connect your Twitter account stream, so that all your LinkedIn updates are tweeted. I do that. Saves a step. There's a vast amount of information you can cull to paint a portrait of who you are, and you can do it one step at a time as you get more comfortable with steering around the site.

Recruiters look at the summary of your LinkedIn profile for a snapshot of your career history, connections, and recommendations, and that can make or break their decision whether to call you for an interview. This is your big chance to pitch yourself in your best possible light.

Add your LinkedIn profile hyperlink address to the bottom signature line on your outgoing e-mail, too. (I put my Twitter handle and my web site on mine as well.)

Basic accounts are free. You fill out your profile, listing key words and skills that apply to the job you're searching for. Those words help recruiters find you online in a snap. Add a professional headshot. Ask ex-colleagues, previous bosses, and clients to write recommendations. You can research companies and individuals you want to target, connect with former associates, and let them know when you're looking for new opportunities.

To help you get rolling, LinkedIn has a Learning Center that offers a new-user guide and plain directions for creating a profile. There are special guides to help a myriad of users from small businesses to entrepreneurs, job seekers, students, and nonprofits.

LinkedIn also has an "Apply Now" button in the Jobs section that makes it easier for you to connect with companies that have open positions. From any job listing, click on the button that appears in the top right corner, and it will zap your

LinkedIn profile and contact information to that business. You can also send along a cover letter and resume.

If you're a freelance writer, you might join Media Jobs or LinkEds & Writers discussion group. Starting your own business? Check out groups like Baby Boomer Business Owners.

2. **Try SimplyHired's "Who Do I Know?" tool.** When you've identified a potential company you want to work for, the Who Do I Know tool on SimplyHired, a job-board search engine, finds your Facebook and LinkedIn connections who currently work at the company, worked there in the past, or are connected to a person who works there. To set up the tool, you give SimplyHired permission to grab data from your Facebook and LinkedIn accounts.

3. **Sign up for a Twitter account and apps.** I'm a Twitter fan for a bunch of reasons, but one selling point is that there's no need for a personal introduction or recommendation, which you need with LinkedIn. Just by following their

tweets, you can get the scoop on people you may wind up interviewing with or tapping for mentoring advice. You can also share ideas and tips with other job seekers and pros. Plus, you're always expanding your network. (You don't have to follow everyone who follows you — choose those who interest you).

I chat daily with Twitter friends whom I've never met or worked with, but we share ideas and information and send private messages. We help each other out. In my case, they might suggest sources for stories I'm reporting, or point me toward research on a topic.

As with LinkedIn, you'll want to add a headshot that looks professional. For your username, always use your actual name or a shortened form. Include where you live and what kind of work you do. It has to be short and to the point — only 160 characters.

You can also download Twitter-related apps that help you job hunt. One to check out is TweetMyJobs. You fill out an online form describing the kinds of job opportunity you're looking for, and TweetMy-Jobs shoots you daily updates via Twitter, e-mail, or text message on your smartphone. Thousands of jobs are posted daily. TwitJobSearch is another one to check out.

4. **Participate in online job real-time chats.** You need to do more on social media than follow people. Especially if you're on Twitter, you need to have regular — albeit brief — online conversations. Check out weekly Twitter chats like #jobhunt-chat, one of the largest regular chat groups on Twitter dedicated to job search, #careerchat, #HireFriday, and #HFChat are others that are currently in vogue.

On these chats, you can find information about employment trends and firms that are hiring and network with recruiters and other job seekers. Several conversations are running at the same time, so hone in on the one that's up your alley. Chats are all live, and you use the hashtag # tied to a certain discussion to keep track of the conversation or ask a question. Sometimes sponsors post transcripts. For example, I did an *AARP Your Life Calling* chat with host Jane Pauley for career changers. If you missed it, you can read the transcript on my AARP Job Expert site.

5. **Tap into virtual job fairs.** It's all there online: company recruiters, experts, and so forth. For example, MBA International held a month-long virtual career fair sponsored by Duke Fuqua School of Business, the University of Virginia's Darden School of Business, Yale, and others. Attending employers included Alcoa, Lilly, and Microsoft. You can find virtual job events like this by doing a Google search.

6. **Join Facebook.** If you set your privacy settings properly and highlight your work experience and education on your profile, the site has lots to offer. Check out *AARP Facebook: Tech to Connect,* by the makers of For Dummies, and *Facebook and Twitter for Seniors for Dummies.*

It's okay to list your hobbies and comment or post articles you find interesting, but keep it in good taste. Think of Facebook as a way to let people learn a little about you. It can open doors to great conversations in a job interview, too. Plus, you might even find you are building your network with people who know you from high school and college. That's been my experience. Trust me, they can turn out to be great sources when you're job hunting. You never know where you might get an introduction to a potential employer, or hear of a job opening.

7. **Use apps.** This is a little more advanced, but you'll get there. You start by adding your accounts on LinkedIn and Facebook to your smartphone. But there's much more for the serious job hunter. There are apps for your mobile iPhone, Droid, Samsung Galaxy Nexus, HTC Rezound, and iPad that you can download for free or a small fee and use to troll job boards or track down someone nearby for a networking coffee klatch.

   If you're really ramped up, you can create your resume on the run. Pocket Resume, for example, costs $2.99. It lets you create and e-mail your resume — right from your phone. 101 Great Answers to the Toughest Interview Question is a free app. And I love the iPhone's Business Card Reader, which costs $4.99. You take a picture of the card and it will store e-mail addresses, phone numbers, and web sites in your phone. The Business Card Reader also supports LinkedIn integration, allowing you to easily import your professional online network.

Two job sites also come with lots of bells and whistles: Indeed.com and the Jobs By CareerBuilder.com apps, which allow you to search millions of jobs by keyword, location, company, and type of job. You can also create resumes, apply for jobs, receive job recommendations just for you, and more.

Two Facebook apps, BranchOut and BeKnown, let you build a network of business contacts that's private and not part of your circle of Facebook friends. Glassdoor.com has an app that lets you pull up comments from people who have interviewed for jobs at certain firms and check for salaries.

8. **Create a video resume.** This can be fun if you're looking for a creative type of job and your personality suits this approach. You can put together your video and share the interactive resume via sites such as GetHired.com, Jobyra, Kareer.me, and Purzue.com.

Want help getting up to speed? Community colleges, adult education centers, the Osher Life Long Learning Institute (with 117 locations around the country), and local libraries offer classes that can help you with smartphones and smartphone apps, among other gadgets. AARP has lots of how-tos on its web site, along with a new Tech to Connect series of books that includes Facebook, iPads, and Tablets. You might also tap into a how-to video on YouTube from CNET, the tech web site.

Bottom line: Using social media helps waylay "older worker" concerns employers may have about you. If you're using LinkedIn and are on Twitter, have a web site, or a blog even, it's darn hard to make a case that you are a Luddite.

Final housekeeping note: Have a professional e-mail address where prospective employers can e-mail you that is your first and last name.

CHAPTER 15
GREAT JOB INTERVIEW TIPS

You can make all the great impressions in the world on paper, but where the rubber meets the road is when you meet someone face-to-face. Once you get the nod for an interview, it's show time.

Here's some interviewing advice that can boost your image and your chances of nabbing the position. There are no do-overs in the interview process, so you have to get this right the first time out of the gate.

Before you start the process, practice your patter. One way is to have a friend or partner act as an interviewer and run through a dress rehearsal in your living room. You can also rig up your own mock interview with Skype (see Chapter 14), a smartphone that has video capability, or a video camera and tripod stand. Ask a friend to lob questions your way. If you have a videotape, you can review it to see where you can improve your delivery and responses.

Some university and college career centers, including Georgetown University's McDonough School of Business and Drexel University's LeBow College of Business's Office of M.B.A. Career Services, offer their alumnae InterviewStream (interviewstream .com), an online interactive simulation program that allows you to hone your interviewing skills. Once you create an account through the center's web site, you can practice answering interview questions at home using a computer with Internet access, a webcam or built-in camera in your computer, and a microphone. There's an iPad mobile app too.

InterviewStream allows you to either select a set of standardized interview questions or customize your interview by choosing from a list of 1,000 varied questions and record your video interview on its platform. You can then use that video to send to a career coach provided by the career center or to trusted friends and colleagues for a critique.

Much of what makes a great interview is intuitive. It's chemistry between two people. Each situation is unique. And regardless of how practiced you are, there's plenty of room for improv when you're in the hot seat.

I'm not going to even try to tell you how to actually answer some of the more bizarre questions that interviewers are tossing out these days. The job web site Glassdoor.com published a list of 25 oddball interview questions of 2011 that interview candidates shared.

Here are a few:

- "Just entertain me for five minutes, I'm not going to talk." Asked at sales and marketing firm, Acosta.
- "What do you think of garden gnomes?" Asked at Trader Joe's.
- "How would you cure world hunger?" Asked at Amazon.com.
- "Does life fascinate you?" Asked at Ernst & Young.

I'm sticking to the old-fashioned nuts and bolts of an interview. The things you can control. The interviewer is leading the dance, but if you're prepared, you can follow along smoothly and with confidence.

Dress appropriately. If it's a "business casual" office, what does that really mean? I lean toward the more formal approach, even if you're told that everyone wears blue jeans and sneakers. Pick something that you feel good in and that's comfortable. Skip the super-high heels or open-toe shoes. You do want polished footwear, though. If you're all scuffed, buy new shoes or pay for a professional's elbow grease. Shoes count.

Take the time to really look in the mirror before you head out. A quick pit stop in the office building's restroom, or the Starbuck's next door, before you enter the firm's actual domain is a good idea. Check for rogue dog hairs, missed buttons, undone zippers, or bits of bagel in your teeth.

True story: I once interviewed for a job with aluminum foil wrapped around all the brass buttons on my red blazer. I had pulled it straight from the cleaner's bag without checking. Yikes. The interviewer never mentioned it. I still laugh sheepishly about it today. I got the job, but ahem, attention to details, please.

Don't be late. Your interview starts way before you shake hands. Arrive 10 or 15 minutes early. It's more than a case of punctuality, too. When you arrive early, you have a chance to take a breath and center yourself. It removes one layer of stress. If you're skating in under the bell, it's probably evident in the tension-taut lines of your face and your damp handshake.

Begin your interview at the door. Greet the receptionist with the same respect as you will the person who is interviewing you. You're on stage from the instant you state your name at the front desk. Most one-on-one job interviews last between 25 and 30 minutes, so your total on-site performance time is precious. Since it's short and sweet, milk every minute of it, from the waiting room onward.

Don't spend your time in the on-deck area gabbing on your cell, for example, or responding to e-mails, or even tweeting. Focus on why you're there. It's okay to review a list of questions you want to ask. Soak up the office atmosphere. Look around. It will give you clues to whether this is a place you might want to hang your hat.

Start with a relaxed meet and greet. Step up with a firm one-handed handshake. Two hands can be a little forthright and maybe even too familiar. Kick off the first few minutes of your interview as you would a conversation with someone you've just met at a reception. Keep it relaxed and conversational, yet professional and not too personal. Direct eye contact is important. My standard advice: Commenting on wall décor or a desk accessory is acceptable, but saying you like someone's tie or shoes may be stepping over the line.

I personally like to scan wall and desk photographs, say, and see if I can find a common bond. A framed image of a Labrador retriever or a horse always sets an instant connection for me. These initial moments are where the chemistry between the interviewer and you can spark. Think speed dating.

Offer your paper resume before you sit down. Presenting an actual resume to an interviewer is akin to bringing a gift to a host or hostess. You're passing along something of value in exchange for the invitation to meet and his or her time. By taking it out in the opening moments of the interview, it becomes an interactive asset. If there are areas or responsibilities that you want to emphasize or explain, the interview is your chance to draw attention to them.

People often think if something is on their resume the significance is clear to the interviewer but those bullet points don't always speak for themselves.

Follow the leader. Synch up with the interviewer's rhythm. It's important to go at his or her tempo. Don't try too hard and talk too fast. Answer concisely and with a confident, calm manner. Pause before you respond — even repeat the question if need be — to buy yourself some moments to gather a measured answer.

Watch your language (body language, that is). Leaning forward can cue that you're interested. Look people in the eyes when you're talking to them. I'm not trying to sound like your mother. But this is important. It's fine to glance upward, or off to the side, if you're forming a thought, but a clear, direct gaze portrays candor and sincerity.

Your body language counts here, so pay attention. No slouching. Sit straight, take some deep breaths, and relax. Stroking your neck and throat unconsciously can make you look nervous. A confident, loose (un-clenched) fist lightly tucked under your chin is okay in small doses. Pressing your finger-tips together in a steeple formation is also a simple sign of self-assurance, but don't overdo it. Be careful about folding your arms across your chest. You might think it makes you look serious, but it can come off as a defensive stance.

If you've got a point you want to play up, a hand gesture is fine, but keep those to a minimum. Your best move is to keep your hands laced together with your thumbs on top, sitting calmly in your lap, or propped lightly on the arms of the chair. Avoid twisting and spinning your pen, rings, necklace, or bracelets. You might even do this inadvertently, so be mindful of what your hands are up to. For an interviewer, it sends off a signal of nerves or even anxiety.

Keep focused on your interviewers and the reality that you're sitting in that chair to sell solutions to their problems or challenges, not what you want to say next about yourself. At the core of a job interview, it's about them, not about you. Listen closely to what they're saying.

Don't make rapid-off-the-top-of-your-head answers. This isn't *Jeopardy.* There's no race to push the buzzer. You might come off as flip without meaning to do so. Don't talk so much that you go on for 10 minutes answering one question. Crisp and to-the-point answers allow interviewers to get to all their questions and gather as much knowledge about you as they can.

Also be sure to ask what they see as the

biggest problem that someone in the job needs to solve. If you have some ideas of what can be done to address that, here is your moment. You can also file it away to slip into your thank-you note.

Be enthused, but not fawning. You're a pro, remember. Act interested and dignified. Interviewers really want to know what interests and intrigues you about their company, too. Be forthright and clear about why you are motivated by what the organization does and the challenges of the position you're interviewing for, plus why you think you would be a good fit with their culture.

It's a two-way street. Yes, you're there to sell yourself, but they're selling the job too. It also makes them feel good about their own good fortune to work there. Even the most jaded hiring manager has a glimmer of insecurity.

Subtly slip into the conversation that you've done your background check — information you've gleaned from the Google news alert for the company and the specific industry you've already set up. This insider knowhow will show that you're aware of the state of their business right now. It will make it easier to respond to questions about why the job is something that's a good match for both of you — that you have the key skills to solve their challenges today and moving forward.

Stick to your main selling points. It's easy to veer off topic in an interview. Write down and practice at home three main selling points about yourself to help you stay focused. Have specific examples that highlight your strengths to share with the interviewer.

I recommend that toward the end of the interview, you click through your mental checklist to make sure you've covered each of your topic points during your discussion. If not, don't leave until you have. If the interviewer is wrapping things up, and you can sense this, politely interject that you want to make sure you mention X, Y, or Z, and why.

Don't be thrown off if asked if you think you're overqualified for a position. You might be. Here's your canned answer: What matters to you at this stage is having the opportunity to work with top people in a firm whose values and products you trust and where your experience can be used in a significant way.

Keep in mind, however, that no one wants to hire someone who will in time resent working at something they feel is less than their talents, or for pay lower than what they believe they merit. You can't blame them. This is a tricky area, and you must be comfortable with the repercussions. It's easy to say it will be okay, but what's that really going to feel like if it comes to pass? Can your ego handle it?

Use your mentoring skills as a selling point. This is often a backdoor way of dealing with the concerns someone might have about how you will deal with the younger boss dilemma. If you can slip it into the conversation, explain how mentoring has always been a part of your work and management style. It's a process that you have benefited from over the years as a mentee and a mentor and hope you can continue to give back by guiding less-experienced co-workers. And, importantly, you're open to learning from them too. Again, mentoring helps both people.

Final questions. In the end, your interviewer will probably ask if you have any questions for them. Be prepared with at least two or three to toss out. Otherwise, you look as if you're not all that interested. But whatever you do, don't bring up salary at this stage. Save that for your next visit — either in person or on the phone, when they're close to making a selection.

Here are a few things you might want answered if they haven't already been covered in the course of your discussion: "What do you think are the key elements of the job? What are the firm's goals for the division the job is in? Why is the position open?"

You may have to use your judgment if this last question is appropriate. It's possible that it will make the interviewer defensive. "Is it a new job or did someone leave the company? Is the interview process just getting rolling, or is it wrapping up? What's a typical day like, or is there such a thing?"

If this person would be your boss, and you feel at ease, you might ask, "What's your management style? Why did you come to work here? What challenges make you excited to come to work each day? What do you like the most about working here?" These kinds of questions let somebody see that you're genuinely attracted to the job, plus, you can get a better read on what's next in the hiring process, and if it's a company you would fit with.

Ask for a business card. In this age of e-mail, a business card seems a little quaint, but it's a tangible gift exchange. You can leave yours, while accepting a card in return with appreciation. It intrinsically shows you're interested in the interviewer's contact information, as well as the job. Ask if they prefer to be contacted via phone or e-mail.

Good manners count. No hugs here. Go for a firm handshake, look your interviewer straight in his or her eyes with a warm smile, and offer genuine thanks for their time. And call me old-fashioned, but never forget to write a thank-you note to everyone you interviewed with.

I'm a stickler for thank-you notes in all aspects of my life. I learned the power of a proper note from a book, *White Gloves and Party Manners,* that my mother gave me when I was a child. It's an etiquette guide for young people, first published in 1965, that was written by Marjabelle Young Stewart and Ann Buchwald (wife of Art Buchwald).

A thank-you note is simple and classy, and just might make you stand apart among a roster of applicants. I personally like a handwritten one, but an e-mail works today, if you shoot it off within 24 hours. In many cases, the immediacy is welcomed and effective. It's not wrong to do both, particularly if there's additional material you'd like to share with the interviewer, or if there were any questions you stumbled on or didn't answer well before you left. Use your correspondence to wrap up and leave a positive impression.

And while I'm thinking of it, thanks for taking the time to read my book. I appreciate it.

CHAPTER 16
WHY PART-TIME OR CONTRACT WORK IS WORTH IT

Today was the day. I put away the last vestige of the ho, ho, ho season — the festive bowl of holiday cards with pictures of smiling kids and pets, along with the occasional annual letters detailing whirlwind lives.

As I was taking a final gander, one caught my eye. It was sent by Gwenn Rosener. I interviewed Rosener last year about her firm, Flexforce Professionals, a recruiting and staffing company in the Washington, D.C., area that focuses on helping professionals — including retirees who want to continue working — find part-time work with competitive pay. The job seekers she places are typically college-educated workers with 10-plus years of professional experience, who are eager to work 20 to 30 hours a week at hourly rates ranging from $20 to $70. The companies she works with are generally small, and fast-growing, and looking for experienced employees who can tackle a range of duties.

Rosener, who was once an Ernst & Young senior manager and holds a Harvard MBA in her back pocket, and her partners, Sheila Murphy and Ellen Grealish, all have executive-level management and consulting backgrounds. Grealish worked at Hewlett-Packard and Andersen Consulting (now Accenture), and Murphy held consulting posts, mostly with government clients, including the U.S. Department of Housing and Urban Development.

The three partners started their business in 2010 and reeled in revenues of $140,000 with a profit of $47,000 that first year, placing CFOs, HR managers, business development and proposal writers, web designers, analysts, bookkeepers, and office managers — all in part-time or temporary jobs. Gwenn wrote in her holiday card:

Dear Kerry,

Enjoyed connecting with you. Thank you for letting us share our story. A quick update since our last talk. We actually ended up quadrupling our sales this year and surpassed the $500k mark. It surprises even us.

It didn't surprise me. Part-time and contract staffing is on the rise. Recently, the big online job site CareerBuilder released a Harris Interactive survey that showed that more than a third of U.S. companies are operating with smaller staffs than before the recession.

To keep business trucking along, roughly one-third of companies hire contract or temporary workers, recently, according to the survey of more than 3,000 hiring managers and human resource professionals. "It's an easy way for employers to get great experienced staff and save money at the same time," says Art Koff, founder of RetiredBrains.com, a job search site for older workers. That can be good news for many of you, and it's especially true if you're a retiree and need some extra money to boost your current retirement income.

Under those circumstances, part-time or contract jobs are often perfect. They can pay enough to bolster income from investments and Social Security, often without exceeding the limits that would require a reduction in Social Security payments. Even if your Social Security payment is reduced due to earnings, those benefits are not truly lost. At your full retirement age, your payment will be increased to account for the benefits withheld. For more about working while receiving Social Security, see *AARP Social Security for Dummies* or contact the Social Security Administration (ssa.gov).

For all types of job seekers, though, there are scores of reasons why part-time or contract work is worth it. Here are a few to ponder:

- It gives you something to do. Don't discount this. Having a sense of purpose is a great thing for all kinds of reasons.
- It gets you in the door. It may lead to full-time work with an employer eventually. Don't miss the opportunity.
- It gets you decent pay. You can make your experience a plus. Employers are typically willing to pay you generously, providing you have the chops and solve their problem or need quickly. It lets them bypass the hand-holding and learning curve stage that a younger, less experienced, but lower-paid worker might require.
- It builds your professional network. Nurture relationships with co-workers during your assignment. You never know where contacts may lead you, and whom they might be able to refer

you to for future jobs.

- It lands you new and *au courant* references for future employers to contact about what you've been up to lately.
- It keeps your resume alive. It's a bone to stave off the disgrace of those gaping holes of idleness in your resume.
- It keeps your skills sharp. You know the mantra: Use it or lose it.
- Contract work, particularly, lets you get psyched about a work project without the pressure of long-term expectations. No job is forever, anyway. This one just might be shorter than most, and that can be tremendously freeing.

You can't expect that part-time or contract positions will lead to a full-time or ongoing position. I know that. If it is a job or a company that turns you on, though, you can subtly let it be known that you'd love an opportunity to be considered for a full-time position should things change. And, please, don't take it personally if it doesn't.

Even if it's just what it claims to be, a part-time or short-term job, you still win, in my experience. First, it might be just the flexible work schedule you're looking for. Second, if it's a permanent, full-time job you really want, it still has your back.

What I mean by that is when you're making money, the truth is you feel better about yourself. You feel valued, and that's cool. It builds confidence. That's far healthier than shooting out resumes and not getting a single response. And seriously, you never know what might come your way when you back away from the computer screen.

Contract Work Is Hot

Contract work typically offers a variable schedule, perhaps lasting a week per month, or a few months each year. It usually offers decent pay, flexible hours, and taps into your professional-level skills. For those looking to switch careers or land a new position, there's an upside here too, as I will explain below. From the employer's perspective, hiring temporary workers simply makes sense in many circumstances. They can staff up for short-range projects without the price tag of health care and other benefits.

And in this employment market, they can attract the crème de la crème. These are often workers who have been downsized or taken early retirement packages.

I have little doubt that employers' shift to hiring contract workers is not so short-term. For older workers who are willing to change their mindset about the security of a permanent, full-time position in the corporate world, these can be a win-win. Nothing is secure these days; if you've been downsized, you're well aware of that.

Moreover, from talking with thousands of 50+ job seekers, I know that plenty of you don't have that burning desire to throw all your energy into a new position in the way you once did anyway, lip-service aside. You want work–life balance. Employers might sense that. Your age and compensation demands may pose an obstacle, too.

The pay for contract positions though, can be top-notch. As a contract worker, you can make your years of experience an asset. In many situations, a younger worker isn't going to get the job done quickly and capably without some hands-on training. So employers are typically willing to pay you handsomely, on an interim basis, that is. You don't have to roll over and work for less money, phew.

People who are genuinely seeking a permanent, full-time job, especially those who have been out of work for several months, are missing an opportunity by not accepting contract jobs as a means to an end. This is not a time to be a snob about it, or wear blinders and be trapped by the quaint notion of nailing a full-time gig "just like your old job."

Those days of velvet handcuffs and cushy benefits are virtually gone. This may be your time to weave together your future, perhaps with a patchwork of contract assignments.

Let's call you self-employed, a consultant, a freelancer, an entrepreneur — You, Inc. Mine is Kerry Inc. It has a nice ring to it, doesn't it?

As an aside, in fact, I always counsel workers of all ages to consider themselves the CEO of their own small business — even if you have a full-time job. Your primary employer is simply your largest client. I always did side jobs when I had a full-time position. That prepared me for my current self-employed status and gave me a ready list of clients. Not everyone can do this, and you have to be careful not to run amiss of employer rules about outside work, or using company time or supplies in your moonlighting endeavors.

As a career transition expert, I view contract assignments as a perfect opportunity for a range of job seekers, particularly career switchers. If you're looking to get into a new field, for example, the opportunity to try on different hats, work in various types of businesses, even add new skills and experience, is worth pursuing. With a short-term "dip in the pool" assignment, you can find out if this is something you really want to do.

I always tell people who ask my advice on changing careers — do the job first: moonlight, apprentice, volunteer. If you can get paid for it, go for it. That's the only way you'll know if the new career is all you dreamed it would be.

A final tip: Hone your yarn-spinning. Even if the assignment was the pits, and that's always possible, find a clever way to use the experience in a positive way. It can be a great example of your work ethic, or your ability to helicopter in and solve a problem, or fill a professional need for a company. Make the time spent part of your personal career story. Poetic license.

Replacing a lost income stream today is challenging, even more so if you were financially and psychologically unprepared for your pink slip. But as Henry Ford, founder of Ford Motor Co., said: "Nothing is particularly hard if you divide it into small jobs."

So Gwenn, well done and congrats!

Kerry

CHAPTER 17
HOW TO PREPARE FOR
NONPROFIT WORK

As an Encore Fellow, John Arnold, 64, a former senior finance executive at Pepsi and Levi Strauss, is creating cash-management procedures for La Clínica de La Raza of Oakland, California, a large community-based consortium of clinics that provide health care to low-income and uninsured patients. Arnold is one of 15 former corporate professionals in the Encore Fellows in California Community Clinics program, financed by the California HealthCare Foundation.

Cheryl Edmonds, a retired Hewlett-Packard marketing manager, took on a 12-month fellowship assignment in Portland, Oregon, with Metropolitan Family Service. As a Volunteer Services Fellow, she leads a program to enhance volunteer development within the agency, working specifically with local businesses to promote volunteerism — focusing on boomers age 55-plus with better professional volunteer opportunities.

And take note, these are paid positions. Encore Fellows are paired with nonprofits, where they typically work 1,000 hours over a six- to 12-month period, through either a part- or full-time schedule, and earn a stipend of $25,000.

The Encore Fellowships Network was created by the research group Encore.org, which launched the original Silicon Valley Encore Fellows program in 2009, backed by the David and Lucile Packard Foundation and Hewlett-Packard.

In 2011, the California HealthCare Foundation launched Encore Fellows in California Community Clinics in the greater San Francisco Bay Area and Central Valley. This California Encore Fellows program matches experienced workers like Arnold to community clinics who need a hand with strategic planning, financial management, process improvement, IT, and human resource development. In 2012, the program doubled in size, adding 32 new fellows and beginning service in San Diego and in new sites in the Central Valley.

"Matching experienced professionals with clinics hungry for organizational and managerial expertise is a win-win for everyone," Sophia Chang, MD, director of the Foundation's Better Chronic Disease Care program, says.

Corporations are getting Fellow-friendly, too. The decline of corporate retirement benefits is an old story. The rise of retirement benefits, well, that's worth some hoopla.

Meet one contrarian company — Intel Corp. The Santa Clara, California-based chip maker is offering all of Intel's U.S. employees who are eligible to retire the chance to apply for Encore Fellowships, yearlong assignments working at local nonprofits. The beauty of it is twofold: The fellowship delivers corporate firepower to a nonprofit that can't afford to bring on board someone with the experience these retirees offer. For Intel's retirees looking to continue working in their next act, it's a perfect training ground in the ways of the nonprofit arena, and a possible try-out for a new job. No promises, of course, but fellowships could lead to a more permanent position, or at the very least, it's a chance to learn about nonprofit work and open the door to develop a network of contacts and resources.

Reportedly, roughly 7 percent of Intel's workforce fits the eligibility requirements to apply — or close to 7,000 employees nationwide. Hewlett-Packard and Agilent have also sponsored Encore Fellows, but Intel is the first company to make this type of extensive commitment.

I hope more companies find ways to offer this kind of opportunity to their retirees. Boomers are clearly hungry for training and entree into the nonprofit world. Workers who end their midcareer for-profit jobs often eye the sector as their next stomping grounds either for full-time or part-time jobs.

If you're 50+ it may be the time in your life when it feels right to give back to society. And getting paid for lending your expertise makes it even better. New research from Encore.org and MetLife Foundation shows that as many as 9 million people, or 9 percent of all people ages 44 to 70, are currently in encore careers, having made major career changes after age 40 or come out of retirement to do work that combines personal meaning, continued income, and social purpose.

"Intel offers those who aren't ready to wind down a new option: Gear up for the greater good," says Encore.org's Freedman.

Today, the Encore Fellowships Network has opportunities in programs via various funders and company sponsors in Silicon Valley, the San Francisco Bay Area, Sacramento, and Central Valley, California; Portland, Oregon; Maricopa County, Arizona; New York; Albuquerque, New Mexico; Hudson, Massachusetts; Seattle; and Washington, D.C.

East Coast nonprofit hosts include Ashoka, Washington, D.C.; Center for Employment Opportunities, New York; Community Environmental Center, New York; Credit Where Credit Is Due, Inc., New York; New York City Housing Authority, New York; and Women in Need, Inc., New York.

In addition to Intel and California Health-Care Foundation (CHCF), big supporters behind the growing Encore Fellowship effort include the Packard Foundation, Agilent Technologies, and H-P.

To learn more about the Encore Fellowships, go to Encore Careers' web site (encore.org/fellowships).

At the site, you'll find an application to fill out with basic information — where you live, who referred you, how you heard about the fellows — then press the "submit" button at the bottom. Once you have submitted the form, your information will be added to Encore's database and routed to appropriate Encore Fellowships programs for their consideration.

A note of warning though. There are a limited number of fellowships available and a large number of applicants, so the application and selection process is competitive. For more information, you can e-mail info@encorefellowships.net.

Encore fellowships are just one type of nonprofit training program emerging. Denver-based Rose Community Foundation (rcfdenver.org), for instance, trains older adults as navigators or community health workers.

ReServe (reserveinc.org), a nonprofit agency based in New York City, connects professionals over 50 who have experience in marketing, accounting, and other areas with government agencies and nonprofit groups. These are usually part-time projects that pay a modest stipend, say, $10 an hour. You might work 15 or 20 hours a week. Reservists come from all backgrounds, from marketing managers to social workers, HR professionals, and financial analysts, and many use their experience to launch new careers in the nonprofit sector.

Leadership Pittsburgh Inc. (lpinc.org) offers a nine-month educational program that bolsters civic engagement. You spend roughly 10–12 hours each month learning and exploring ways to make a difference in the Pittsburgh region's economic development, education, human needs and human services, arts and culture, criminal justice, and quality of life issues in the community. Afterwards, graduates gain first-hand experience with nonprofit boards for ten-month stints. They're matched based on their interests and skill sets with the needs of local nonprofit organizations, including United Way agencies and state commissions that serve the region.

Recent surveys from Idealist.org and others indicate that the doors are swinging open in the nonprofit arena. But the jobs aren't suited for everyone. You need more than an altruistic bent. To succeed at nonprofit work, you must have a certain mental mojo, work style, and tenacity for the move to be a win-win for both parties.

Here are some ways to prepare.

Review your expectations. You might not be welcomed with open arms just because you were a star in the for-profit world. It can be a culture clash. Hello humility.

Play nicely with others. Decisions are generally made by group accord. If you're a take-charge type who gets turned on by making things come to pass fast, this can be exasperating. Team players need apply.

Make do with less. In the nonprofit world, you go all out, often lacking resources to get things done as swiftly or professionally as you wish for. Are you prepared to put up with that?

Narrow your search. What causes are you serious about? Can you genuinely show that you have a passionate interest in a certain nonprofit's mission and care deeply about the challenges and pressing issues on its agenda?

Follow your passion. "Your passion and commitment for the organization and cause is the thing that sets you apart from other candidates," says Laura Gassner Otting, president of Nonprofit Professionals Advisory Group, an executive search firm.

For the last decade, her Boston-based firm has helped fill the shoes of chief executive officers, chief financial officers, directors of communication, vice presidents of development, and project managers for a panoply of nonprofits, including the Kellogg Foundation, Civic Ventures, Boston College, the National Urban League, and Special Olympics International.

Volunteer. Join boards and get involved by volunteering for the organization or other, similar nonprofits serving the same community: "If you have an interest in making a switch to nonprofit work, getting active now in the causes that interest you will show your commitment to making the transition," Gassner Otting advises. It also builds your network in the sector, increases your knowledge about trends, and helps you get a feel for the culture of the sector. You'll find more on volunteering in the next chapter.

Work as a consultant. If you aren't in a position to work for free, you might be able to land a position part-time on a reduced consultant fee basis, ReServe's president, Mary Bleiberg, suggests. "Most nonprofits would jump at that. Plus, it's a great way to prove yourself in the nonprofit world and get the credentials that you have done it," she says. "If you've been a controller in a small manufacturing company, for example, and have been let go, you should be willing to take on a position in the nonprofit sector at a reduced rate, even working two or three days a week. Then, after a year, you can say 'I was a controller at the Evergreen Childcare Agency and managed a budget of $15 million,' " she advises.

Don't be the first one in. Just because nonprofits say they want to bring in best practices from businesses, it doesn't mean they necessarily know how to or are sold on it, Gassner Otting advises. Nonprofits might think they want someone from the business world, but that might be because they are getting pressure from a funder or board member and haven't really bought into the idea. So do your homework to find out if there are others like you in staff and leadership positions.

Wear your heart on your sleeve. Do so, and the nonprofit sector will applaud your fashion sense, Gassner Otting told me: "A desire to give back in general is good, but it won't cut it alone. And a proclamation that you have deigned to lend your business thinking to save the nonprofit sector is a deadly sin. We want to hear why you want this specific job for this specific cause. The work is going to be harder; pay is going to be less. Your story matters, and makes credible your intended major life shift."

Look at other factors, too. What size organization suits you? Do you favor a small group with a tight focus and a smaller amount of resources, but a greater chance to make a difference? Does a start-up appeal to you? Or are you drawn to a bigger organization, which might offer training to help you get started in the nonprofit arena but less hands-on work? Do you want to be out in the field working directly with people, or would you rather strategize in an office? Are you willing to travel?

Know what you have to offer. Consider your expertise. This can run the gamut from legal to financial management/bookkeeping (can you say shoestring?) to computers, to writing skills that can shore up grant writing efforts.

A financial background for example, is in demand these days. Nonprofit boards are increasingly focused on bottom-line results for money spent and invested. Agencies need someone to help make decisions about benefits, insurance, grants, purchasing, and staff salaries. And the best people for these jobs are those who have done this kind of work in the private sector.

As a result, nonprofit organizations are more willing to hire people from the for-profit world who get the bean counter bottom-line approach. Donors often see themselves as investors these days, too, so they want to see that the organization is run like a business and hitting its financial goals.

"Cash flow is a huge issue for many non-profits," Bleiberg says. It's the people who have fiscal and operation management skills whom ReServe gets the most calls for, according to Bleiberg. "If you have a background as a chief financial officer, controller, accountant, they're looking for you." One caveat: You'll need to have your Internet-based accounting skills up-to-date. Most nonprofits rely on QuickBooks and Fund E-Z to manage the books, she explains.

She's onto something here. According to the Bureau of Labor Statistics, the demand for accounting positions will increase 22 percent between 2008 and 2018. If this holds true, it means that approximately 500,000 accountant jobs will be created. For both nonprofits and for-profits that are trimming back, accountants are needed to help control spending and make the best use of resources. For those outfits that are now bouncing back, too, accountants are needed to monitor that growth.

Bleiberg practices what she preaches. She is heading up one of those growing organizations. In 2011, she hired a retired corporate controller to step in as the chief financial officer at ReServe. Fifty-nine-year-old

Liam Carlos had retired after 30 years from his position at the New York Times Company. "We yanked him out of retirement," she says. "He's a godsend."

Be realistic about your salary, vacation, and benefits requirements. Nonprofit work usually comes with a lower salary. But can you put a price on the potential reward? Only you will know.

Add credentials. You might think about taking a course to fill in any gaps in your background. There are master's degree and certificate programs in public administration, philanthropic studies, and social work — some can even be earned completely online. Coursework includes nonprofit marketing, fundraising, campaigns, corporate philanthropy, ethics, and law.

Institutions that offer training include Case Western Reserve University, Columbia University, Indiana University, New York University, the University of San Francisco, and Seton Hall.

There are a number of organizations and community college programs designed to help experienced professionals transition into nonprofit jobs via training programs, fellowships, and part-time assignments. Re-

Serve, of course, is one. So is Encore!Hartford, if you live in Connecticut.

Research jobs and job-hunting resources online. Check out nonprofit-oriented web sites to help you make the transition. See the resource section for some ideas. These sites offer employment resources; volunteer opportunities, which can lead to paying jobs; board opportunities; and full- and part-time openings.

Read the job descriptions carefully. You will need to translate your skills in the corporate world *literally* to their lingo.

If you've worked in marketing, advertising, or even journalism and know how to be an advocate in prose, that's extremely important, Bleiberg notes. "Anyone really comfy sitting down in front of their computer and blogging, tweeting, and pulling articles that relate to the organization to highlight on a nonprofit's web site will get a hiring manager's attention," she says. That's because web content marketing is the primary vehicle for communication to potential donors for many nonprofits these days. So don't call it public relations or marketing, call it, say, blogging.

It's all about figuring out how you can advance the mission of the organization, whether it is tweeting, writing grants, or managing its financial affairs. LinkedIn (see Chapter 14) also has a job search section dedicated to nonprofit positions.

Use nonprofit work as a springboard. Working for a nonprofit might not be your ultimate goal. By offering your services for a period of time, though, you can get the flavor of that type of work, or an overview of the industry. If you yearn to be a landscape designer, for example, volunteer at your city's botanical gardens or lend your hand to a grounds committee for a historical home known for its manicured gardens.

CHAPTER 18
VOLUNTEER YOUR WAY TO A JOB

Go volunteer has become my mantra when doling out advice on career transitions for job seekers of all ages. If you don't know what you want to do or should be doing, or your stomach is in knots because *NO ONE* is calling you back for a job interview, then get up, get out, and *do* something for someone else.

The payback is plain when you volunteer for the charity that's near and dear to your heart. And chances are, you've already been devoting your time to one or two for some of your working years already. Nearly half of all Americans age 55 and over volunteered at least once in the past year, according to Encore.org.

Volunteering — for a charity or a for-profit — can shape the next chapter of your life and lead to a specific job. It might spur an idea for a job to pursue, or open a door to meet someone who can help you in your hunt.

Simply put, doing good makes you, well, feel good — even if you're just singing songs with patients in an Alzheimer's unit at an assisted-care home on Sunday afternoons. It's a warm glow of giving back to others, and for a brief time you get out of your own brain that's perhaps riddled with anxiety if the job market has you down. It gives you a perspective on the world outside your private worries. It's a confidence booster. You're needed. You make a difference. You're engaged.

You also make new acquaintances. I'll say it again: You make contacts, get fresh ideas, and perhaps get a spark of inspiration from these unexpected and sometimes unlikely connections. Sorry, it's worth repeating. Get out of your weatherman Phil's *Groundhog Day* routine. It may also be a test run for a potential job. If you choose a volunteer post with an eye to your future, you may be able to take advantage of the chance to do a job before you actually "do" a job, if you get my drift. Volunteering is a way to get inside and see what goes on behind the scenes. It's not unusual for this kind of undercover detective work to lead to a paying job with the organization, or one involved with a similar cause.

The underlying job-seeking strategy: If you pick a volunteer opening that's in line with the type of job you want, you might run into people with the same interests or someone currently working in areas similar to the one you're seeking.

Volunteer Checklist

When you're hunting for a volunteer job, there are some important things you should think about. Here's a checklist:

- For starters, are you ready to go after a volunteer job with as much determination as you would a paying job? To apply for volunteer work, you don't just call up and show up. You need to apply, send a resume, go in for an interview.
- What type of business or nonprofit is in line with your job interests?
- Would you choose a small organization with a clear mission or assignment where you can really play a big role? Or would the lure of potential skill-building and training at a bigger organization be better for you in the long run?
- Are you an out-in-the-field kind of person, or would you rather be back in the office working on strategy?

- How much time do you practically have to offer? Don't overcommit; you may not be able to bring your best effort. Volunteering more hours than you can rationally afford can also be a losing proposition if it takes away from time you need to spend job hunting. Both of these mistakes can create resentments within you and from your fellow volunteers, too.
- How long of an obligation do you want to make? Don't get roped into a yearlong project if you really have only a few free weeks to focus on the project.

Where can you find a project that actually puts your skills and talents to good use? Skill-based volunteering is the new rage. A growing number of web sites try to match your skills with a volunteer project. Promising stuff.

In addition to ReServe, which I told you about in the last chapter, I recommend you check out Hands On Network (Handson network.org). This is the volunteer action arm of Points of Light, a network of 250 volunteer action centers that extend to 16 countries around the world.

Another free site is Catchafire.org, which is based in New York City. The site sets you up with a nonprofit or social enterprise, where you can volunteer a handful of hours a week over a period of a few months.

After you file your professional profile and check your expertise, the site pops you a personalized list of potential projects, so you can pick a volunteer opportunity and organization. And while a sizeable percentage of the 10,000 volunteers who've signed up with Catchafire are in their 20s and 30s, Catchafire's chief executive and founder, Rachael Chong, says she's eager to attract professionals in their 50s and 60s as volunteers.

According to the Bureau of Labor Statistics, about 64.3 million people volunteered for an organization in 2011. "Individuals with higher levels of educational attainment engaged in volunteer activities at higher rates than did those with less education," the report found. To break it down, a whopping 42.4 percent of all volunteers held a bachelor's degree or higher. So your chances of meeting professionals in the volunteer pool are promising.

Based on U.S. Census data, the number of volunteers age 65 and older will increase 50 percent over the next 13 years, from fewer than 9 million in 2007 to more than 13 million in 2020.

Baby boomers today have the highest volunteer rate of any age group. They also volunteer at higher rates than past generations did when they were the same age, according to a report by the Corporation for National and Community Service.

Volunteering offers chances to advise, teach, arrange events and activities, do bookkeeping, and charm potential donors, among other options. Whether it is working with clients directly, say, serving meals at a homeless shelter, or helping out in the office, you're touching peoples' lives, and making a difference.

Moreover, for you retirees reading this book, volunteering may increase your life span. In a study of U.S. retirees, researchers from the VA Medical Center and The University of California, San Francisco found that volunteering may improve health outcomes by expanding retirees' social networks, increasing their access to resources and improving their sense of self-worth. Another often overlooked benefit to lending a hand gratis is that you can gain actual work experience that can train you for your new line of work. If you're interested in moving into work as a nutritionist, or even opening a restaurant, for example, at DC Central Kitchen (dccentralkitchen. org), in

Washington, D.C., you might volunteer at the organization's Nutrition Lab to help prepare healthy meals cooked from scratch.

If you're having trouble seeing how donating your time is a good use of your day, try viewing it as a skill-building exercise. Believe me, if you've been in charge of the silent auction at a nonprofit's fundraising event, you can surely add event planning or event marketing to your resume and online professional profile. Tackling a fundraising job or chipping in to organize an entire event for a nonprofit shows off your sales, marketing, and management skills. Managing a team of volunteers is sometimes a paying job at a nonprofit (see my chapter on great nonprofit jobs), so being able to show that you have done this type of work is valuable information for a hiring manager.

Moreover, volunteer experience can pique a potential employer's interest. Many corporations have a soft spot when it comes to social responsibility. Do-gooders are valued. Volunteering also draws attention to your willingness to learn new things, contribute creative ideas, and provide hands-on help in situations where organizations are understaffed and lacking resources.

In fact, 41 percent of the 2,000 professionals that LinkedIn surveyed stated that when they evaluate candidates, they consider volunteer work equally as valuable as paid work experience. If you already have a history of volunteering, list on your resume and LinkedIn profile the specific charity or business and the dates you worked. Don't, however, use the word "volunteer" in the title. List it as "fundraiser" or "project manager." Highlight the bottom-line results, returns, special awards, or accolades you received for your efforts. Of course, in the actual job description, you can mention that it was a pro bono project. This highlights your altruism, but by defining it as a professional job, you give it the cachet and respect it deserves.

In the final tally, volunteering builds out your resume with a new dimension and shows you in a positive light.

There can be a downside: Many organizations do a pretty lousy job of managing their volunteer pool, so it may be up to you to find ways to donate your time productively. Importantly, though, don't present yourself as a great resource who has condescended to land in their laps and silently wait on the sidelines for someone to recognize that. Be willing to respectfully do what's requested, but don't be shy about speaking up about other talent you might be able to bring to the party.

If you have volunteered in the past, you probably know that it can be maddening. It's hard to believe they don't tap all the skills you have to offer. You feel as if you're wasting your time. So take action.

My insider tip: Give 100 percent to your volunteer effort. Show up when you're asked to and do what you promise you'll do. Be proactive. Anything less has the potential to reflect badly on your work ethic and level of commitment.

Not Just for Charities

It doesn't always have to be volunteering for a good cause, though. To figure out if a certain type of business is going to be a good fit for you, give it a test run by working as an unpaid helper. And yes, volunteering at any type of business is a viable path to a full-time engagement. Here's why: An employer gets a chance to size you up with few consequences and visa versa.

If that employer doesn't suit you, you're still able to get the essence of that type of work, or a general idea of the industry. If you want to open a restaurant or start a chocolate-making business, or even get hired to work in one, for instance, you might start out by volunteering in the kitchen behind the scenes. You'll chop carrots and turnips, dip strawberries in gooey chocolate. You'll discover pretty fast how glamorous those tedious and long hours can really be.

You may love it. Hopefully so. And while you're doing the job for free, you have the pleasure of working alongside some pros, who may very well turn out to be super mentors for you. They can be great sounding boards, introduce you to others in the field, and offer advice that can smooth your way into that line of business.

Why Volunteer?
- It feels good.
- It offers a peek at whether a certain career field is right for you.
- It keeps your professional skills current.
- It broadens your resume.
- It adds networking contacts.

If you want to be invited to volunteer at a company, make an appointment with the hiring manager or owner and meet face-to-face to present your offer of free labor. If it's a small business, say, a gourmet chocolate shop or neighborhood restaurant, introduce yourself to the owner and explain what you're looking for and what hours you're available to work. Offer a trial work schedule, perhaps a few hours a day for several days, so they don't feel that they need to get tied down with a commitment to you. Be willing to do the grunt work. Then stay loose and see where it leads.

Some Places to Look for Volunteer Projects (for more, see Helpful Web Sites)

- Ashoka.org (Ashoka.org) supports the work of social entrepreneurs. Volunteers are needed to translate documents. Ashoka and Ashoka Fellows are sometimes in need of experienced translators to be "virtual volunteers" and translate documents such as articles, newsletters, surveys, brochures, reports, and proposals. Volunteers are also needed to assist with fundraising, marketing, web site design, research, writing, graphic design, and technical support. You fill in the Ashoka Volunteer Form, attach a resume if possible and send it directly to the contact listed on any posted opportunity to which you would like to respond.

  When traveling abroad to volunteer,

you should be prepared to cover travel, housing, and living expenses, and feel at ease in "rustic" environments.

- BoardnetUSA.org (Boardnetusa.org) helps individuals interested in board service or a nonprofit looking for a new board member. Over 12,000 candidates and nonprofit boards are currently using BoardnetUSA. You fill out a profile of your interests and professional skills; nonprofits then choose whether to interview you for their board positions. There is no fee for an individual to register as a candidatee.
- Create The Good (Createthegood .com) is AARP's site that lets you find good works to do in your community and posts volunteer opportunities. Learn from how-to videos how to start your own volunteer project.
- Doctorswithoutborders.org (Doctors withoutborders.org) provides aid in nearly 60 countries to people whose survival is threatened by violence, neglect, or catastrophe, primarily due to armed conflict, epidemics, malnutrition, exclusion from health care, or natural disasters. Volunteers are doctors, nurses, logistics experts, administrators, epidemiologists, laboratory

technicians, mental health professionals, and others.

- Hands On Network (Handsonnetwork .org) features skills-based volunteer opportunities. This is the volunteer-activation arm of Points of Light. Hands on Network includes 250 community action centers that deliver 30 million hours of volunteer service each year and extend to 16 countries around the world. These centers focus on helping people plug into volunteer opportunities in their local communities, partnering with more than 70,000 corporate, faith, and nonprofit organizations to manage volunteer resources, and developing the leadership capacity of volunteers.
- Idealist.org (Idealist.org) offers leads to thousands of volunteer opportunities nationwide, plus internships and jobs in the nonprofit sector. Go to the volunteer resource center on the site for more.
- Lawyers Without Borders (Lawyers withoutborders.org) and Judges Without Borders direct legal pro bono services and resources to human rights initiatives, legal capacity-building projects, and rule-of-law projects

around the world. It seeks volunteers with a legal background — practicing or retired lawyers, judges, law students, and others who have worked as legal support staff — to manage projects and sustain home and branch office operations.

- Operation Hope (Operationhope.org) seeks volunteers with a background in the financial industry (mortgage brokers, bankers, tax consultants, etc.) to work as virtual volunteers. For instance, in one program, volunteers provide free financial literacy empowerment programs for youth ages 8–24; this program has reached over 640,000 students in more than 700 schools and community-based organizations in the U.S. and South Africa. The Mortgage HOPE Crisis Hotline (MHCH) and the HOPE Consumer Credit Crisis Hotline (HCCCH) provide toll-free services to assist homeowners and consumers needing answers and guidance for mortgage, credit, and financial problems.

- Senior Corps (seniorcorps.org) The Corporation for National and Community Service offers a RSVP (Retired Senior Volunteer Program) service for those 55 or older to match them with volunteer opportunities. These programs are typically sponsored locally by area nonprofits. Some offer compensation or a small stipend, too. For most of the programs, health insurance is available for the volunteers, according to the site.

- Serve.gov is a national online resource for not only finding volunteer opportunities in your community, but also creating your own. It's managed by the Corporation for National and Community Service.
- Taproot Foundation (Taprootfoundation.org) places teams of business professionals who are doing pro bono consulting to help a local nonprofit increase its impact via marketing, design, technology, management, or strategic planning on issues like the environment, health, and education. Since its inception in 2001, the nonprofit has engaged professionals in over 780,000 hours of pro bono service on over 1,300 projects. It operates in five U.S. cities — Chicago, Los Angeles, New York City, San Francisco Bay Area, and Washington, D.C. — in a variety of fields, including finance, mar-

keting, and information technology.

- Onlinevolunteering.org is a database to find online volunteering opportunities with organizations that serve communities in developing countries. There are opportunities in educational institutions, grassroots organizations, international NGOs, local governments, and United Nations agencies.
- Volunteer.gov (Volunteer.gov) is a one-stop shop for public-service volunteer projects sponsored by the U.S. government. It's searchable by agency, city, and state.
- VolunteerMatch.org (Volunteermatch .org) allows you to search more than 73,000 listings nationwide.

CHAPTER 19
BE YOUR OWN BOSS

For many 50+ workers, the entrepreneurial path is the ticket. It's the American Dream. And with years of experience, you're far more prepared to launch than a twenty-something. I have interviewed hundreds of entrepreneurs and profiled some of their success stories in my book *What's Next?* and I am always struck by entrepreneurs' confidence, tenacity, and hope. No one questions how challenging it can be, but for most people, the reward is an inner payout that blows right by the financial struggles and setbacks.

An increasing number of workers age 50 and older are starting new businesses. A new AARP/Society for Human Resource Management (SHRM) survey of 50+ employed workers shows that one in 20 plans to start his or her own business. Nearly one in five unemployed workers would like to do the same.

For the most part, we're not talking Silicon Valley start-ups here, but one-person shops that might employ a handful of helpers.

Older entrepreneurs can have a lot of things working in their favor — a strong work ethic, management experience and well-established networks of potential customers. But be forewarned. Running a business usually takes more than a simple passion for what you're doing. You may need to go back to school and get certifications.

You'll definitely need a list of pros to help you, from a lawyer to a tax accountant. And, it's always good to try out the job first as an apprentice or moonlight to be sure it's right for you.

To learn more about what it takes to succeed in business when you're over 50, I visited with Randal Charlton. On a sun-kissed California day last winter, I tugged my chair across the porch of the Cavallo Point Lodge in Sausalito and pulled it up next to 71-year-old Charlton, a newly minted 2011 Purpose Prize winner. He had already sunk into a chair for a brief break in a whirlwind weekend of meetings and celebration.

As we gazed up at the sweeping span of the Golden Gate Bridge nearby, we talked about new beginnings. Something he knows a lot about.

Charlton's efforts at Detroit's business incubator TechTown, where he was the executive director from 2007 until the end of 2011 — and the turnaround in his personal life — landed him one of five $100,000 Purpose Prizes, which honors Americans over 60 who are developing new ways to tackle social problems.

The award, given annually, is part of a program of Encore.org, which aims to engage millions of boomers in careers that combine personal meaning, income, and social impact. One observer I know dubbed the prize, sponsored by the Atlantic Philanthropies and the John Templeton Foundation, "a sort of Oscars" for social entrepreneurs.

Charlton plans to use the money to support baby boomers who want to go the entrepreneurial path via a new arm of TechTown called BOOM! The New Economy. The start-up aims to help adults 50+ in southeast Michigan transition to new careers, entrepreneurship, and volunteer service. It's a collaboration between AARP Michigan, Community Foundation for Southeastern Michigan, Corporation for a Skilled Workforce, Luella Hannan Memorial Foundation, Operation ABLE of Michigan, and TechTown.

He knows the demand is there. At TechTown, more than a third of the entrepreneurs coming to the incubator for conferences and training were over age 50. Consider this:

- AARP national Boomer surveys — the most recent in 2011 — have consistently shown that about one-sixth of those surveyed expected to go into business for themselves at some point.
- Federal statistics show that, in 2011 there were 7.4 million self-employed workers in the United States who were 50 or over.

As a result, AARP and the U.S. Small Business Administration have recently formed a multi-pronged collaboration to promote entrepreneurship as a career option for older Americans. The aim of the joint effort is to link 100,000 Americans over age 50 with small business development resources, including live workshops, conferences, and mentoring programs. "Millions of Americans keep dreaming of owning their own business as a second or third career, using their creative talents to do productive work that also helps them gain economic stability as they move toward retirement," AARP CEO A. Barry Rand says.

Recent research released by Encore.org shows that approximately 25 million people — one in four Americans ages 44 to 70 — are interested in starting businesses or nonprofit ventures in the next five to 10 years.

The findings support research from the Kauffman Index of Entrepreneurial Activity, which shows that in 2010, entrepreneurs between the ages of 55 and 64 accounted for 23 percent of new entrepreneurs, up from 15 percent in 1996. And, in fact, over the past decade, the highest rate of entrepreneurial activity belongs to the 55 to 64 age group, according to the Kauffman Foundation, a Kansas City, Missouri–based entrepreneurship institute's study.

Aspiring entrepreneurs report an average of 31 years of work experience and 12 years of community involvement, according to Encore.org. Five out of six (85 percent) report having management experience — 15 years on average.

Encore entrepreneurs also want work that they "are passionate about" (84 percent) and that gives them "a sense of meaning and a feeling of accomplishment" (83 percent), the group found. They're interested in social services (37 percent), poverty alleviation (28 percent), working with at-risk youth, economic development, and health care (all at 24 percent), the environment (19 percent), and human rights or social justice (18 percent).

Moreover, it's interesting to note that the Encore.org study found:

- Two out of three potential encore entrepreneurs (68 percent) would consider their businesses or nonprofit ventures worthwhile if they earned less than $60,000 a year.
- Two out of three (67 percent) report that they need $50,000 or less to get started, and only one in five (20 percent) say they need more than $100,000.

"There are many obstacles to building successful enterprises at this stage in life," says Encore.org's Marc Freedman, "But, as we've seen with the Purpose Prize, many have been able to make a living while making a difference. We need to help many more do the same." Even if you think you're prepared, I urge you to proceed with caution. If you've over 50, building a successful business can have some downsides. The most obvious being you don't have time on your side. And if you go belly-up, you run the risk of doing some serious damage to your retirement savings since you don't have as much time to rebuild as you might have when you were a decade or so younger.

That said, you do have something on your side: Launching a business later in life has some secret weapons. It allows you to take advantage of the treasure trove of business experience you have built up, your road warrior honed skills of how to be competitive and navigate your way from failures to success. Finally, you've probably grown out of any impetuous streak you might have had in your youth. And my guess is you will take the time to think it through before you make the leap.

Your ultimate success in running a small business will come from having clear vision of what it is you want from the very beginning. How much time can you really devote to it? How flexible do you want it to be? Is it too late to really make a go of it?

To get a lay of the land, I asked Elizabeth Isele, co-founder of Senior Entrepreneurship Works (seniorentrepreneurshipworks .org), the nonprofit venture dedicated to

399

helping workers over 50 start their own businesses, for her take on this growing trend.

"Talk about power and promise," Isele said. "Today's senior entrepreneurs are dynamic economic engines. America's independent spirit is thriving in today's swelling ranks of senior entrepreneurs. As they launch new businesses and create jobs, they're becoming the economic engines revitalizing our economy and solving some of our society's most pressing social problems. They are not, as some would have it, draining Social Security and Medicare reserves but are actually bolstering those funds with their increased tax dollars."

And then she said something, when she noticed me flinch at the repeated use of the word senior, that caught my attention. (As you have probably gathered as you've read along, I'm a little sensitive to thinking of 50+ workers as "seniors.") "Come on now," she said quite seriously. "Kerry, when did the word senior, become a bad thing? When we were in high school and college, we couldn't wait to be seniors. When we went to work, one of our goals was to become a senior partner, or senior vice president or senior something. It was a good thing. Being a senior meant you were someone to look up to, someone to respect, seek counsel from, someone who was an achiever."

Ahh, so true, Elizabeth. And then she started spinning stories of senior entrepreneurs from one-person e-commerce to main street small business, and from small scale social enterprises to major cultural festivals. I was inspired. Senior entrepreneurs rock.

Purpose Prizewinner Randal Charlton is the quintessential senior entrepreneur. His is a story worth telling. You will learn important lessons from it. He knows first-hand how to bounce back when the rug is pulled out and start over. It's about believing in yourself, as I have discussed in other chapters, and staying in the game. If you've been laid off, or are struggling to figure out what to do next, read on. I think we can all learn valuable lessons from each other's journeys.

Charlton is the quintessential senior entrepreneur. He has bought and sold 14 different companies during his career and been an executive for several global biotech companies. But his path has been twisty. A native of England, Charlton kicked off his career as an agriculture journalist, worked for an agricultural export company, and lived for weeks in a Saudi Arabian desert tending a Saudi sheik's herd of dairy cows.

He has been a consultant for cattle breeding associations and for the European Development Fund, too.

Not all of his endeavors have been hits. He lost money on a cattle-ranching operation to produce low-fat beef, for instance. And when he was 53, his Cajun-tinged jazz club in Sarasota, Florida, went belly-up.

And when I say belly-up, I mean kaput. Not only did he lose his club, but also his luxurious waterfront home was signed over to creditors to pay his debts. His marriage ended. Then in 1998, one of his four daughters, Kate, who suffered from schizophrenia, committed suicide at the age of 28. His world had exploded.

He floundered. Charlton spent a year in his native England with his other children. Not knowing what to do next, he wrote a book about women's World Cup soccer in 1999. Kate had played soccer. The book didn't make him any money. "It was good therapy, though," he says.

His life spun back around in his 60s. He remarried and moved to Detroit, where he developed an idea he had for a biotech company. He co-founded the firm Asterand, a human-tissue research business, and successfully attracted investors to get it off the ground. The firm merged with a UK competitor, and then went public in 2006. Shares now trade on the London Stock Exchange.

The writing was on the wall. It was time to retire. He was over 65, and at that time it was "expected that CEOs of big UK publicly listed companies retire at that age," he recalls. But he wasn't ready to really retire, so before he handed over the business to a new CEO, he started job hunting.

"I went to see my friend Irv Reid, the president of Wayne State University, to ask him if he had anything useful for me to do," Charlton recounts. And the door to Tech-Town swung open. TechTown was established in 2000 when Wayne State University, General Motors, and the Henry Ford Health System convened to fight Motor City's economic blight by creating an engine of economic growth with both local and statewide impact.

Reid made Charlton an adviser on economic development. When the director of TechTown resigned three months later, Reid asked Charlton to take on the job. "I had no experience of running an incubator," says Reid with a modest but self-assured smile of someone who has spent a lifetime jumping into the unknown.

It clicked. In four years, he raised $24 million from foundations and government and assembled a remarkable array of resources for training and start-up funding in a city hit hard by the economic downturn. To date, TechTown has invested $700,000 directly in early-stage businesses through the TechTown Loan Fund and the Thrive One Fund, and helped clients raise $14 million in seed funding.

More than 250 companies have taken advantage of entrepreneurial support at TechTown. Some 3,000 people have attended TechTown conferences, and more than 2,200 entrepreneurs have graduated from training programs.

As we sat soaking in the rays and blue skies above, Charlton graciously doled out astute advice for entrepreneurs over 50. And with refreshing honesty and a twinkle in his eye, he shared some of his personal saga, too. This is what he told me:

What motivates me to help other entrepreneurs and build BOOM at my age? I grew up on a farm in Devon, England, and was milking cows at six. My life's culture is work. That's important to me. It doesn't have to be important work. But it has to be work. I have to contribute.

I lost a daughter, and that changed my

approach to life in a lot of ways. I think what I am trying to do is give back something to society. I can't get back my beloved Kate, but I am trying to get more purpose to my life.

I reached the age of 60 having had a wonderful career, having been involved in 14 different companies, always doing something that fascinated me, and always being quite well rewarded. During the 1990s, I made a few mistakes both from a business and personal perspective, and I ended up broke at 60. Completely broke. I had to go to the library to read the newspaper because I couldn't afford it. I lost my house. But I learned six crucial lessons that can help people who want to start their own business.

Here's his key advice:

- **De-risk your personal life.** If you are a risk taker, as all entrepreneurs are, it doesn't help if you also add risk into your personal life. This is the biggest single lesson Charlton says he has carried through the last decade. He made a conscious effort to de-risk his personal life. Stress in your personal financial life ruins your ability to make good business decisions. You can't be nimble.

In other words, do not build up credit card debt, do not have a big mortgage, and do not buy a car with big monthly payments. Charlton's house is the smallest house on the block. He doesn't have a mortgage. His Subaru Outback is 10 years old. "I do not feel I suffer in any way," he says. "I love the good life just like everybody else. I will go out and have a nice dinner with my wife and friends, but I pay with money I have already earned."

- **Don't bet your retirement money.** Do not put your whole 401(k), or even half, into this great idea. It doesn't matter if you have to have nine partners and you only get a tenth of your great idea. Better to do that than risk your financial future.

- **Be disciplined.** Men more than women, particularly when they are young, do not understand that they are mortal, Charlton says. "Like a lot of people, I burned the candle at both ends when I was young. I worked hard and I played hard. I decided that the only way I was going to function and be successful post-60 was to be ruthlessly disciplined. Picture Muhammad Ali. He won some of his best fights with phenomenal discipline and training."

People over 60 have got to train for that period of their life. Before a business meeting, he makes sure he is mentally and physically fit. He watches what he eats and drinks. He has had joint replacement and clearly he is not going to run too many marathons, but he walks two or three miles every day. If you look at successful businessmen and women, they're pretty fit, and physical fitness helps your mental fitness.

- **Always overdress.** This is something he says he learned at the airport. He asked himself, "Would I be less confident if the pilot were sitting in the cockpit wearing a Grateful Dead T-shirt with a ring in his or her nose and spiked colored hair?' The answer is I wouldn't feel as comfortable. There is a reason they wear a uniform. I knew I wasn't going to be a dashing young man when I engaged in my business activities, but I determined that I would always dress as well as I could."

He wears nice suits, ties, and shirts,

big designer labels even, but his wife buys them at a resale shop. Some have never even been worn before. He does have one pair of dress shoes he had to buy new, though. He arrived at a conference in Kalamazoo and had forgotten to pack any.

- **Network without fear.** Who do you know? Who do they know? State what you are looking for. Be upfront about it. Is it money? Advice? A job until your business gets up and running? Don't worry about rejection. It's not about you. It's about them.
- **Get out in the marketplace.** If you don't, what happens is you shrink, shrink, shrink back into your own little world and your confidence goes. "You have got to be in the game," he says. "It doesn't matter how you are in the game. You need to stay out there."

Charlton loves to tell his tale of regaining his traction.

When I was in my 60s, struggling financially and waiting to see if I could find anyone to fund my venture, I did a gig for a month delivering phone books, the big ones. I used them to get fit. It was a wonderful mental exercise, too, figuring out what was the optimum number to carry. How many houses forward to go before I would need to go back and move the car.

I worked delivering flowers and driving a van. People might say, "Well, that's below you. You've been a CEO of a public company or two and worked for British Petroleum." But for me it was like exercise, you know. It was a thing of joy. It wasn't about the money. It was about keeping me mentally fit and engaged.

I remember one day in 2000, I applied for and got three jobs. There was an advertisement for a zookeeper at the Detroit Zoo in the paper. I happen to have been brought up on a farm, and I know a little about animals. [He had also earned an agricultural degree from England's Wye College.] I went down to City Hall and I sat for the zookeepers test and I passed it, and I got the job. I also got a job making sandwiches in a deli. That very same day, these venture capitalists in Boston told me they would give me $500,000 to start a life sciences company.

And on that note, Charlton looked at his $10 watch, straightened his $2 designer tie, and stood up. It was time to go to lunch and shake some hands.

There is something intrinsic in the American spirit that makes the idea of being your own boss a dream worth fighting for, regardless of your age. I get it. Working for ourselves is often what so many of us really want to do at this stage of our lives. It harks back to that entrepreneurial mindset that I think most of us have en*gin*dered in us, as my Irish grandmother, Ellen Nolan, would say.

I work for myself. My brother does. My father did — on a much larger scale. I suspect one or two of my eight nephews and nieces will too.

Being an entrepreneur can produce teeth-grinding anxiety when you take on too much work, or when there is too little of it, or when your invoices seem to have slipped into a black hole.

It can be hard to juggle that whole work/life balance thing when your work is your life. I don't think I've ever met entrepreneurs who say they aren't working harder than they ever have, but . . . they are okay with that. I suspect it's because when it is your own business, your own money at risk, your own dream up for validation, your work becomes your life in many ways. It's who you are at this stage of your life. Of course, not everyone is hardwired for this kind of adjustment, but for those that are prepared, the ride can be truly worth every ounce of perspiration and aspiration.

The Going Solo Economy

I spend a great deal of time in the small Virginia towns of Culpeper, Sperryville, and Warrenton, all about an hour-plus drive from Washington, D.C., and close to the breathtaking Shenandoah National Park. My husband and I have a tiny cottage out that way. The vistas of the Blue Ridge Mountains, rolling fields, and mountain streams are the lure. And of course, there's the awe of star-strewn night skies.

This is the land of small business and sole proprietors. A small business owner operates every place I shop or dine. I'm on a first-name basis with most of them. They are grocers, coffee roasters, innkeepers, organic farmers, veterinarians, antique dealers, silversmiths, winemakers, dairy operators, bakers, restaurateurs, and more.

There's a tack shop for the horsey set, with saddles and stylish riding boots, that smells enticingly of rich English leather and liniment. (As a horse-addled adult, I'm biased, of course.) One bakery, in particular, makes me instantly hungry just by opening the door. And don't get me started about Janet's pies. Then too, dozens of artists have studios here and market their goods privately by word-of-mouth. Farmers raise sheep and cattle, and stable owners board and train horses for a living.

Despite the rise of big-box and online stores, this small-town Virginia world is a network and community of small business bravehearts with entrepreneurial drive and a belief that they will make it, and the lion's share are making it . . . for today. And that's what small business is often all about, the present. It's frequently tenuous, living on the edge.

It can be a struggle when the leaf peepers and park hikers are gone, and the short, cold days of winter set in. But year after year, the entrepreneurs keep at it. Of course, there are those that fall by the wayside, and we mourn the loss. We root for them to succeed and put our money where our mouth is by supporting them.

These towns depend on small business to thrive. More than a few of the owners are mid-life entrepreneurs, who have switched careers to do something they love. Rick Wasmund is one. The 53-year-old sells Wasmund's Single Malt and Rye Whisky, produced at his Copper

Fox Distillery in Sperryville, Virginia.

Wasmund had dreamed of running his own business since he was a kid in upstate New York. But until he took a leap of faith and started his distillery, he spent his days selling insurance policies for Northwestern Mutual and doling out financial planning advice to many small businesses, as well as accountants and physicians. "I saw first-hand the challenges of running a small operation, and went for it anyway," he says.

He took his time and did his research, including a six-week internship at Bowmore Distillery on the island of Islay in Scotland. He experimented with the flavoring of the malt using the smoke of selected, smoldering fruit-woods (instead of peat), and using hand chipped and toasted fruitwood chips in the aging process to add a range of natural flavors that was not only new, but "fantastic" to the taste, Wasmund exclaims. Six years ago, he sold his first bottle of single-malt. This year, Copper Fox will produce more than 3,000 cases.

The challenge, he says, is turning a profit: "You would like to think at some point that money is not going to be an issue."

Going solo isn't for everyone. You need business chops — an understanding of the whole kit from marketing to sales and finance, or the willingness to learn those integral facets. At the heart of it, though, is something that can't be taught. It's what keeps Wasmund trucking his whisky for tastings up and down the East Coast and sometimes sleeping in his van: a dream, powerful self-motivation, and inner drive.

In today's economy, more and more workers are exiting the once secure realm of corporate jobs — many because of layoffs — and starting their own businesses. In 2011, more than 600,000 small firms were started in the United States, according to the Small Business Administration. Trouble is, only half will survive beyond five years.

It takes far more than a brilliant idea or a hankering for wonderful whisky made by using special fruitwood peat to succeed. Here are some basic business steps I recommend to help you land among the winners.

Do the prep work. Find a mentor. Whom do you know who might be able to guide you along your new path? In the next chapter, you will learn more about the importance of having a mentor. You may have to study marketing, finance, and employment law. Sign up for a community college or certification program to get the necessary skills. You can begin by contacting your town or county's Small Business Development Center. A three-hour course in the essentials of starting a business or e-mail marketing might cost as little as $15 to $30.

Take inventory. The checklist for launching a company from the Small Business Administration (SBA.gov) is a great place to begin. It helps you review your situation, identify a niche, analyze the market, and get a sense of your financial picture.

Write a business plan. There's no strict model to follow, but in general, a simple plan — which you'll have to submit to get a loan or other financing — should be about 20 pages. Here's what you'll need:

- An executive summary that explains what your company will do, who the customers will be, why you are qualified to run it, how you'll sell your goods and services, and your financial outlook.
- A detailed description of the business, its location, your management team, and your staffing requirements. You'll

also need to include information about your industry and competition.

- A market analysis that targets your customers more specifically, including age, gender, and geographic location. The analysis also will describe your sales and promotional strategy to reach them.
- A realistic forecast of start-up outlays — cost of raw materials, equipment, employee salaries, marketing materials, insurance, utilities, and fees for attorneys and accountants — and how much you expect to sell and to earn.

Line up sources of funding. Here are some ways to find the money to get started:

- **Savings.** Most start-ups are funded with personal savings. (This is where a severance package comes in handy.) It's advisable to set aside at least six months of fixed living expenses, though. Try not to dip into your retirement savings: You'll be subject to withdrawal penalties and income taxes and lose the tax-deferred compounding that could serve you well in retirement.
- **Friends and relatives.** Money is

often lent interest free or at a low rate. Be sure to put the terms in writing so that there are no misunderstandings about interest and repayment. When Bill Skees, 58, needed funding to open his independent bookstore, Well Read, in Hawthorne, New Jersey, he turned to his six siblings. The rate on his family loans: 3.5 percent. "At the time I was starting up in 2010, small-business bank loans were hard to get," says Skees. He raised $124,000 from them, borrowing on a three-year term. He and his wife, Mary Ann, tapped savings for the remaining start-up costs of $78,000. Be forewarned: Money can wreak havoc on relationships should things not work out as planned. That hasn't happened to Skees, but I want you to tread lightly if you think it might have the possibility of turning ugly. See Chapter 22 for more on borrowing.

- **Banks and credit unions.** A tight lending environment has made borrowing a struggle. A solid business plan and a shiny credit record are prerequisites. You might try a bank that's familiar with you or your industry, or one that is active in small-business lending. To find a bank that offers SBA-guaranteed loans, check the "Local Resources" section of the agency's web site (sba.gov). An SBA-guaranteed bank loan can keep your down payment and monthly payments low. Keep in mind that a lender will still want you to put up collateral, usually in the form of a real estate asset. Plan to have some capital or equity that you personally put into the business. Lenders want you to have some skin in the game, so to speak. Business.usa.gov is the federal government's site for entrepreneurs seeking short-term microloans and small business loans. Search this site for info on all programs available in your state.

- **Angel investors and venture capital firms.** These individuals and firms invest in exchange for equity or partial ownership. But they are typically overwhelmed by requests for financing. Another source of venture capital is the SBA's Small Business Investment Company Program.
- **Economic development programs.** This type of financing will take a little homework, but it's worth pursuing. For example, if you're a woman, you

might consider getting your firm certified as a woman-owned business. That can help you qualify for money that's only available to companies with that designation.

- **Certification can also help you land government clients.** Small-business certifications and verifications confirm a company's status, like whether the principal owner is a minority group member or whether the firm is located in an economically disadvantaged area. The SBA's economic development department can help you determine if this might be an avenue for you. If you're a veteran, the Department of Veteran Affairs, for instance, can provide you with information on how to get certified.
- **Corporations.** Some corporations offer assistance. For example, Michelin North America, based in Greenville, South Carolina, has provided low-interest financing — loans range from $10,000 to $100,000 — to certain minority-owned and disadvantaged businesses, including women-owned firms, in parts of South Carolina.
- **Grants.** Grants.gov lists information on more than 1,000 federal grant

programs. Female entrepreneurs should check out the SBA network of nearly 100 Women's Business Centers around the country. They offer state, local and private grant information to women interested in starting for-profit or nonprofit businesses.

- **Online seed money.** These "crowdfunding" sites have been cropping up like wildflowers. Financing for the incredibly successful Pebble smartwatch was ramped up via Kickstarter, a crowdfunding web site that entrepreneurs use to find people who'll invest small amounts of money in tech projects or creative endeavors like music or video games. Pebble's founders hoped to raise $100,000 through Kickstarter; they ended up bringing in more than $10 million. One of my friends' kids' band, the Shields Brothers, launched a Kick starter.com campaign to help finance the recording of a new rock and roll album. I donated to help the 20-somethings. I love this duo. They were featured on this season's *The Voice* reality competition on NBC, and I instantly wanted to help them reach their $4,000 goal.

It was easy. I agreed to donate, and the site clicked me over to Amazon to complete my transaction via credit card. I felt good about helping them out and expect nothing in return. You can donate anywhere from $1 to the sky's the limit. It's not an investment. They did say I could have my name listed as an associate producer, and they would send me a personal thank-you video. Plus, I will get a free download of the first single released.

It's a fun concept if taken in the right spirit. It's free to list your project. You simply post a description of what your project is with a video, a target dollar amount, and a deadline. You send out a mass e-mail to friends, family, and colleagues and ask them to share your project and funding invitation with their friends, and so on.

When you reach your goal, Kickstarter takes 5 percent, and you pay 3 to 5 percent to Amazon.com's credit card service. If you don't raise the money by the deadline, the pledges are canceled. Your contributors aren't charged for their donation, and Kickstarter takes nothing.

It's a grassroots financing method

that seems to be working. If you're just getting your project or home business started, you might want to check it out. The categories include music, film, art, design, food, publishing, and technology. Some other sites to help you raise seed money online include Rock The Post (rockthepost.com), a free network that helps entrepreneurs meet professionals and investors who can help via funds, time, or materials; Indiegogo.com; and AngelList (angel .co), which can help link you up with angel investors. You post your company's information, and the angels call you. Since these are all fairly new, be sure to do your own background check on these sites. In the past, small businesses couldn't sell shares of their company through crowdfunding sites because that violated Securities and Exchange Commission rules. But this spring, Congress passed the JOBS Act, which will allow such equity-based crowdfunding, when the SEC's new rules kick in.

- **Home equity loans.** This may be an option because the funds are usually taken as a lump sum that you can pay off over time. In this housing market, though, qualifying for such a loan can be tough. If you have equity in your home and a credit score well above 700, it may be worth exploring. You may also qualify for a tax deduction on the interest on a loan up to $100,000. Consult a financial adviser.

- **Credit cards.** This might be tempting, but avoid tapping plastic at all costs. Most cards have double-digit interest rates, a very high cost of capital to carry on your new company's books.

Purchase health insurance. Compare plans available in your area at the federal web site, Healthcare.gov. Check your state insurance department web site, too, since it might list health insurance choices for residents. If you hire employees (your spouse, for example) you may be eligible to buy coverage through a small-business group insurance plan; you need at least two employees to be considered a group. This type of plan could come in especially handy if you have a pre-existing condition, since some states require insurers to offer coverage to small groups regardless of whether any employees have health issues. You'll probably need a health insurance agent to help set up this type of plan. Look for one at the National Association of Health Underwriters web site.

Hire an accountant. It's critical to know which business expenses are deductible and more. Careful record keeping is essential, and having a pro to guide you will come in handy. I haven't met a new business owner who hasn't moaned about tax compliance worries, and it's more than simply withholding taxes for employees.

There's a broad sweep of taxes to consider, ranging from personal income tax to sales and payroll taxes. Hiring a knowledgeable tax professional makes sense. That can take some legwork. You need more than tax software to guide you, and someone who is adept at running individual tax returns isn't necessarily well versed in the intricacies of small business tax law.

Search for someone who is available to you all year round to answer the inevitable questions that arise. You might hire someone on a retainer basis, say, $200 a month, who can hold your hand and make sure the filings get sent in a timely fashion. Go to the source for more details: IRS Publication 334, "Tax Guide for Small Businesses." Useful information is available at the IRS

Small Business and Self-Employed Tax Center on the agency's site.

Don't neglect retirement savings. You have two basic ways to set aside pretax savings: a simplified employee pension, or SEP IRA, and an individual 401(k). See Chapter 21 for more on this.

Do the paperwork. The majority of small businesses require permits and licenses from your town, county and at the state level, too. These vary by location, and typically need to be renewed annually, so you will need to keep good records. Check out online resources for details. It's also smart to touch base with your town officials and local business owners to get a grip on the current local regulations.

Prepare to wait for income. You should expect that it will take three years before your business gets on its feet financially, but be prepared for it to take longer. There are exceptions, of course. Since its first year of business, Linda Waitkus' pet shop and grooming salon, Great Dogs of Great Falls, in Virginia, has turned a profit, and the 57-year-old has been able to pay herself a salary. "I saved and planned carefully for more than a year before I opened the store in 2009, and the gift I gave to myself is freedom of doing what I love — playing with dogs," Waitkus says.

CHAPTER 20
HOW TO FIND A MENTOR

Whether you're currently hunting for a new job, just getting started in one, or planning a change into a new field, it's a good idea to have a mentor or sponsor at your side. You need someone in your corner to calm you, focus you, and push you beyond your comfort zone.

The term "mentor" reportedly originated in the mid-18th century from the Greek word *Mentōr,* the name of the adviser (Athena in disguise) of the young Telemachus in Homer's *Odyssey.*

Under the guise of Mentor, an old friend of Telemachus's father, Odysseus, Athena gives him the confidence and support to embark on his epic journey to learn about his father's fate. She even collects the ship's crew for him. Although Telemachus has little experience with public speaking, for example, Mentor gives him the encouragement that he needs to approach Nestor, the king of the city Pylos, and ask him about his father.

Your mentor isn't likely to set you on such a bold course, but he or she may get you on board the boat and sailing ahead — even in rocky and unfamiliar seas, to keep the analogy rolling. We all need someone with experience and gravitas of whom we can ask questions without fear of looking stupid or putting our position in jeopardy.

Finding an unpaid advisor who has the time available to listen and counsel takes time and patience. A good mentor is not a career coach per se, though they may play that role at times. And unlike our lovely Greek goddess, your mentor is unlikely to appear out of thin air to help you set your course.

A good mentoring relationship grows organically over time. It takes nurturing, but a relationship often lasts for years, and a friendship grows that is priceless. Almost universally, the workers I know who have made a successful transition to new work after 50 had at least one person they could turn to when the ground got shaky. It was inevitably someone who was experienced with the ins and outs of the new line of work and could lend a verbal hand.

These workers tapped into a great mentor

for constructive advice, a "you can do it" pep talk. Sometimes it was a tough love kick in the pants or brutal honesty. In the best scenarios, the mentor opened up a broad network of contacts that gave back tenfold as resources, even as investors in a new venture, or leads to future job opportunities.

It makes sense. Most people like to help each other out when we can, provided we have the time and think we can really make a difference. There are tangible and intangible benefits to having a mentor. Someone with a mentor is more confident and self-aware and often more of a risk taker, according to a recent Gallup survey based on its consulting practice.

By absorbing advice from people who have been successful in a field you want to jump into, you can get a sense of what the work is like on a day-to-day basis. You learn what has worked for them in the past and what stumbling blocks to avoid.

Like most things in life, finding a mentor is a process. The right chemistry takes some trial and error. And there's no law that says you can only have one. Remember, you aren't looking for yes-men and -women, who support you no matter what. You want them to believe in your mission, but you need to hear the good, the bad, and the ugly. No lip-gloss.

Landing the right person to have in your corner may take some work on your part. But the resulting relationship can truly impact your life. A study published by economist Sylvia Ann Hewlett found that both men and women who have a mentor behind them are more likely than those without one to ask their boss for a raise, or an assignment that pushes them out of their comfort zone that they haven't tackled before.

Ask yourself what you want in a mentor. Is it an expert who can help with a specific goal — finding a job, planning a second career, asking for a raise, say, or suggesting ways to spiff up your image with the proper dress for success attire? Do you want someone at your workplace who can be an advocate for your project or promotion, or someone on the outside who can act as a more general sounding board and big-picture guide?

Where to look for a mentor:

- Your employer may have a mentoring program. Check with the human resources department. Many big corporations — American Express, Cisco, Citi, Deloitte, Ernst & Young, General Mills, Intel, Morgan Stanley, Procter & Gamble, and Time Warner among them — offer sponsorship and mentoring programs.

- Outside the office, you can find mentors you have met through activities you're involved in. Consider neighbors, friends, and relatives. One person I call for guidance is my older sister. This works for me. She's smart, successful, and a good listener with clear advice and no hidden agenda.
- Your high school, college, or university's alumni association may offer a mentoring program.
- Professional associations often have mentoring programs to match members with experienced mentors. For example, local chapters of the National Association of Women Business Owners (nawbo.org) offer mentoring programs. You can search for a local chapter on the site.
- Your local Rotary Club, the U.S. Small Business Association (SBA) in your town, and the Chamber of Commerce near you are good resources. There are

often lunches and other events sponsored by these groups who have guests whose wisdom you need. You might discover someone who is looking for a protégé and has expertise to lend free-of-charge and time to devote to lending a behind-the-scenes hand without seeing you as a competitor. The SBA also offers a Mentor-Protégé program designed to help small businesses compete for federal government contracts.

- SCORE (Score.org), a nonprofit association dedicated to educating entrepreneurs and to the formation, growth, and success of small business nationwide, is a resource partner with the U.S. Small Business Administration (SBA.gov). Both working and retired executives and business owners donate time and expertise as business counselors. SCORE mentors will advise you for free, in person or online.
- The Association of Small Business Development Centers, a joint effort of the SBA, universities, colleges, and local governments, provides no-cost consulting and low-cost training at about a thousand locations. You might find a mentor in the mix.
- The U.S. General Services Administra-

tion (GSA.gov) offers a GSA mentor protégé program that focuses on small business growth and development and subcontractor partnering relationships. An Advanced People Search on LinkedIn can lead you to a mentor. You might search for someone from your alma mater. College ties do bind. You type in a title and your university, for example, current vice presidents of marketing and attended Duke University. You can focus the search on your zip code or town, so you can connect with someone nearby.

Now it's time to narrow that field of dream possibilities down to the individual most likely to take you up on your offer. This is a stage that can be a little touchy-feely. So here's my advice.

Consider a mentor younger than you. 50+ workers might want to tap someone who may be junior in age but can offer more experience and guidance when it comes to new fields and areas like technology, where you might not be quite as fluent.

Practice your "Why Me" speech. This is a sales job. Landing a mentor calls for self-promotion. You often must brag about your accomplishments to get a higher-up's attention. A potential mentor may not want to back someone who doesn't have the potential to be a winner and make *them* look good. Skip the modest approach.

Steer clear of the formal request. The "Will you be my mentor?" invitation can be stiff and off-putting. Sounds like way too much work and responsibility. This is an inner undertaking. The main reason most mentors and sponsors say they take the time to counsel and help is the intangible satisfaction they get in paying it forward. Start by simply asking for advice on one action or problem.

Show them how to help. If you truly have a pressing need, take the plunge and make a specific request when you want someone to speak up on your behalf. Most people don't know where to start to help you.

Make it fun. When asking, don't make it sound like work. Exude a sense of excitement, smile, and laugh a little. Mentorship and sponsorship is an energy-boosting opportunity for both of you, and it often turns into a friendship. Find ways to meet regularly, even without an urgent agenda. Nurture the relationship.

Do something for them. Show your gratitude. Make the relationship reciprocal by serving as a source of information and support for your mentor in some way. It's the proverbial two-way street.

Be a mentor. This will give you a better idea of how to work with a mentor yourself. Even if you are at the bottom of your hierarchy at work or in your field, you might find mentees through alumni associations or nonprofits where you volunteer.

Listen. Whether you are the mentor or mentee, you can cultivate the relationship by asking questions and sincerely listening to the answers. Sometimes a mentor's most important input is to give practical feedback. Purpose Prizewinner Randal Charlton told me, "As a mentor, you have to listen to the person you are mentoring very carefully and try to figure out what they have got out of focus. As I have grown older, I've tried to resist the temptation to give instant advice. You don't have to solve their problem that precise minute. Think about what you've heard."

Men, Women, and Mentoring

LinkedIn surveyed nearly 1,000 female professionals in the United States and found that most women feel that it's important to have a mentor.

But most boomer women don't actually have one.

About two-thirds of boomer women — between 45 and 66 years old — say they never had a mentor, according to LinkedIn's study.

The statistics for younger female professionals are better: More than half of the Gen Y women — between 18 and 29 years old — say they're being or have been mentored by women.

LinkedIn asked the women who hadn't had a mentor why that was the case. More than half of the women say they hadn't had a mentor because they had "never encountered someone appropriate."

I know that for men, mentoring has been entrenched in the corporate world. I have often thought that is a result of growing up in a culture of team sports. Unlike today's generation of women who grow up playing soccer and basketball and lacrosse, many of us boomer women did not have that opportunity. It wasn't as encouraged as, say, Little League, was for our male peers. So we never learned the importance of working together, teamwork, and so on. Just my soapbox, but I think there is a grain of truth there. This may be one explanation for why boomer women are less likely to have mentors. When we were getting rolling in the work world, there weren't as many women in senior slots to look up to or ask for guidance. And those who were there could be pretty guarded about supporting other women. When I began my career, I was eager to find a woman I admired who would go to bat for me, help me up the ladder, teach me, even help me figure how to dress appropriately.

Financial journalism was still a male-dominated cadre at the top of the masthead. Male editors were more willing to offer advice, but that could be tricky. Office politics generally don't cotton to an older man mentoring a younger woman, no matter how well intentioned.

I never did find a female mentor in those early years, and I regret that. Now in my 50s, I work diligently to form these kinds of relationships, and it's happening. I can feel the impact both psychologically and concretely in the way my work life is progressing.

As a mentee, resist the knee-jerk urge to respond defensively. That's easier said than done. But hit the pause button and give yourself time to absorb the message and consider if it works for you.

My advice is to never stop trying. It's worth the effort. I also recommend that you have male and female mentors, depending on the corporate environment where you work, or your field. It just makes sense. These kinds of bonds will help you tremendously whether you're in a part-time or full-time position.

Desktop Mentors

In addition to the nonprofit Senior Entrepreneurship Works, the organization that I mentioned in the last chapter, and SCORE, there are also for-profit "virtual" mentoring services cropping up. For example, one that has caught my eye is PivotPlanet, a new virtual mentoring service founded by VocationVacations' Brian Kurth, author of *Test-Drive Your Dream Jobs: A Step-by-Step Guide to Finding & Creating the Work You Love*. PivotPlanet lets you connect with expert advisors via one-on-one video and phone conferences or in person.

The mission here is to offer easy access to

expert advisors in hundreds of fields to people looking to "pivot" from an existing career to another, looking for a hand to hold from someone who has done the job and knows what lurks beneath the surface. "It's networking and counseling for job seekers of all stripes — from aspiring entrepreneurs to people burned out in the corporate cubicle, and baby boomers planning encore careers," Kurth says, "at a fraction of the cost of hiring a career coach."

If you want to learn how to start a tech company, you tap into PivotPlanet's expert database and sign on with an entrepreneur in Palo Alto — no plane ticket or hotel room required. If you want to learn how to transition from the corporate world to nonprofit, you get the scoop from a nonprofit founder in New York. Unlike Kurth's VocationVacations, it's not just a two-day, get-your-toes wet sampler; it's designed to help build a more concrete mentor relationship that can evolve over a series of sessions at regular intervals and on an as-needed basis. These meetings are billed hourly and can range in price from $50 to $200. For more information, go to PivotPlanet.com. I have had a chance to use it and was impressed.

Chapter 21
The Best Retirement Plans
for the Self-Employed

For the self-employed, even if the will to save for retirement is there, the way can be problematic. If you've made the transition to being your own boss — whether as a freelancer, contract worker, or a small business operator — you probably need to ramp up a retirement account.

It's easy to get tripped up on some of the things you took for granted when you worked for your old employer, for instance, a no-brainer, 401(k)-type retirement plan handed to you in a tidy package that didn't require a lot of heavy lifting from you.

But once you're out of that ready-to-go retirement plan, it's really tough to get one started on your own. One of the biggest mistakes entrepreneurs make is not planning adequately — or at all — for their retirement.

This isn't all that surprising. If you're self-employed, it's a squeeze to set the money aside, even if it is tax-deferred. There's a fear that you may need those funds to keep things rolling if the business doesn't grow the way you expect, or clients are lax on paying your invoices. What might be shaved off for a retirement savings account instead becomes your cushion to protect again cash-flow mishaps.

And if you've been focused on funding your start-up costs, it's even more likely you have put retirement on the back burner. I wouldn't be surprised if you tapped your existing retirement accounts for funds to launch your enterprise, or to pay living costs while you build up your income. You may even rationalize not saving for retirement with the dream that ultimately you'll sell your rip-roaring business and live off the proceeds in your old age.

Few people actually sock away the maximum allowed by the IRS in retirement accounts. Most surveys, for example, indicate that a mere 5 percent of an estimated 60 million 401(k) participants do so.

The reality is that planning for retirement is not as tricky as you may think. Uncle Sam offers a variety of relatively painless plans to help self-employed small-business owners, freelancers, and contract workers save for retirement in tax-favorable accounts.

Here's a round-up of the three main options:

1. SEP-IRA. If you're a one-man or -woman band, this account is a good bet. A simplified employee pension (SEP) IRA is a basic way to set aside pretax savings. A SEP Individual Retirement Account (IRA) plan provides employers with a simplified method to make contributions toward their employees' retirement and, if self-employed, their own retirement.

Contributions are made directly to a traditional (not Roth) IRA or annuity set up for each employee (a SEP-IRA). See Publication 560 for detailed SEP information for employers and employees.

You can contribute as much as 25 percent of compensation or 20 percent of your net earnings from self-employment, up to a maximum of $50,000 in 2012 (subject to annual cost-of-living adjustments for later years). Compensation considered would include bonuses and overtime.

Similar limits on contributions made to employees' SEP-IRAs also apply to contributions made to a self-employed individual's SEP-IRA. Special rules apply, however, when figuring out the maximum deductible contribution. See Publication 560 for details on determining the contribution amount.

Best features: Flexibility. There's no need to fund the account until you file your return. So if your net income turns out to be higher than expected, you can make a larger contribution and trim your tax bill. If you have a bad year, you can reduce your contribution.

Another plus: If you're building your new business on the side while still working for an employer, you can contribute to both its 401(k) and your SEP.

Caveat: This plan may be costly eventually if you have employees, as opposed to contract workers, because the money you put into a SEP counts as an employer contribution. You must make the same percentage contributions for all covered workers, or those who are 21 and older who have been employed by you for at least three of the last five years and are expected to earn $550 in 2012 (this number is subject to cost-of-living adjustments annually). Your spouse is exempt.

Generally, you can deduct the contributions you make each year to each employee's SEP-IRA. If you are self-employed, you can deduct the contributions you make each year to your own SEP-IRA.

Filer tip: You have until the due date for the business's tax return, including any extensions, for that year to both set up and fund the plan.

You can open a SEP-IRA at practically any financial service company including banks, mutual fund companies, or brokerage firms. Firms such as Fidelity, Schwab, T. Rowe Price, or Vanguard will set up an account gratis, and account fees are low or nil.

Keep in mind, the IRA minimum withdrawal rules also apply to SEP accounts as well as simple IRAs, since they're both considered IRAs for this purpose. (Roth IRA owners are exempt from the minimum withdrawal rules as long as the original account owner is alive). You can take your first minimum withdrawal during the year you turn 70 1/2, or you can take it by April 1 of the year after you turn 70 1/2. Then for each subsequent year, you must take at least the required minimum withdrawal by Dec. 31 of that year. There is a 10 percent early withdrawal penalty, and you'll pay federal and state income taxes. You cannot take loans.

2. Solo 401(k). This is a solid choice if you're self-employed or a business owner with no employees except a spouse. With a solo 401(k), also known as an individual 401(k), a one-person 401(k), or single participant 401(k), you can stash away 25 percent of a salary or 20 percent of net earnings up to $17,000 in 2012. If you're 50+ at any time in the tax year (even if you turn 50 on December 31), you can contribute an additional catch-up contribution, $5,500 in 2012, for a total of $22,500. In 2012, the total maximum contribution combined for employer and employee together is up to $50,000, plus $5,500 if you're 50+, for a maximum contribution of $55,500.

As with all qualified plans, withdrawals prior to age 59 1/2 (age 55 if you are terminated) are subject to a 10 percent penalty tax, and required minimum distributions must begin at age 70 1/2 for retired individuals.

Best features: Generous contribution

limits and low or no set-up or annual fees. Fidelity or Vanguard, for example, have no set-up fees. Other institutions charge a low set-up — say, $100 or less — plus an annual fee of $10 to $250.

Contribution amounts are optional, so you can save the top figure in flush years and zilch in leaner times. That's because salary deferrals are optional, so contribution levels can be adjusted to the fluctuations of business income. If you already have an individual retirement account funded by money rolled from a previous employer's 401(k), you can roll those retirement savings into your new solo 401(k). Some accounts such as T. Rowe Price and Vanguard also offer a Roth option — you put in after-tax money that grows tax-free.

It may also be possible to take out a loan against a solo 401(k), but you pay a price. Loans can be useful if you need funds in a pinch. You can borrow half the account's balance, up to $50,000, and normally you can take up to five years to pay it back (provider rules differ). Not all solo 401(k) plans, however, allow loans. For example, Fidelity, T. Rowe Price, and the Vanguard Group don't allow loans. Oppenheimer and TD Ameritrade do.

Loans must be repaid according to the terms of the loan amortization schedule, which is provided when you take the loan. Typically, the loan interest rate charged is the prime rate or prime plus 1 percent or 2 percent, but that will vary by provider. Failure to pay the loan according to the loan terms can trigger taxes and early withdrawal penalties, since the IRS considers the unpaid loan as an early distribution from the retirement account.

I don't recommend borrowing from your plan unless it's a serious situation. But having the option can make it easier to get over the psychological hurdle of opening a retirement account.

Caveat: No extra employees can participate. This savings vehicle is only for self-employed business owners and a spouse. This is not the best option if you're still working a day job. If you contribute to an employee 401(k) at your day job, you might already be saving the max. You get only one combined contribution of $17,000, or $22,500 for 50+.

Filer tip: The deadline to open a new plan is typically December 31 (or fiscal year end) and must be funded by your tax return due date, plus extension. This is a traditional "qualified" pension. That means once it's worth $250,000 or more, you must file an annual Form 5500 report. So you may have some paperwork here. Fidelity and Vanguard, for example, provide the information you need for the form but do not complete or file it for you.

3. A Simple IRA. A simple IRA is designed specifically for small businesses and self-employed individuals.

If you have a few employees who each make more than $5,000 but far from six figures and you want to offer a plan for them as a perk, this is probably the one for you. It was designed for firms with no more than 100 employees. Employers as well as employees can contribute.

For 2012, as an employer, you can make an employee contribution of up to $11,500 pretax, or $14,000 if you're 50 or older. There isn't any percentage of income restrictions. Your contributions are tax deductible, and your investments grow tax deferred until you are ready to make withdrawals in retirement.

A simple IRA is a little burdensome if you're a fledgling firm. You're generally required to make a contribution to match each employee's salary reduction contributions on a dollar-for-dollar basis up to 3 percent of the employee's salary, no matter what the employee contributes to the account. An employer may choose to make a matching contribution of less than 3 percent, but it must be at least 1 percent and for no more than two out of five years.

Best feature. Easy paperwork. It should take about 15 minutes or less to fill out the forms.

Caveat: This one isn't for moonlighters — you can't contribute if you've already maxed out employee contributions to a 401(k) at your day job. Also, if you need to make a withdrawal from a simple IRA plan within two years of its inception, the 25 percent penalty is significantly higher than the 10 percent fee you'd be charged for early withdrawal from a SEP IRA.

Filer tip: You must set one up by October 1 to make contributions for that tax year, and all employee contributions must be made by December 31.

For additional guidance on retirement plans for the self-employed, see IRS Publication 560 and Publication 4334, *Simple IRA Plans for Small Businesses.*

CHAPTER 22
PAYING FOR YOUR CAREER SHIFT EDUCATION

I was sitting toes in the sand on a New Jersey beach talking to my friend Larry Schmidt, who has spent more than 30 years working for one company, Meditech, based in Westwood, Massachusetts. It's a fast-growing medical software firm. And he has been there as it has grown by leaps and bounds, enjoying and being an integral part of the ride.

Now in his late 50s, he is beginning to think about what's next for him. Not any time soon, but eventually, when he retires in a decade or so. His kids already graduated from college. But what struck me most about our conversation is how much he likes his work — the challenges, the opportunity to mentor and coach younger employees, and the overall work environment.

He's a marketing and communication guy. His off-site passion is painting and drawing, and his employer is all for it. When Larry wanted to take classes to hone his painting technique, Meditech paid the tuition to support his "creative development," particularly since he manages a group of designers and writers.

There's even a "creativity lab" at the office for workers to zip into for a respite during the day. It's stocked with canvas, paints, brushes, and more — all available to encourage folks to take a few brush strokes and recharge. The creativity labs are set up, Larry explains, "to promote team building through creative activities (such as collaborative drawings), rather than for individual recreation. It's more in the context of working collaboratively on a fun activity and carrying this back to the workplace, rather than for individual recreation."

Who knows? His next act may very well flow from this artistic passion in some incarnation. He's not sure.

The creativity lab intrigues me, but the fact that Meditech paid for his art classes really made me take notice. Under federal law, employers can offer tax-free education-assistance benefits for undergraduate or graduate courses up to $5,250 in 2012. Depending on your employer, you may not need to be working toward a degree. Beware, however, that employers can impose a variety of restrictions such as taking courses that relate to the employee's duties, taking courses as part of a degree program, and requiring you to work a certain length of time after taking the course — or requiring repayment of tuition if you leave early.

The number of students ages 50 to 64 has been climbing steadily. To meet the demand for continuing education, colleges are creating retraining and certificate programs aimed squarely at the demographic. The American Association of Community Colleges, for example, offers a "Plus 50 Initiative" on campuses across the country.

If going back to school is on your mind, check your employer's education reimbursement program. This one is probably best if you're planning several years ahead for your "working in retirement" job. You might need to show your boss that your course of study will be a help, even tangentially, with your current job duties. Not too many managers are ready to invest in their employees' post-retirement careers. They're interested in how continuing education will make you a more valuable worker now.

With or without employer assistance, paying for your career education doesn't have to cut too deeply into your wallet. Community college courses are usually a few hundred dollars per credit, and certificate programs are generally cheaper and more focused on the professional skills you want to add now than a degree program. Online webinars and workshops offered by industry associations are other avenues to consider.

Potential costs. If you sign up for a course at a public four-year college near you, you can expect to pay upwards of $700. A single course at a private college can top $2,700. A master's degree can set you back anywhere from $5,000 to more than $40,000 annually, depending on the school. A certificate program in financial planning or career coaching, however, might run the gamut from $3,000 done entirely online to $15,000 for on-campus credit hours. New York University, for example offers an online course to be a certified financial planner for as little as $2,495. If another 10 to 15 years of work is on your dance card, then it might be worth it. If not, you need to do the cost-reward analysis with a sharp pencil.

In the ideal world, you can rev up training and necessary degrees or certificates while you're gainfully employed, adding a few at time and spreading the cost over a few years. Even if you have just an inkling of what interests you and enroll in one class, you are starting to smooth the way for a transition to new work.

Don't be caught flat-footed by the realization that you will need different skills to transfer to a new field, even part-time. It will take time, money, and discipline to pursue a certification or add classes. It can mean weekends and evenings, and most people are leery of making that kind of commitment.

Smart Ways to Help You Afford Your Education

Tax breaks. There are several tax moves to consider for your career education that can help — even if you don't itemize deductions on your 1040. For example, there are student loan interest deductions and deductions for tuition. To see whether you qualify, check irs.gov or talk with your tax advisor. Tuition to add job skills may qualify for the Lifetime Learning tax credit, or the above the line deduction for tuition and fees, both of which have limitations and income restrictions that are explained in IRS Publication 970.

Loans. Borrowing money to pay for education can be tricky. You don't want to fall into a trap of graduating with a mound of debt in your 50s or 60s. Make sure the pay scale for the position you are training for warrants it.

The good news is that age is not a factor in determining eligibility for the Federal Student Aid programs. Low-interest Stafford loans (staffordloan.com) are the main federal loans for students. The loan doesn't require repayment until you graduate as long as you meet certain income requirements and are in school at least half-time. For graduates who work in public safety, public health, education, social work, or the nonprofit sector, however, the Education for Public Service Act lets you lower monthly payments on federal student loans. There's also a debt-forgiveness program for borrowers who spend ten years in relatively low-paying jobs in government or charities after graduation. Many private lenders also offer loans, though rates will be higher. Go to FastWeb.com and FinAid.org for details and a list of education lenders. Both are free sites for information on school loans and grants. Federal Student Aid, (studentaid.ed .gov), an office of the U.S. Department of Education, is another excellent resource.

Federal grant for undergraduates. If you're going back to school for an undergraduate degree, you may qualify for a federal Pell Grant. To get a Pell Grant, you must complete the free Application for Federal Student Aid (FAFSA). A federal Pell Grant, unlike a loan, does not have to be repaid. The maximum Pell Grant for the 2011–2012 award year (July 1, 2012, to June 30, 2013) is $5,550. The amount depends on your financial need, costs to attend school, status as a full-time or part-time student, and plans to attend school for a full academic year or less. For more information, go to the U.S. Department of Education's website, ed.gov.

Intrafamily loan. Like funding a start-up, you might see if your parents or one of your siblings is in a position to help out. Offer to pay, say, 3 percent interest, which is more than double what they can score now with a five-year CD.

To steer clear of family trouble, be sure to put the loan and its terms in writing. And if it is for more than $10,000 total, unless it is a gift, the IRS sets minimum rates of interest depending on the length of the loan period. That's because the interest you pay will become taxable income to them. Currently, the IRS minimum interest rates range from around 2 percent to less than 4 percent for loans longer than nine years. You can purchase standard loan forms, for instance, through Nolo.com, and Legal zoom.com.

Scholarships and grants. Besides Pell Grants, look for scholarships and grants available specifically for older students that are offered by different associations and foundations. There is a wide range of scholarships or grants available if you do some sleuthing. You'll find those earmarked for individuals below a certain income bracket, minorities, or veterans, to name a few categories.

The American Association of University Women (aauw.org), for example, offers grants between $2,000 and $12,000 for women who hold bachelor's degrees and are going back to school to advance their careers, change careers, or re-enter the work force. Look under "Career Development Grants" on the group's web site.

The AARP Foundation's Women's Scholarships Program offers scholarships between $500 and $5,000 for low-income 50+ women to fund education, training, and skills upgrades that can lead to better employment. AARP scholarships pay partially or in full for tuition, fees, and books;

they may be used for part-time as well as full-time study; and they are distributed directly to the institution. Online coursework is eligible, too. Institutions must be accredited by the U.S. Department of Education.

For more scholarships and grants, you can also check out FastWeb.com and FinAid.org.

Paying for your adult education is no day at the beach, but don't forget you're building more than a castle in the sand.

CHAPTER 23
HOW TO WRITE OFF
YOUR JOB HUNT

March Madness means more than basketball. Can you say tax time? If you spend a chunk of time and money on the job-hunting trail, you'll probably have a tidy pile of receipts stashed in an envelope or file to show for it.

Anyone who has put together a natty new resume on high-quality paper, mailed it out the old-fashioned way, bought new business cards, traveled back and forth to job interviews, or attended a networking event is painfully aware of the price tag. The simple nuts and bolts of marketing yourself can be pricey. Believe me, those $15 parking garage tickets do add up to a sizeable sum.

You'll be grateful for rigorous record-keeping. I recommend keeping a journal with notations of what you did each day toward your job hunt and what money you spent, even if you don't have a paper receipt.

"When you're looking for a job you're

probably short on cash and will want to reduce your tax bill as much as possible," CCH Tax Expert and Analyst Mark Luscombe says. "So you should claim all the deductions you can, if you're eligible."

And that's the trick — knowing what is and what's not acceptable by The Internal Revenue Service. There are restrictions.

The biggest one is job-hunting deductions apply only to job searching in your current occupation. If you're switching careers, they're off-limits. And if you're looking for your first job, you're also out of luck. Moreover, the IRS does not allow deductions after a "substantial break" between your last job and your current job. No explanation, though, of what the agency means by "substantial break."

Here's how it works: The allowable job search costs can be deducted only if you itemize expenses on Schedule A of your Form 1040 tax return (so you get no deduction if you claim the standard deduction). They are counted as itemized deductions.

Importantly, I must emphasize, it is critical to have detailed records. You must be able to show with documented receipts and logs of mileage that the expenses were directly a result of your job search efforts, and receipts for all expenses.

These are some of the major items you might be able to write off on your return.

Outplacement and employment agency fees. These are includible whether or not a new job is landed, assuming, of course, that you are looking for a job in the same line of work. Career coaching fees can usually be deducted, too.

Resume. Preparation fees, paper, inkjet cartridges, and printing costs for your resume and postage are all job write-offs. But again, don't get sloppy; detailed records are key, especially for expenses such as paper and inkjet cartridges, since the IRS could question the connection to your job search, which once again, has to be for a job in the same line of work.

Travel and meals. Meals as well as lodging can be included in travel costs, if the job search (present occupation, of course) trip is away from home, which basically means you are traveling outside of the area where you usually work. The 2012 IRS standard mileage rate is generally 55.5 cents per mile, which the IRS in Publication 529 says you can use to figure your job search expenses if you use your car. However, this per-mile rate varies. Check www.IRS.gov for the latest rates and restrictions on using the standard mileage rate. Airfare, train tickets, and taxis, too, are deductible, providing they're strictly related to your job hunt. You can't, for instance, take a five-day trip to New York City to catch some Broadway shows, enjoy the nightlife, and spend a day interviewing, and then consider the entire trip a write-off, Luscombe warns. Be careful not to try to make a pleasure trip a business one.

Internet costs. The big ones here are work-related Wi-Fi charges, online jobs sites that charge a fee, and networking services like LinkedIn's fee for upgraded professional access that you can honestly say are directly used as a tool in your job hunt. In today's market, these costs are standard, and Luscombe says while they aren't specifically listed in the IRS guidelines, they are an acceptable cost of the job-hunting process.

Skill-building. If you pay to take seminars, job-training courses, or attend networking events, the charge is usually deductible, but again, you must be certain you can prove that it's connected to your job search. Tuition to acquire or improve job skills may qualify for the Lifetime Learning tax credit, or the above-the-line deduction for tuition and fees, both of which have limitations and income restrictions that are explained in IRS Publication 970.

Professional dues, subscriptions, and association fees. These can be deductible if you use the services provided by the groups to help your job search, Luscombe says. If challenged, you will need to show documentation that a job board at your professional association, for example, was a direct source of leads for you.

Moving costs. If you accept a job in another state, you might be able to write off all expenses associated with your move, from packing boxes to shipping. Brace yourself — the moving rules are a little wacky. Unreimbursed moving expenses may be written off even if you don't itemize deductions. There is an illustration of the distance test in the publication 521. You'll want to study the graph. For details, see IRS Publication 521.

What's generally not on the allowable deduction list? Haircuts, Botox treatments, and face lifts, new interview clothes, and a briefcase.

You might be happy to know that your expenses that pass the IRS tests are deductible whether or not the job search is successful. However, if a subsequent employer reimburses you for any of the expenses deducted, you must include that amount in your gross income in the year of the reimbursement.

For some taxpayers, it might not be worth the hassle. If you haven't itemized deductions in the past, you might be better off skipping all the paperwork. The IRS says most taxpayers use the standard deduction. The standard deduction amount is different for each filing status and is higher if you're 65 or older and for blind taxpayers. The amounts adjust for inflation each year. In 2012, for instance, the standard deduction comes to $11,900 for married couples filing jointly or $5,950 for single filers.

I recommend that you add up all of your job hunting out-of-pocket expenses and combine with other miscellaneous itemized deductions — not only job search ones — such as mortgage interest, real estate taxes, tax preparation fees, certain medical bills, charitable deductions and more (IRS Publication 529 provides a more complete list of miscellaneous itemized deductions) and compare to the standard deduction. If all of those itemized are higher than the standard deduction, and exceed 2 percent of your adjusted gross income, you can typically deduct those job search costs.

You'll use Schedule A, Itemized Deductions. For more information about job search expenses, see IRS Publication 529, Miscellaneous Deductions. This publication is available on IRS.gov or by calling 800-TAX-FORM (800-829-3676).

Some important caveats. If you fall under the alternative minimum tax, you won't have any deductions. Then too, these deductions might not help you much if your spouse is pulling in a healthy income, or you have a substantial severance payout. If your adjusted gross income (AGI) is $100,000, your miscellaneous deductions must exceed $2,000; if they add up to $2,200, you can deduct $200. See IRS Publication 17, *Your Federal Income Tax,* for more information.

On a related note, I know that many people who are job hunting are also receiving severance packages from previous employers or on unemployment. You should be aware of what the government considers taxable.

- **Severance pay is taxable.** If you accepted a severance package and benefits when you parted ways with your former employer, or you were paid for unused vacation and sick leave, that's considered taxable income. Be sure enough taxes are withheld from these payments by your former employer, or make estimated payments. See IRS Publication 17, *Your Federal Income Tax,* for more information.
- **Unemployment pay is taxable.** Go to IRS Publication 525 for help, as well as the IRS publication, *The Tax Impact of a Job Loss.*

Bottom line: When filing your taxes, step up and take all the deductions you are legally allowed to. If you're on the job hunt now, be obsessive about saving all those receipts. The IRS may let you deduct some expenses. I highly recommend you seek professional tax help if you are at all unsure. You never know — with a little assistance, you might sink a three-pointer. Swish.

CHAPTER 24
WAYS TO CONQUER YOUR FEAR
OF CAREER CHANGE

When it comes to changing jobs and certainly entire career paths, there are plenty of things to be afraid of. You might not call it fear. But let's face it. That's what stops you from making the move out of a miserable job, starting over in a new field, or picking up the phone to make a networking call, no matter how right the time is to do just that. It's paralyzing.

The biggest worries: failure, loss of money, loss of pride, rejection, and feeling undervalued. And obviously, if you're starting over no matter where it is, being the new kid on the block, when your ego isn't prepared, can be daunting. These are all honest and true gut-level fears. They are fears that we can put down to simple human nature.

It's okay to be afraid. But it's not okay to let those fears stop you from following a new path that might make your life a heck of a lot better in many ways — personally and financially. If you don't fall into the trap of second-guessing your decisions, you'll develop an inner confidence that keeps you going when things take a turn for the worse.

It happens. It's being able to keep your head down and barrel on through the hard times to get to the other side that's a secret ingredient for starting new careers and jobs at any age.

You must be able to take action when faced with a challenge like finding a job when you've been pink-slipped at age 57 like my friend Randy was. You can't get waylaid by anger or let grief (it is a genuine emotion when you leave a job whether by choice or not) overwhelm you.

You've got to stay open to new ideas and be willing to take sacrifices if you want to be a successful rebounder, *U.S. News & World Report* business correspondent Rick Newman writes in his book *Rebounders: How Winners Pivot from Setback to Success.*

"It's important to keep in mind that anxiety, depression, discouragement, fear, worry, and many other challenges we face today are nothing new," Newman writes, "They've been part of every generation in modern history, and all along, there have been people with the grit needed to sur-

mount challenges and keep pressing forward."

You can be one of them.

The fact is, there's a bulging file drawer
full of fears that come along with the notion
of interviewing for jobs, changing jobs, or
starting a new business, no matter what age
you are or how much experience you have
under your belt. Fear is far from a one-size-
fits-all opponent to face. Each person has a
unique challenge, and fear plays out in different ways in how we go about looking for
a new job, the kinds of work we explore,
our willingness to make mistakes.

To get some advice on what you can do
to address your fears, I sat down with business and work coach Patricia DiVecchio,
author of *Evolutionary Work: Unleashing Your
Potential in Extraordinary Times* and president of International Purpose, based in Ar-
lington, Virginia. She has been helping
people for more than 25 years to manage
fear and uncover their work potential and
purpose.

KH: *What are some basic ways to conquer fear?*
PD: First, think about these three concepts:

    ○ See fear as an ally.

○ Don't fear what you want most.

○ Embrace your resistance.

KH: *Fear as an ally? Are you serious?*

PD: It can be a great motivator, a great teacher. We don't see it like that. We tend to run away from fear, back or shy away from it, instead of stepping into it. You need to recognize it as something you can learn from. You need to shake hands with your fear and enlist it as a friend — a force to encourage forward movement, rather than something to hide from.

KH: *Why are people so anxious about work transitions even if they know it's time to do something different?*

PD: It should be exciting to do something you've always wanted to do or are passionate about, but we fear change, even if it is positive change. It's the unknown. We are afraid of the conflict that it might create within and outside of ourselves when we stand up for our true wants and needs. There's the fear of greater responsibility.

Or if you are starting over in a new field, there's the fear of a downgrade in status, at least initially. That can come with a fear of a loss of power, respect, acceptance, and money.

Funny, those same things can be scary in the reverse too; people are sometimes afraid of the gain of power, respect, acceptance, and money.

KH: *Fear of success? Sounds so counter-productive. What's that all about?*

PD: Getting what we want most in life can be scary. There's a huge responsibility to success. You have to keep it up and stay successful. Then too, success means change and often transformation. Our mindsets are typically based on the past and how things have always been. So if we are looking at changing our career, or looking at moving into a business, it's difficult to comprehend, again, the unknown. And it sounds funny, but we also fear success because we fear it's going to be more work, and we don't want to work that hard. One way to get a handle on this is to write down what emotions you feel when you start to visualize your new work life. What surfaces?

KH: *Any other lurking fears that surface for career switchers?*

PD: The final fear, or what I call door number three, is the fear that when you really start the internal digging to find your passion, you are not going to find anything there. You aren't going to unearth unique skills and talents — this can be pretty scary. That's when you really need help.

KH: *Okay. So what actions can you take to break through to the other side?*

PD: Here are six ways to help embrace fear and learn to say, bring it on:

1. **Draw your fear.** One client saw himself in a rickety old car, the only one on a pothole-filled road heading up a huge mountain. When you give a form or image to your fear, it makes it more concrete. Otherwise, fear is very nebulous and has us by our neck.

2. **Write about it in a journal.** For my client in that car, when he wrote about the image, he concluded it meant he could see there was no end in sight. He felt discouraged. Fear has something to teach you. It's telling you something. When you try to interpret your drawing, it brings it to the surface. Is the broken-down car out in the wilderness all about being afraid to ask for help? It can be that obvious.

3. **Draw what it would look like**

without the fear. This shifts your perception. Maybe the road is smooth for my client. The sun is out. When you visualize the fear and act on it, you can conquer it.

4. **Do small things.** Do one thing different every day that you are afraid to do. Keep track of them in a journal. This practice starts to build your "risk" muscle. You might make a phone call, for example, that you have been hesitant to make. Before you call, write what you want to say and your goals for the call, and visualize the person on the other end as being as human as you are. People are always willing to talk about themselves and their work. Engage them. Make the conversation valuable for them.

5. **Write about what comes to you easily and effortlessly that is exciting (the three E's).** If you can recognize your innate skills and talents, you can package that and create work from it. You're going to be the most successful, the happiest, and probably better rewarded financially because you are doing work based on your strong skills

and talents. I believe our innate skills are our strongest — more than what we gain from education and experience.

6. **Interview four or five people in your life — friends, family, or colleagues — and ask them what they think you are good at.** Sometimes we are the last to get our true value. Look at the patterns that emerge from their responses. Look at what's repeating itself. If everyone says you have wonderful communication skills, pay attention to that.

CHAPTER 25
BEST PLACES TO FIND A JOB

Ever thought about moving for a job? Seriously, picking up stakes and going where the getting is good. I have found that many great towns for working in your 50s and beyond are college towns with thriving medical centers — both good omens for job seekers. Then, too, state capitals, where government jobs are plentiful, or regions where world-class health care centers dominate have often bypassed economic declines and are good job-hunting grounds.

Physically moving could be a good career move. If you're starting an encore career, you've lost a job, have accepted an early-retirement package, or are a retiree or soon-to-be retiree facing a smaller retirement account than you need to see you through, this may be worth taking into consideration.

Even if you've just barely passed the big 50, this might be your time to get a jump-start on finding a place where you might

476

like to live in retirement. Sure, relocating now to where you want to live in 10 or more years from now might seem like jumping the gun, but if work is what you're after, it's worth doing some research. You'll want to job hunt in regions with below-average unemployment and a steady record of job creation over the past decade. Consider, too, the cost of living, access to top-notch medical facilities, and leisure activities.

College towns in particular are great places to live and work in retirement. They're typically lively entertainment and sports hubs and make good job-hunting grounds. That's because these communities tend to be recession-resistant.

Each year, a new crop of students rolls into the area, and, along with them, visitors, to keep the economy humming. Plus, many towns are tucked into regions with booming health care centers that are also a good source of jobs.

Better yet, many are home to employers who are friendly to older workers. Check out AARP's recent "Best Employers for Workers 50+ Winners," for example. Some of the leading employers on the list are universities and health care providers in college towns.

Winners include Cornell University in Ithaca, New York; Blue Cross and Blue Shield of North Carolina in Durham, North Carolina, hometown of Duke University; West Virginia University in Morgantown; the University of Pittsburgh; and Virginia Commonwealth University in Richmond.

If you're looking to relocate, the opportunity to find work in an economy buoyed by a top-notch university is a lure for those not yet ready to clock out completely. Consider Ames, Iowa, a town that buzzes around the happenings at Iowa State University and the schedules of its Cyclones sports teams. Iowa State boasts over 28,000 students and employs around 9,000 people.

Just two hours from Chicago, Madison, Wisconsin has a healthy economy, supported by the University of Wisconsin and its growing research centers.

Penn State University, for instance, has made an effort to appeal to those who fall into this category. It even has a retirement community on campus that gives residents access to free college classes and priority tickets to games. For culture buffs, the Penn State Center for the Performing Arts presents music, dance, and theater.

One good way to learn about campus job openings is to tap into a college or university's human resources section on its web site for postings. Another good spot to search, especially if you're willing to relocate, is higheredjobs.com. You can screen by location, institution, job title, category, and full-time or part-time. The big job board Indeed .com also lists university-oriented opportunities.

Some possible part-time jobs range from a researcher for an academic or scientific study to staffing ticket services for the athletic department. You don't have to dress up as the team's mascot, but you will be front and center. You'll be the one juggling ticket requests to sports and athletic-related events. Those sometimes urgent pleas will come from well-heeled donors, eager alumni, university staffers needing a last-minute favor, students, and, importantly, fanatic fans who may or may not be regular season ticket holders. At The University of Virginia, for example, the hiring range for a recent posting was $10.65–$11.50.

Alumni event planning is another job that might appeal to you. This work requires lots of behind-the-scenes advance work leading up to a major event, say, a class reunion or campus conference. You might put on your travel shoes from time to time to take the show on the road to alums in their hometowns. The job usually comes under the banner of alumni affairs at most schools, and can be part of a broader job description, for instance, assistant director of alumni relations.

Other around campus jobs include career center counselor, university bookstore retail specialist, and shuttle bus driver.

I've had the opportunity to collaborate with two organizations that crunched the numbers to find the best places for 50+ workers: *U.S. News & World Report* and *The Daily Beast.* These lists change year to year, of course, with towns dropping on and off as the winds of change prevail. Nonetheless, they do provide a starting point for a job search in a new region.

When I run my eyes down the lists they spat out, I smile. Several of the cities that appear on the lists are ones I personally have visited or lived in, and I really do know people over 50 who have found rewarding work there. So perhaps there is something to these lists. Some of the cities that cropped up — Nashville, Madison, Wisconsin, Chapel Hill, North Carolina, Washington, D.C., and Pittsburgh, Pennsylvania — get my personal, slightly biased vote for good job-hunting venues, and they're lively entertainment and sports hubs too.

Washington, D.C., for example, is home

to several colleges and health care centers, and it has those ever-present government jobs going for it. Pittsburgh, of course, has long left the steel trade, even if the Steelers still remain, and has a huge health care economy buoyed by UPMC, western Pennsylvania's largest employer, with almost 50,000 employees.

One of the cities that made the *U.S. News* roster is Ames, Iowa, as I mentioned above. In addition to the college, pasta and sauce maker Barilla runs its U.S. operations from a base here, and Post-it maker 3M has a strong local presence as well. "The benefits that a university offers really can't be beat," says former journalist Jackie King, 59, who took a position as a program assistant in the university relations office at Iowa State. "A lot of my former jobs didn't have 401(k)s or a retirement program." Biotech and agriculture round out the job market.

Madison, Wisconsin, is a hot dog of a spot for a second stage of work life, according to the *U.S. News* list. Since the early 1990s, the state capital has undergone continual economic growth and even in recession boasts low unemployment, a low crime rate, and a healthy economy nurtured by the University of Wisconsin and its expanding research centers as well as state government jobs. High-tech and biotech ventures have created opportunity as well. And Oscar Mayer has been a Madison fixture for decades.

Madison — also known as the City of Four Lakes (Mendota, Monona, Waubesa, and Kegonsa) — has also earned a status as a kind of groovy "Berkeley of the Midwest," home of politically liberal voters and birthplace of the satirical newspaper *The Onion.* The University of Wisconsin Badgers sports teams help take the chill off the local winters. Architect Frank Lloyd Wright, who spent much of his childhood in Madison and briefly studied civil engineering at the university, is responsible for several local buildings.

And how about Oklahoma City? Among U.S. metro areas with a population of at least 1 million, this state capital has the lowest business costs, in part because of tax incentives, according to KPMG's "Competitive Alternatives" analysis of 112 cities in 10 countries. It also has a low unemployment rate. "People can find jobs here, period," crows Roy Williams, president and CEO of the Greater Oklahoma City Chamber of Commerce.

Energy companies are big employers, and Tinker Air Force Base provides a stream of consulting work for retirees, particularly military folks. Plus, the University of Oklahoma Medical Center generates growth in health care jobs as well as bioscience startups.

Among workers in the country's 52 largest cities, Oklahoma City residents deal with the third-shortest commutes, according to the Census Bureau's most recent American Community Survey. Drivers spend an average of 21.35 minutes behind the wheel on their way to work, with only drivers in Rochester, N.Y., (20.37 minutes) and Buffalo–Niagara Falls (20.78) arriving quicker.

Love the cold weather? If you're familiar with the famed Mayo Clinic, you already know much of what you need to know about Rochester, Minnesota, or "Med City." Mayo employs more than 30,000 people, and there's no denying that health care rules this town, which is a draw for people from around the country seeking care. Older workers with health care and social assistance backgrounds will find that the fast-growing jobs include registered nurse, home health aide, and medical assistant. IBM, the town's second-biggest employer, has more than 4,000 workers at its life sciences division.

Situated along the banks of the Zumbro

River, Rochester has plenty of green space in its 3,500 acres of parkland — or white space, depending on the time of year. The city averages 48 inches of snow annually.

What Else to Consider When Relocating

After more than three decades of living and working in New York City and environs, Jerrold Footlick, a magazine editor, and his wife, Ceil Cleveland, an author and New York University English professor, retired to Durham, North Carolina. It had nothing to do with lower taxes or a cheaper cost of living or jobs. "That was happy happenstance," Cleveland says.

That's not so unusual. About 40 percent of boomers expect to move to another state at retirement, according to a survey by Del Webb, a retirement housing corporation. And while a smart relocation decision will bolster a financial plan, the reality is that money matters often take a back seat to lifestyle issues in retirement.

Not that money doesn't matter (more on that later), but what's really key is living in a place that makes you feel comfortable. "Sure, the cost of living is very important," says Tom Wetzel, president of Retirement Living Information Center, a web site. "But family, social networks, and other things often come first." Several criteria can trump financial concerns: climate, access to health care, crime rates, recreation, and culture — even shopping.

For Cleveland and Footlick, moving to the Tar Heel State had everything to do with culture and climate. The couple was pulled in by the dynamic arts, sports, and intellectual scene around Durham's Duke University and the nearby University of North Carolina–Chapel Hill. But something else also struck a chord. "The area was Southern enough for me," says Cleveland, who grew up in West Texas, "and Midwestern enough for Jerry, who was raised in Ohio, and offered other things we loved about living in the Northeast — like changing seasons."

Plus, the couple knew the area and people living there. Footlick's daughter, Robbyn, is a Duke grad, so they had spent time visiting there while she was studying there. Footlick had also been on one of the university's editorial boards for well over a decade. So it was easy to fall in with a group of short-story writers, novelists, and journalists who had already migrated to the Research Triangle. "We don't consider ourselves retired," Footlick says. "We just write full-time now, like practically everyone else we know here."

Living near their children and grandchildren

wasn't a prerequisite for the couple, as it is for many relocating retirees. "We have five kids in five different states," Cleveland says. "We figured they chose where they want to live. Let's choose where we want to live."

There is plenty to be said for that. But where you live will be the key to a big chunk of your retirement budget. And if basic living costs like gas prices, utility bills, and groceries keep rising, moving to a more affordable area will pay off.

"Happy happenstance" is nice if it happens for you, as it did for Footlick and Cleveland. But if you have a few locations to choose among, making a strategic money decision can bulletproof your future retirement budget.

While heading to a job-friendly town may be your motivation, keep in mind the five key financial factors to consider when planning to relocate.

1. **Cashing in:** One big reward of relocating is cashing in the equity you've built up in your home and moving to a more affordable area where you can buy a nice place for less. You might even be able to go further upscale. That's what Footlick and Cleveland did. They snagged a home half again as large as the one they

sold on Long Island's North Shore.

And if your timing is right, you might have cash left over. That's great news for those looking to pay down or eliminate credit card and other consumer debts. You might also choose to pay cash for your new digs and wipe out your monthly mortgage payment.

If you do opt for a home loan, a clean credit record and cash in hand for a fat down payment will get you a better interest rate. That will let you take advantage of today's relatively low fixed rates on most mortgages, which economists expect to hold steady for the next year or so.

If your expected income from Social Security, pensions, and other sources isn't going to be enough, you may need the cash generated from selling your house for living expenses.

2. **Tax-free gain:** Married couples can exclude up to $500,000 in capital gains from the sale of a primary residence (single homeowners can exclude $250,000). This rule can be a windfall for retirees who own highly appreciated residential property, as long as they have owned and used

the house as a primary residence for two of the past five years. Home flippers, if there are any left, need not apply.

3. **Tax consequences:** Moving from a high-tax state to a low-tax state is key. Look at income, sales, property, estate, and inheritance taxes. Many people pick a retirement destination purely because there is no income tax. "This is a serious mistake, since higher sales and state and local property taxes can more than offset any lack of a state income tax," says Bill Stromsen, accounting and tax professor at George Washington University. Florida, for example, imposes no income tax but makes up for that with sales and property taxes. State sales taxes vary greatly, with some at 7 percent or more. Only five states — Alaska, Delaware, Montana, New Hampshire, and Oregon — have no sales tax. In the state of Alaska, however, some local jurisdictions impose local sales taxes.

Property taxes are generally the heaviest tax burden for homeowning retirees. States with low median real estate taxes, according to Kiplinger

.com include Alaska, Alabama, Louisiana, Mississippi, and West Virginia. Those with high real estate taxes include New Hampshire, New Jersey, and Texas.

Most states give breaks to residents over a certain age, and there may be property tax credits or homestead exemptions that limit the value of assessed property subject to tax. But it's usually not up to the state to judge the total taxable value. That's in the hands of a local assessor.

Best advice: Check out the total tax picture of your possible destinations and compare them side-by-side, advises Stromsen. "There's no free ride from any state. You may win on some taxes and lose on others. And you certainly don't want the tax tail to wag the dog. Go where you want to go," he says.

4. **The Medicare mix:** Medicare premiums vary by market. Each place has its own blend of medical facilities and insurers. For the prices and terms of carriers that serve your future community, check the federal web site Medicare.gov and the web site of the

state's department of insurance.

5. **Utilitarian thinking:** Daily living costs fluctuate from place to place. Moving to a smaller residence will immediately save you money on utilities and maintenance costs. Depending on the climate where you settle, you might not even have to shrink your living space to slash utility bills. That was Footlick and Cleveland's surprise. Even in a larger home, their energy bills are down considerably from what they paid up north.

With Raleigh-Durham International Airport just 15 minutes down the road from their lakeside home, those savings make trips back to Manhattan for a splash of bright lights easy to work into their retirement budget.

Chapter 26
Couples and
Career Harmony

Most of my musings, advice, and expert brain-picking have been aimed at finding a good job when you're over 50, planning for retirement, and creating work that's financially rewarding and mentally engaging. But there's a big piece of boomer life after 50 that's often ignored.

Making a job change or retiring at different times can be a nightmare if one partner is at loose ends trying to figure out a new non-career-based identity, while the other is still in the same work mode. Or, say, one partner has taken an early retirement package and is launching a new career post-50 that requires a financial risk and dips into joint savings.

What if you want to keep working in retirement and your partner doesn't? What if your partner takes a severance package and opts to start a consulting business out of the house, a house where you have been firmly ensconced for a decade or more working as a freelance writer, thank you?

Have you thought and talked about how this stage will play out in your lives? I have my own theories about how to tiptoe through this awkward stage of our lives when kids are grown, first or primary careers are winding down, and new ones are emerging. I, however, turned to the real experts in this emerging field of counseling — Roberta K. Taylor and Dorian Mintzer, relationship psychotherapists and retirement coaches specializing in life transitions, for guidance.

The two women have written a terrific book called *The Couple's Retirement Puzzle* to help couples piece together a road map to deal with this potential dilemma.

This is uncharted territory. If you're part of a couple, you start by talking about it, they tell me. Gulp. This sounds hard even from where I stand peering over the ledge.

It begins with a frank conversation about how you want to live the next part of your life. You need to begin to prioritize and make decisions. You may not have a choice about whether to work into your 70s but "there may be creative options for how to work and what you can do, given your interests, experience, and skills," Taylor and

Mintzer tell me.

That's precisely why you need to be on the same page. Having someone to grow old with is great and helps defray stress. It frequently provides financial support, and, of course, a human bond that's priceless. But unless you have a general plan that you're both following, it can get pretty complicated.

Taylor and Mintzer hit on some key concerns:

- How do dual-career couples make decisions about when to retire, whether to retire together or separately, or if they can afford to retire at all?
- What if you're out of sync? A woman who has put her career on hold until children are grown might be reentering the job force as her husband is thinking about leaving his job and winding down, or transitioning into something less demanding.
- What do you do if you're used to working out of your home office as a freelancer, and suddenly your spouse is underfoot 24–7? Resentments can build.

How can you successfully meld two individuals' innermost needs, desires, and dreams for the next chapter? You want to live in the country, say, with your dogs and horses. He's a city boy and enjoys being able to walk to the grocery store and slip into a theater for the latest movie, and has a hankering for public transportation.

After years of individually coaching couples in their third stage of life, Taylor and Mintzer realized that many couples and partners just "don't want to talk about it now" when it came to all things related to retirement issues. Taylor and Mintzer's task is to present a strategy to start the conversations that help couples tackle pieces of the puzzle. Most couples aren't going to agree on everything. But if you can communicate, you can find solutions, they say.

The duo provide practical questions to get you started:

- What are my goals for the next stage of life? Have you always wanted to learn Italian or buy a vacation home in Maine?
- What are my options if I decide to continue working?
- How do financial decisions get made in our relationship? Do I want that to change?

- How do my family relationships and current or anticipated obligations and responsibilities affect my partner and our relationship?
- Have we talked about our current and future health care needs?
- Do I want to explore a different lifestyle?
- What is important for us to do as a couple?

Each of you answers a variety of questions within a specific area. These range from finances to health and wellness, time together/time apart, and changing roles and identity. Then you sit down and compare your responses together, making a list of what you agree on.

You eventually draft a "shared vision," which should be revisited at least once a year. You might review your plan, much as you do your investment portfolio, and rebalance priorities as things shift.

It makes sense. What couples are thinking about and planning for at age 46 or even 50 is very different from what it is at age 60 or 70. Moreover, "relationships are always a work in progress," Taylor and Mintzer explain.

Getting these hot-button topics out front

is uncomfortable and awkward, but step-by-step, the two relationship coaches direct a thoughtful conversational process to ease you along. The serious exercises that they dole out in their book help jump-start these discussions. They are balanced with some fun to keep things flowing. Learn to tango, for example, is one suggestion to improve your health and wellness together.

It's ultimately freeing to have these conversations about money matters and dreams, but lack of smooth communication tools trip us up. Simply put, it's hard to get started. Even when you do, it's easy to become frustrated and angry when your partner doesn't share your future goals.

But you've got to push on through. Make a date to talk. Set a time limit for it. Avoid such words as "always" and "never." Then set a time for your next conversation.

The takeaway: Couples need to start talking about the next stage well before they get there, and reassess as circumstances change.

"There is no magic wand," the coaches concede. How to put it together is up to you.

Some people are better at it than others, but Taylor and Mintzer promise that if you practice being a good listener, are open to concessions, and remember to share something positive that you learned about each other after each conversation, it will make the process a little easier.

How an Encore Career Can Be Like an Affair

In an interview with me, Roberta Taylor talks about great ways couples can get on the same page.

KH: *What's the biggest stumbling block for couples facing retirement?*

RT: Lack of planning for postretirement life. Many couples don't start planning for retirement until late in the process, when important decisions end up getting made by default. Communication issues often get in the way of planning for retirement. Even when couples want to be able to make decisions together, they may have difficulty knowing how to bring up difficult issues and problem solve together.

KH: *What makes these conversations so tricky?*

RT: It can be scary to open up unresolved issues from the past or talk about differences that may cause conflict or threaten the relationship. It's easier to avoid a difficult conversation than risk having an unsettling argument. It can also be hard to look ahead to the future when the present is so consuming.

KH: *What are your top conversation tips to help couples move into retirement together gracefully?*

RT: Begin the conversation by talking about the things you agree on. Use "I" statements, learn to listen, and avoid blaming. Make sure you understand your partner's perspective and why it's important to him or her. If you're not on the same page, agree to disagree.

KH: *Second careers and working in retirement — this is new territory in many ways for this generation. How has this reality impacted couples and retirement issues?*

RT: Getting absorbed in an encore career can be like having an affair. If one partner is spending the majority of time involved with something new, the other partner is probably going to feel left out, hurt, and threatened. Sharing the engrossing project with your partner can go a long way in helping him or her to feel included and supported rather than excluded.

KH: *"Are you saving enough for retirement?" is the key question that everyone focuses on, but beyond money, what else should couples be discussing when creating a* *"shared vision"* for this stage of life?

RT: Here are some to get you going.

- How will your roles and responsibilities change?
- How much togetherness and separateness does each of you want and need?
- What about physical space in the home?
- What health and medical considerations need to be factored into decision making?
- Where to live: geographic location, proximity to family, climate, what is the importance of nature, culture, and other preferences? What about social life, friends, and community?
- What responsibilities and obligations do you have for adult children, aging parents, and grandchildren or other relatives and friends?
- How can you live a fulfilling life with purpose and meaning?

KH: *How important is revisiting your "shared vision" once a year? It's a little like rebalancing your investment portfolio at regular intervals, isn't it?*

RT: Absolutely! Reviewing your vision on a regular basis will help to maintain open communication and a realistic perspective.

KH: *What surprised you the most about couples and retirement from the people you interviewed?*

RT: For many couples, avoiding conflict was more important than having important conversations.

KH: *Were there any common issues that they shared?*

RT: Money, but from a different perspective. Women were more concerned about security, and men worried about maintaining the standard of living. In addition, the most common issues for women were:

- 24/7 with their partners.
- Fear that their partners would be too reliant on them.
- Changing roles.

For men the most common issues were:

- Loss of identity as a professional.
- Lack of purpose and meaning.
- Not feeling appreciated.

AFTERWORD

Finding a great job is within your power. As you've heard from the people who've shared their work lives with you in these pages, great jobs come in all different forms. At the root of what makes a job search successful and a job *great,* is our attitude.

We have the ability to control how our mind confronts and responds to trying something new, to learning new skills, or to adapting to new work environments. At this stage in our lives, we've developed knowledge and capability about a vast number of subjects. We've worked alongside a diverse group of people in a variety of workplaces. We have swag.

Even if you have had only one employer to date, which is less likely than it was in our parents' generation, you've probably shifted from divisions or departments over time and taken on new job responsibilities. You've pushed outside your comfort zone.

We aren't beginners. We come to the challenge of job seeking with an inner compass that has steadily given us direction. Our accumulated expertise allows us to quickly get up to speed in fields that may seem worlds apart from where we've started.

Consider the culture shock, for example, of moving to a small nonprofit from a large insurance company, as Cheryl Champagne did when she left the Hartford. But when you look below the surface, you find that you, like Cheryl, can succeed.

It's a process. A great job rarely falls in your lap. It takes some detective work and preparation.

In review, there are three major actions that will contribute to your success.

1. **Pause and take the time to explore what you're good at.** What have you enjoyed in jobs and work experiences from your past? What are the pastimes you're passionate about, even those that sparked you as a child? Those personal questions will guide you to your next endeavor. They are your clues to what will make a job your great job. Dream a little. This could be the opportunity you've been waiting for

to try something new.

2. **Do your homework.** Read books like this one about a wide variety of jobs. Learn about which jobs truly fit this stage of your life — from a financial, intellectual, and psychological perspective. Check into all the resources available in your town for you to add new skills, volunteer, or moonlight.

3. **Network.** Ask people who know you well and people you've worked with over the years for advice on what kinds of opportunities they think you would be good at. Who else do they suggest you talk to?

If you've reached the end of this job-hunting guide with an enthusiasm for a new kind of work and some fresh tools for your kit, I've done my job. After two years of researching the job market and the types of careers and jobs available for 50+ workers, I feel encouraged by the possibilities.

As I've said throughout this book, no two people are looking for the same ingredients in a job. Each person I interviewed had different skill-sets, backgrounds, and goals. Many took the time to go back to school to prepare for a new kind of work.

Others simply let their heart lead them to a job that makes clocking in turn them into a kid again — as Rich Bartkowski did. It makes me smile to picture him heading over to Camden Yards to lead tours of the Baltimore Orioles ballpark.

The common bond: a happy, healthy state of mind.

Batter up!

HELPFUL WEB SITES
FOR 50+ WORKERS

If you're job hunting, planning a career change, or thinking about working in your "retirement" years, here's a list of resources to help you get going. The number of web sites dedicated to job search is in a state of constant growth and change. I have cherry-picked some to get you started. It is by no means a definitive listing, and subject to change after publication.

Job-Hunting Sites

AARPWorksearch.org is AARP Foundation's WorkSearch Information Network, which covers each phase of the job search in detail, from beginning a search to accepting a job.

AARP.org/work has a complete channel with news, resources, and how-to help, plus the biennial list of Best Employers for Workers Over 50.

CareerBuilder.com is an extensive overall career site.

CareerOneStop.org offers career resources to job seekers.

CoolWorks.com is a database of seasonal jobs, amusement park jobs, and more.

Craigslist.com provides a wide range of job listings.

Enrge.us (The Employment Network for Retirement Government Experts) helps retired government employees — federal, state, and local — find new employment.

Erieri.com (The Economic Research Institute) provides free salary information for both for-profit and not-for-profit organizations by industry and geographic location. It also offers cost-of-living data.

ExecSearches.com is a job board that focuses on government, nonprofit, education, and health openings.

Execunet.com is a network of senior-level retired executives.

Flexjobs.com is a subscription-based job board with fee starting at $14.95 a month for listing of prescreened openings for freelancers, telecommuters, and more.

Glassdoor.com is a free jobs and career community that offers an inside look at jobs and companies, salary information, and so on.

Greenbiz.com is a comprehensive green business news and information site with a section dedicated to friendly job openings.

Indeed.com is an online jobs listing and search engine that aggregates thousands of jobs listings from multiple sites.

JobMonkey.com is a site that features seasonal and summer gigs.

LinkedIn.com/job allows you to search for jobs and contacts at potential employers at this social networking spot.

Monster.com is a large general jobs web site with a special section for older workers.

Payscale.com offers salary data for a broad sweep of jobs.

PrimeCB.com is Careerbuilder.com's section for experienced workers.

Ratracerebellion.com is a site that is geared for work-at-home opportunities.

RetiredBrains.com is run by Art Koff, a 70-something retired ad executive, who is the dynamo behind this online job board that connects to thousands of jobs for those over 50. It's also a resource center on other retirement-related issues, from continuing education to health care to dealing with grief.

RetireeWorkForce.com provides job postings and resume services, plus a database with flexible, seasonal, and full-time positions specifically for more experienced candidates.

Retirementjobs.com is a site geared toward 50+ job seekers.

Salary.com is a free source for salary comparisons by city and job.

Seniors4Hire.org is a site where seniors can apply for jobs, submit a resume, or post a description of their model job.

SimplyHired.com is a large jobs database.

WorkForce50.com offers employment and career change resources.

Vault.com is a job-hunting site with a range of postings and help.

Nonprofit Web Sites

Here is a listing of web sites aimed at those looking to work or volunteer in the nonprofit sector. It is by no means a complete selection, but a sampler to help you start your research. Also see the resources listed in Chapter 18.

Ashoka.org has a program that provides fellows living stipends, professional support, and access to a global network of peers in more than 60 countries.

Boardnetusa.org is a great site for individuals interested in board service.

Bridgestar.org is a nonprofit job board listings and more.

The Center for Productive Longevity (ctrpl.org) is a nonprofit created by Human Resource Services, Inc. (HRS) in 2006 with the mission of stimulating the substantially increased engagement of people 55 and older (55+) in productive activities, paid and volunteer.

Change.org Search allows you to search for jobs with nonprofit organizations; there's a specific section for experienced workers called "Sector Switchers."

CharityChannel.com is a subscription-based online social network for professionals working for nonprofit organizations, and includes job listings at U.S. nonprofits if you search under professional growth.

Commongoodcareers.org gives you a sense of where the jobs are and who is hiring.

Councilofnonprofits.org is a national network of state and regional nonprofit associations serving more than 20,000 organizations.

CreatetheGood.org is AARP's site for links to community volunteer projects.

Encore.org is a nonprofit that promotes second acts for the greater good and provides free, comprehensive information that helps people transition to jobs in the nonprofit world and the public sector.

Experiencecorps.org is a national AARP program that engages people 50+ in tutoring and mentoring activities in 19 cities across the country, providing literacy coaching, homework help, consistent role models, and committed, caring attention.

GuideStar.org is a leading source on nonprofit organizations.

Idealist.org provides leads to more than 14,000 volunteer opportunities nationwide, plus internships and jobs in the nonprofit sector.

Independentsector.org provides research and resources of over 600 charities, foundations, and corporations.

LinkedIn.com includes positions at nonprofits when you go to the "Industry" section of the jobs search area, and type in "Nonprofit Organization Management."

The National Older Worker Career Center (nowcc.org) is a national nonprofit organization dedicated to promoting workers 55+ in full- and part-time positions for two federal agencies — the Environmental Protection Agency and the Natural Resources Conservation Service of the U.S. Department of Agriculture.

NationalService.gov is the web site for the Corporation for National and Community Service.

Nonprofitjobseeeker.com has a fast-growing job board for job seekers reports on charitable organizations' salaries and benefits.

PeaceCorps.gov offers some paid volunteering overseas in areas such as education, health, business, and information and communication technology.

Philanthropy.com/jobs has a listing of jobs primarily in foundations from The Chronicle of Philanthropy.

ReServe (reserveinc.org), an innovative resource that matches continuing professionals 55+ with the nonprofits that need them.

SeniorServiceAmerica.org runs federally funded programs that put people into temporary or full-time jobs with local, state, and federal government agencies.

General Information

I have listed below a few sites, in addition to aarp.org, where you will find a broad range of information on employment and other issues of interest to the 50+ crowd.

The U.S. Department of Labor

(Dol.gov) has a trove of information for job hunters and employer benefits.

The Employee Benefits Research Institute (ebri.org) offers insight into today's trends in employee benefits and retirement confidence.

NextAvenue.org provides timely news and insight for baby boomers.

Northeastern University (encore.org/find/resources/after-recovery-help) predicts the occupations that will have the most job openings for older workers in the coming decade.

RetirementRevised.com is a highly respected site for information on retirement planning, jobs, and resources for entrepreneurs.

Sloan Center on Aging and Work (bc.edu/research/agingandwork) conducts original research and maintains an extensive library on age-related subjects.

Thetransitionnetwork.org has a variety of resources for women over 50 in transition.

2young2retire.com offers resources and articles for those 50+.

Whatsnext.com provides information on career coaches and mid-life job transition, articles, and life assessment tools.

Small Business

If you're itching to start a small business, here are some great resources to get you rolling.

SBA.org provides small-business resources from loans to franchising to tips on starting a small company from the U.S. Small Business Administration.

Score.org is a nonprofit association dedicated to educating entrepreneurs nationwide via 13,000 volunteer counselors, who include working and retired business owners and executives. Type in your ZIP code to find a local office.

Seniorentrepreneurshipworks.org is a nonprofit organization designed to engage, empower, connect, and celebrate seniors 55+ who choose to become entrepreneurs.

Continuing Education

Encore.org/colleges is a listing of Plus 50 programs at community colleges around the country.

FastWeb.com is a search engine for research scholarships and grants for older students offered by associations, colleges, religious groups, and foundations.

IRS.gov provides information about educational tax breaks in Publication 970.

NASFAA.org is the site of the National Association of Student Financial Aid Administrators.

Osher.net is the home of Osher Life Long Learning network site.

Plus50.aacc.nche.edu is the site of the Plus 50 Initiative by the American Association of Community Colleges aimed at students over 50.

Studentaid.ed.gov is a source for information on federal student aid.

Volunteering

There are thousands of organizations that provide volunteer opportunities from your local hospitals and hospices to small non-profits in your community. I have listed a few large national organizations below that can help you track down opportunities that are in your area and will aim to match your skills with projects.

Catchafire.org matches professionals who want to give their skills with nonprofits and social enterprises that need their help. We match professionals and organizations based on a variety of characteristics including skills, cause interests, and time availability.

Createthegood.org is AARP's site for community volunteer projects.

Doctorswithoutborders.org provides aid in nearly 60 countries thorough the efforts of volunteers who are doctors, nurses, logistics experts, administrators, epidemiologists, laboratory technicians, mental health professionals, and others.

HandsOnNetwork.org is a skills-based volunteer activation arm of Points of Light. Including 250 community action centers.

Hands.org is the site of All Hands Volunteers and provides opportunities for volunteers to help survivors of natural disasters and communities in need.

LawyersWithoutBorders.org provides legal pro bono services around the world.

Onlinevolunteering.org is a database to find online volunteering opportunities with organizations that serve communities in developing countries, sponsored by the United Nations.

OperationHope.org seeks volunteers with a background in the financial industry to work as virtual volunteers to victims of hurricanes and other disasters, offering financial and budget counseling via the Internet.

NPS.gov/volunteer is the National Park Service volunteer channel.

Taprootfoundation.org places teams of professionals who are doing pro bono consulting with nonprofits and operates in seven U.S. cities in a variety of fields, including finance, marketing, and information technology.

Volunteer.gov is a one-stop shop for public-service volunteer projects sponsored by the U.S. government.

VolunteerMatch.org allows you to search more than 73,000 listings nationwide via an extensive database of projects that lets you screen for everything from board opportunities to communications positions based on your interests and geographical location.

IDEAS FOR FURTHER READING

There are scores of great books aimed at boomers and work. Here are a few I recommend, but it is by no means the ultimate list. There are always new ones coming along. No doubt, I have inadvertently neglected some titles. But the ones you will find below will certainly get you started on your research and provide you with innovative ideas, inspiration, and guidance for finding your next great job.

The Big Shift: Navigating the New Stage Beyond Midlife (Public Affairs, 2011) and **Encore: Finding Work That Matters in the Second Half of Life** (Public Affairs, 2008) by Marc Freedman. Freedman is the founder and CEO of Encore .org, a nonprofit that promotes second acts for the greater good.

Composing a Further Life by Mary Catherine Bateson (Knopf, 2010). In her latest book, the famed anthropologist focuses on the newly emerging period of active engagement that falls roughly between ages 55 and 70. She calls this period Adulthood II.

The Couple's Retirement Puzzle: 10 Must-Have Conversations for Transitioning to the Second Half of Life by Roberta K. Taylor and Dorian Mintzer (Lincoln Street Press, 2011). A great resource for dealing with a working retirement for couples.

Diary of a Company Man: Losing a Job, Finding a Life by James S. Kunen (Lyons Press, 2012). An inspiring story of being fired after two decades with Time Warner in a corporate downsizing, and finding a new beginning teaching English as a second language.

Do What You Are: Discover the Perfect Career for You Through the Secrets of Personality Type by Paul D. Tieger and Barbara Barron-Tieger (Little, Brown, 2007). This job-hunting classic helps midlife and other job seekers consider careers that suit them based on their personality type. This revolves around the Myers-Briggs Personality Indicator (MBPI), which categorizes people into types.

Don't Retire, Rewire, 2nd Edition: 5 Steps to Fulfilling Work That Fuels Your Passion, Suits Your Personality, and Fills Your Pocket by Jeri Sedlar and Rick Miners (Alpha, 2007). A bestseller on making the transition to new work after retirement.

Drive: The Surprising Truth About What Motivates Us by Daniel Pink (Riverhead Books, 2009).

Escape from Corporate America: A Practical Guide to Creating the Career of Your Dreams by Pamela Skillings (Ballantine Books, 2008). Advice on where and how to find career coaches, health insurance, and jobs.

Escape from Cubicle Nation: From Corporate Prisoner to Thriving Entrepreneur by Pamela Slim (Portfolio, 2009). Life coach Slim shows readers how to navigate the transition from corporate worker bee to entrepreneur.

Evolutionary Work: Unleashing Your Potential in Extraordinary Times by Patricia DiVecchio (Pearhouse Press, 2010). Great advice on bringing passion to your work life.

The Hard Times Guide to Retirement Security: Practical Strategies for Money, Work, and Living by Mark Miller (Bloomberg Press/Wiley 2010). Miller is an expert on aging and retirement and publishes RetirementRevised.com. Miller offers ways to build long-term retirement security and boost knowledge on a broad array of topics from money issues such as 401(k) plans to ways to navigate the 50+ job market.

How to Change the World: Social Entrepreneurs and the Power of New Ideas by David Bornstein (Oxford University Press, 2007). This has become the bible for social entrepreneurship. It profiles men and women from around the world who have found innovative solutions to a wide variety of social and economic problems.

How to Speak Money: The Language and Knowledge You Need Now by Ali Velshi and Christine Romans (John Wiley & Sons, 2011). Authors and CNN financial experts Ali Velshi and Christine Romans have penned an easy-to-read, practical book.

A Long Bright Future: An Action Plan for a Lifetime of Happiness, Health, and Financial Security by Laura Carstensen (Broadway Books, 2009). Carstensen is a professor of psychology and founding director of the Stanford Center on Longevity. For more than twenty years, her research has been supported by the National Institute on Aging.

Me 2.0, Revised and Updated Edition: 4 Steps to Building Your Future by Dan Schawbel (Kaplan Publishing, 2010). Savvy help for shaping your personal brand. There's a great chapter on job hunting with help navigating online job boards, Facebook, and Twitter job chats.

One Person/Multiple Careers: The Original Guide to the Slash Career [Kindle Edition] by Marci Alboher (Hey-Marci, 2012). Innovative take on the core of today's worklife as we weave together a variety of jobs.

The Pathfinder: How to Choose or Change Your Career for a Lifetime of Satisfaction and Success by Nicholas Lore (Fireside, 2012). A top-notch best-selling guide to being your own career detective and finding the right work for you.

Rebounders: How Winners Pivot from Setback to Success by Rick Newman. (Ballantine Books, 2012) Setbacks can be a secret weapon, writes the chief business correspondent for *U.S. News & World Report* in his book. He analyzes how people react to stressful events and succeed by being open to new ideas, taking action, and not squealing with outrage if they have to make sacrifices in order to accomplish something important.

The Savage Truth on Money, 2nd Edition by Terry Savage (John Wiley and Sons, 2011). The author shows you how to gain control over your financial future, setting you free to truly enjoy the present.

The Secret of Shelter Island: Money and What Matters by Alexander Green (John Wiley & Sons, 2010). The author explores the complicated relationship we all have with money.

Shock of Gray: The Aging of the World's Population and How it Pits Young Against Old, Child Against Parent, Worker Against Boss, Company Against Rival, and Nation Against Nation by Ted Fishman (Scribner, 2010). Fishman is a big-picture writer who commands a profound understanding of global economic and social trends.

Smart Women Don't Retire — They Break Free by the Transition Network and Gail Rentsch (Springboard Press, 2008). A must-read for women over 50 who are making life transitions.

Social Networking for Career Success: Using Online Tools to Create a Personal Brand by Miriam Salpeter

(LearningExpress, 2011). Step-by-step help with job search and social media coach Salpeter, owner of Keppie Careers.

Social Security for Dummies by Jonathan Peterson (For Dummies, 2012). Peterson is Executive Communications Director at AARP and an award-winning journalist who expertly makes sense of Social Security for all of us.

Sparkle & Hustle: Launch and Grow Your Small Business Now by Tory Johnson (Berkeley Books, 2012). The founder and CEO of Women For Hire and Good Morning America contributor lays it out from writing a one-page business plan to finding the money to get going.

Switch: How to Change Things When Change Is Hard by Chip Heath and Dan Heath (Broadway Books, 2010). Who doesn't want to know how to make a winning change? Chip Heath and Dan Heath discuss a common quest in their book.

Test-Drive Your Dream Job: A Step-by-Step Guide to Finding and Creating the Work You Love by Brian Kurth with Robin Simons (BusinessPlus, 2008). The founder of VocationVacations and Pivot-Planet offers a guide to finding mentors and your own dream job.

The Third Chapter: Passion, Risk, and

Adventure in the 25 Years after 50 by Sara Lawrence-Lightfoot (Farrar, Straus and Giroux, 2009). The author approaches this stage of life from her perspective as a sociologist. The book's premise is that life's third chapter is one of substantial growth and change.

Unbeatable Resumes: America's Top Recruiter Reveals What REALLY Gets You Hired by Tony Beshara (Amacom, 2011). The title says it all.

What Color Is Your Parachute? for Retirement, Second Edition: Planning a Prosperous, Healthy, and Happy Future by John E. Nelson and Richard N. Bolles (Ten Speed Press, 2010). Useful insights and exercises so you can make the best choices for all facets of your life from work and leisure to health and where to live.

What Should I Do with the Rest of My Life? True Stories of Finding Success, Passion, and New Meaning in the Second Half of Life by Bruce Frankel (Avery, 2010). A must-read if you've been laid off, downsized, or are just ready for a change.

What's Next? Follow Your Passion and Find Your Dream Job by Kerry Hannon (Chronicle Books, 2010). This is a collection of inspiring career switcher profiles. It's an essential guide to those hoping to pull off a midlife reinvention or looking for a job that brings meaning to their lives and those whose lives they touch.

Your Credit Score: How to Improve the 3-Digit Number That Shapes Your Financial Future (4th Edition) by Liz Pulliam Weston (FT Press, 2011). Key advice on getting financially fit.

ACKNOWLEDGMENTS

I am grateful to many people for their assistance, support, and knowledge.

I send a special wave to my 50+ workers who shared their stories, motivation, and valuable time with me.

I owe boundless gratitude to the career and transition experts who gladly offered thoughtful guidance. These include Encore .org's Marc Freedman and the Encore.org team's Marci Alboher and Stefanie Weiss, The Transition Network Executive Director Betsy Werley, Nicholas Lore, Maggie Mistal, Patricia DiVecchio, Dorian Mintzer, Roberta Taylor, Tony Beshara, Beverly Jones, Miriam Salpeter, Mary Bleiberg, and Laura Gassner Otting.

My Great Jobs column, which has appeared at AARP.org since 2010, would not have become a reality without the vision and skilled editorial touch of Mike DeSenne, who tapped me to write the column in the belief that this kind of job help was precisely what AARP members were craving in a tough job market.

The indomitable Tara Coates, editor at AARP.org, has been my column's chief strategist, cheerleader, and editor extraordinaire since May 2011. My heartfelt thanks, Tara, for your great editorial judgment, support, cool patience, and keen sense of how the system works and making me smile when I'm crashing deadlines.

If not for *Forbes* media Vice President and Investing Editor Matt Schifrin and Executive Editor and Washington Bureau Chief Janet Novack, my Second Verse column would not have taken flight on Forbes.com back in November 2010. Nor would I be back writing for the print magazine, where I cut my teeth from 1985 to 1990 as a staff writer and editor. You both have given me an opportunity to share my career transition, retirement, and personal finance advice with an ever-growing body of readers. Thank you for your friendship and for showing me that you really can go home again.

I send my deep appreciation to my agent, Linda Konner, whose gusto and guidance made it possible for this book to be published and much more. It's a true pleasure to work with a pro like you.

My admiration to John Wiley & Son's Editorial Director Debra Englander, whom I have known since our *Money* magazine days, and onward through three previous books together. And as we do it again, your belief in my work means more than you know.

Special thanks to AARP Books Managing Editor Jodi Lipson, who put her heart into this project and worked in tandem with John Wiley's hard-working editorial crew — Editorial Assistant Tula Batanchiev; Development Editors Kimberly Bernard and Judy Howarth; and Production Editor Melissa Lopez — to diligently shape this book and bring forth the kind of no-nonsense job help that 50+ workers are seeking.

I extend a hearty shout-out of appreciation to the Gerontological Society of America's Linda Harootyan and Todd Kluss and the New America Media's Paul Kleyman. I'm indebted to all three of you for the honor of being chosen to be a fellow in the MetLife Foundation Journalists in Aging Fellows program. This experience has opened my eyes and mind to the sober challenges of work and of aging in our society.

I also want to thank A.J. Campbell of CoSynergy.com, my go-to web designer and consultant. AJ, you are a "Creative Genius."

On a personal note, there are those in my life whom I could not do my great job without. Here goes . . .

To the Bonney family — Paul, Pat, Christine, Mike, Caitlin, Shannon — Sassy, and Piper, too — for your never-ending ballast in my life and always keeping the door open.

To the Hannon family — Mike, Judy, Brendan, Sean, Conor, and Brian — for your boundless energy, competitive spirit, and love. You inspire me.

To my brother, Jack, for never failing to answer my calls for help and advice and to his wife, Charmaine, for those special hugs.

To Jonelle Mullen Stern, my friends at TuDane Farm, and my lovely mare Saintly (a.k.a Brinkley), for helping me gallop from deadlines into the magical world of horses.

To my dear friends Marcy Holquist Duff and Lisa Williamson, for unselfishly sharing your artistic spirits with me.

A special nod to my mother, Marguerite Hannon, for always being there as my best friend.

Finally, my husband, Cliff, for your unwavering love and support and for being my biggest fan. Thank you.

Of course, without Zena, my road manager, I would be lost.

INDEX

401(k), solo, 445–48

American Institute of Professional
    Bookkeepers, 40, 156
American Marketing Association, 199–200
American Medical Association, 242
American Speech-Language-Hearing
    Association, 249
American Translators Association, 145
American Veterinary Medical Association,
    224
amusement parks, 83–84
apprenticing, 273–75
apps, using, 335–36
Aramark, 74
Arnold, John, 362
Ashoka, 366, 387
assistant
  medical, 221–23
  virtual, 159–60
Association of Fundraising Professionals,
    154, 202
Association of Medical Technologists, 223
Association of Small Business
    Development Centers, 432
ATA. *See* American Translators
    Association
athletic coach, 53–56
athletic event ticket services, 88–89
audiologist, 249
Audiology Foundation of America, 249

G

General Services Administration, 432–33
George Washington University, 255
Georgetown University, 255
gift wrapper, 108–9
goal, working toward, 283
GoHealthInsurance.com, 278
going solo, 411–14
Google, 307
Google alerts, 307
Google+, 280, 306–7, 324
grant writer, 153–54
Grant-Writing for Dummies, 154
grants, 273
  as source of education funds, 456–57
graphic designer, 148–50
Grassley, Chuck, 295–96
Grealish, Ellen, 354
Green Building Certification Institute, 48
green building consultant, 47–48
green conferences, 284–85
green jobs, 284–85
  tips for finding, 284–85
GreenBiz.com, 284, 300
greeter, restaurant, 110–11
Gross, Jack, 294–95
group decisions, 368–69

H

T

ABOUT THE AUTHOR

Kerry Hannon is a nationally recognized authority on career transitions and retirement and a frequent TV and radio commentator speaking about career and personal finance trends and offering advice.

She is the author of the award-winning *What's Next? Follow Your Passion and Find Your Dream Job,* which *USA Today* hailed as "a road map for those striking out on their own." Kerry is AARP's Jobs Expert and is the Great Jobs for Retirees columnist at AARP.org. She is a contributing editor at *Forbes* magazine and the Second Verse columnist at Forbes.com, and she writes a personal finance column for boomer women at NextAvenue.org, a web site launched by PBS stations focused on America's growing 50+ population.

She has been engaged in covering careers and individual career choices for the last decade. In 2006, Kerry developed *U.S.*

News & World Report's "Second Acts" feature — a regular column that looked at people who successfully navigated a complete career change midlife, their challenges, and their motivations.

She has spent more than two decades covering all aspects of business and personal finance as a columnist, editor, and writer for the nation's leading media companies, including *Forbes, Money, U.S. News & World Report,* and *USA Today.* Kerry's work has also appeared in *Business Week, Kiplinger's Personal Finance, The Wall Street Journal,* and *Reader's Digest,* among other national publications. She has appeared as a financial expert on ABC News, CBS, CNBC, NPR, and PBS.

Kerry is also the author of *Getting Started in Estate Planning* (John Wiley & Sons), *Suddenly Single: Money Skills for Divorcees and Widows* (John Wiley & Sons), and the *Ten Minute Guide to Retirement for Women* (Macmillan Publishing).

She lives in Washington, D.C. with her husband, Cliff Hackel, and Labrador retriever, Zena. Follow her on Twitter: @KerryHannon

Visit: www.kerryhannon.com